Searching

by
Daniel J. Schneck

Cover Design by Patti and Geoffrey Rowland

International Scientific Communications, Inc.
Shelton, Connecticut

Published by
International Scientific Communications, Inc.
30 Controls Drive
Shelton, Connecticut 06484-0870

Copyright © 2005 by International Scientific Communications, Inc.

All rights reserved
including the right of reproduction
in whole or any other form.

ISBN 0-9644911-1-7

TABLE OF CONTENTS

page

Preface	vii
Editor's Introduction	xiv
Author's Introduction	xv

Part I: Searching for **Knowledge and Truth**— The "Out There"

On the Seven Elements of Knowledge	3
The Seven Rudimentary Axioms of Reality	6
The Seven Fundamental Laws of Reality	9
Seven Axiomatic Foundations of Analysis	13
Pro or Con or . . . Neither	19
Can We . . . Should We . . . Measure Everything in a Purely Objective Way?	23
Units of Measurement: The Glass and the Spoon	28
Energy	33
Equilibrium	37
Time	41
All God's Creations Got Rhythm!	45
Time Revisited	48
Space	52
Space Revisited	56
Space–Time Reality Variables	61
Entropy	66
Beware of Medical (and Scientific) Fads	70

Part II: Searching for **Self and Identity**— The "In Here"

	page
What Is This Thing Called "Me"? Part 1: Levels of Organization of the Human Body	77
Each of Us Is a Minority of One	83
A Biomedical Engineer Views the Human Body	86
Will the *Real* You Please Stand Up?	90
A Musician Views the Human Body	95
A Society of Intensive Potentialists	100
What Is This Thing Called "Me"? Part 2: Attributes That Classify the Human Body as Being Alive	103
Mind/Body—Both or Neither?	109
How Many Brains Do We Have? It's Not Enough	112
The Physiology of Relativity	116
Creativity	120
There Is No Such Thing as a Learning Disability, Only Teaching Disabilities	124
Scaling "Unreachable" Heights	127
Stay Teachable!	131
Bad Stress	135
Food Allergies	139
Physiological Accommodation	144

Part III: Searching for **Relations and Self-Fulfillment**—Relating the "In Here" With the "Out There"

	page
Simple Wisdom I: Seven Building Blocks to a Healthy Relationship	151
Attitude!	156
Let's *Really* Get Back to Basics	160
Bonding	164
The Seven "C's"	168
Simple Wisdom II	172
The Great Equalizer	175
Ethics	178
Seven "F-Words"	181
To Err Is Human, to Forgive Divine	186
On the Importance of Putting Things Into Perspective	189
The "I's" Have It!	192
"L"-Ementary, My Dear Fellow!	196
There's a Big Difference Between Ruling and Leading!	201
Leadership Skills	204
Decision-Making Skills	208
"Enlightened" Neurosis!	213
We're So Busy Being Busy!	218

Dedication

This book is dedicated to my family and friends, who are a constant source of inspiration; to the thousands of students who have challenged me over the years to keep learning in order to be a better communicator and effective teacher; and to my loyal fans, who continue to encourage me to become a better person. To all of them, I say a sincere "Thank you!"

Preface

This book took five years to write, but it took me more than ten times that long—over 50 years—to formulate and develop the ideas expressed herein. The writing itself dates back to July of 2000, when my first editorial, "Mind/Body . . . Both or Neither?" appeared in *American Laboratory* (32[14]:6–8), and for that, I owe Brian Howard, Publisher and Editor in Chief of International Scientific Communications (ISC), Inc., a very sincere "Thank you!" Without his vision, his willingness to be receptive to my ideas, to publish them, and to encourage me to keep writing, there is a good chance that none of what you are about to read would have materialized in quite the way that it did. I am also indebted to Susan Messinger, Donna Frankel, Sharlene Kehlenbeck, Julie DeMaio, Rachel Domack, and all of the other members of the editorial and production staff at ISC for "keeping me honest," but most of all, for being such a great group of folks with whom to work. They have made my association with ISC a truly rewarding and pleasant experience.

The history of the formulation and development of ideas expressed in this book is best summarized by my dear wife, Judi, who says, "Dan is still trying to decide what he wants to do when he grows up!" I started out as a violinist at age 5, gave my debut at age 7 in New York City's famous Carnegie Recital Hall, was graduated from the prestigious High School of Music and Art in 1958, and then went on to study privately with the renowned Dorothy Delay at the Juilliard School of Music (which is where, incidentally, I met Judi, who at the time was also studying with Ms. Delay, and practicing the violin up to eight hours per day, sometimes more!). Both of us continue to pursue very active careers in music. We have our own music ensemble (the Alleghany String Quartet), teach and administer the music program at the Blacksburg New School (K–8, Blacksburg, VA), and do quite a bit of freelance work with local orchestras and other performing groups.

At a critical time in my life, I was advised that I should do something "more sensible" than become a full-time professional violinist—so off I went to the City College of New York (CCNY), from which I received a Bachelor of Mechanical Engineering Degree in 1963. By the time I was graduated from CCNY—perhaps due to both my intensive and extensive background in the liberal arts—I was convinced that a full-time career as a Mechanical Engineer was not right for me, so I decided to try medicine, which I did at New York University from 1963 to 1967. Upon being graduated from a joint program in Engineering and Medicine, I accepted a faculty position at New York Medical College. It was here that I became involved in some serious medical research, which quickly made me realize that I didn't know enough to do pure scientific research. So . . . armed with a United States Public Health Service Special Research Fellowship, I headed off in 1969 to Case Western Reserve University (CWRU, Cleveland, OH), from which, in 1973 (and again, under a joint program administered through both the College of Engineering and the School of Medicine), I was awarded the Ph.D. degree in Fluid, Thermal and Aerospace Sciences.

By this time, Judi and I had been married for six years, and our family had grown to include twin daughters, Patti and Cyndi. Also, my credentials now included a brief military assignment in the U.S. Army Corps of Engineers, a private pilot's license (with a Single-Engine, Land and Sea Rating), and I had become certified by the Civil Air Patrol as a trained and qualified Mission Pilot for Search and Rescue Operations.

Upon completing my Ph.D. work, I was informed by my major advisor at CWRU that the Engineering Science and Mechanics Department in the College of Engineering at Virginia Polytechnic Institute and State University (a.k.a. Virginia Tech or VPI, Blacksburg, VA) was about to launch a new program in Biomedical Engineering, and they were looking for somebody to help get the program started. He encouraged me to apply for the position, which I did, with eventual success, and following my appointment to the faculty at Virginia Tech, I developed and directed the Biomedical Engineering Program from 1973 to 1993. Then, in August of 2001, after 28 years with the University, and, ultimately, the recipient of its Distinguished W.S. "Pete" White Endowed Chair in Engineering, I retired from Virginia Tech in order to pursue full time a consulting business in the fields of

Forensic Biomechanics and Biomusical Engineering. Shortly thereafter, by a unanimous vote of the Virginia Tech Board of Visitors, I was awarded the permanent lifetime appointment of Professor Emeritus of Engineering Science and Mechanics.

My consulting career as a court-qualified expert witness in litigation matters that involve issues in Forensic Biomechanics has since acquainted me in some depth with still another profession—the field of law. Forensic Biomechanics (see *American Laboratory News* Apr 2005; 37[8]:4–6) deals with such things as accident reconstruction to assess occupant injuries in motor vehicle accidents, medical malpractice involving issues related to clinical instrumentation and medical technology, workmen's compensation claims, and complaints of work-related injuries that are litigated under the Federal Employees Liability Act (FELA). Biomusical Engineering (see Schneck DJ, Berger DS, The Music Effect: Music Physiology and Clinical Applications. London, U.K.: Jessica Kingsley Publishers, 2006) employs principles derived from the engineering sciences to study the physiologic effects on the human body of adequate stimuli embedded in the elements of music, and from such studies, to formulate a protocol and develop a corresponding medical technology that can be used effectively as a clinical intervention (therapy) in diagnosed populations.

Why, you may ask, do I relate to you the detailed saga of my life to date? Certainly, it is not to brag about my accomplishments, or to impress you with my diverse background, because, frankly, I don't take myself all that seriously. And even if I, every so often, so much as *lean* in that direction, Judi always brings things quickly back into proper perspective! (see "On the Importance of Putting Things Into Perspective, *American Laboratory* Jul 2001; 33[14]:6–8). No ... I tell you about myself to make the point that I have experienced life from very many different aspects, among them:

- Linguistic/cultural (being born in Argentina, my native language was Spanish, but I quickly learned Yiddish, since it was the language generally spoken at home between my parents, and, of course, I adopted English when we moved to the United States just as I was about to start kindergarten)

- Music (nearly 60 years and counting)
- Engineering (47+ years)
- Medicine (42+ years)
- Education and teaching (30+ years in the classroom)
- Politics and government (member and, eventually, Chairman of the Montgomery County, Virginia, School Board)
- Religion (raised in the very ethnic neighborhood of Williamsburgh in Brooklyn, NY; seven years of Hebrew School; and married to a "shiksa" [a non-Jewish girl]—hence, considerable exposure to several Christian denominations, Moslem, Hindu, etc.)
- The law (about 10 years through my legal work in the field of Forensic Biomechanics)
- Physiology
- Theoretical physics
- Applied mathematics
- Flying (on and off since age 16; private pilot's license)
- Volunteerism (hundreds of hours of service at the Cleveland [OH] Society for the Blind, Radford [Virginia] Community Hospital, and Rotary International, including being President of the Blacksburg, VA, Rotary Club)
- The publishing industry (over 260 publications, including 18 books)
- The Army (ROTC Corps of Engineers, Fort Belvoir, VA)
- Being a husband (since 1967)
- Being a father (since 1972) and, most recently (within the last four years),
- A grandfather!

Given such a broad base of discovery (I am also, and always have been, an avid sports fan/participant), it is virtually impossible for one to reflect upon all of those experiences and *not* come away having developed a unique perspective on what this thing we call "life" is all about. Over a period of time, one begins to observe sets of "common denominators," if you will, that are shared by all of the manifestations of reality in the human experience, and perhaps even beyond. One also gleans an appreciation for what is *really* important in this life: friends and family, manners and morality, ethics, education (not necessarily purely academic), *ben*evolence, common courtesy, and just plain being a *mentsch* (the Yiddish word for a very special person—one with worth, dignity, and an ethical sense that commands respect). These are as opposed to those things that, in the long run (one comes to realize), *aren't* among the most desirable attributes of a happy, healthy life (even though we often *think* they are!)— things such as power and prestige, glitz and glamour, fame and fortune, professional success, rewards and recognitions, and *mal*evolent, selfish materialism.

Thus, my telling you the details of my background is, quite simply, my way of justifying why I feel qualified to put together a volume such as this one, which proposes to formulate certain basic ideas about the whole of all human experiences. In a word, those experiences involve *searching*:

1. *Searching* for an absolute "out there"—our insatiable and perpetual thirst for knowledge and, through it, truth
2. *Searching* for an introspective "in here"—our continuous pursuit of the elusive "self," and, through it, identity
3. *Searching* for a meaningful conjointment between the "in here" and the "out there"—our need to build bridges, establish connections, pursue *purposeful* and *satisfying* social and familial relationships, and through these, achieve happiness and self-fulfillment.

Indeed, *searching*! Furthermore, the search for truth, identity, and self-fulfillment (happiness) is, in turn, constrained by four basic human needs. Two of these are purely anatomic/physiologic ones: *survival*, of the self, and of the species; the other two are purely anthropocentric: spiritual fulfillment and self-determination (i.e., control of one's own destiny). There are others, of course, and I mention several of them here and there in the editorials contained herein, but the four *basic* human needs drive just about every aspect of the human experience in a very fundamental sense. Thus, I write about one's journey through life (i.e., the *search*) within the context of these four *constraints* ("boundary conditions," if you will), which, effectively, limit the paths one can take from beginning (birth) to end (death). The 52 "search" editorials contained herein are thus grouped according to the above three broad categories: searching for knowledge and truth; searching for identity and self; searching for meaning and self-fulfillment (vaguely associated with happiness). They are then written with the understanding that what drives this search is, basically, the instinct to fulfill four fundamental human needs: survival of the self, survival of the species (sexual fulfillment), spiritual fulfillment, and self-determination.

As much as possible, I have attempted to keep these editorials upbeat and positive... Judi is my conscience in that respect, too! As you will see, she has the gift of *always* being able to find something good about any given situation (the consummate optimist!), and she tries (with modest success) to keep me on track, determined, and headed in the right direction regardless of the obstacles in the path. I would also be remiss in not expressing a deep gratitude to the thousands of students with whom I have come in contact during my career as a teacher. They, too, have always kept me honest, always willing to learn, and always *searching*—for better ways to communicate, better ways to influence them, better ways to let them influence *me*, and better ways to fulfill my role in their lives. Although I don't claim to have always been successful in those attempts, I do hope, as you read these articles, that you will:

1. Glean from them some sense of hope and encouragement
2. Realize that to be human is to fall short of perfection, but that less than 100% is *not* a failing grade—certainly not by comparison to the enormity of the human potential
3. Develop the courage to exploit that potential, bringing it to fruition, and not allowing yourself to be deterred—by *anyone* or any set of circumstances—in the pursuit of your life's dreams
4. Appreciate that there are inherent anatomical and physiological constraints, within which you can still operate quite effectively, if you learn: a) to accept those constraints as givens, and b) to develop skills that help you meet and conquer the inevitable challenges that you are destined to face in life

5. Gain perspectives that might otherwise have eluded you, especially as they relate to formulating a philosophy of what a well-balanced life is all about, and the control that you have over that balance
6. Recognize that we have so much yet to learn, and thus must always "stay teachable" and guard against delusional beliefs or opinions
7. Even laugh (or certainly smile) a time or two.

If I have succeeded in some small way in accomplishing any of the above, it will all have been worth it!

May only good things happen to you!

Dr. "Dan," 2005

Editor's Introduction

Dr. Daniel Schneck has been our editorial writer for nearly six years, and he has been widely acknowledged among the readers of the publications of International Scientific Communications for his erudition, simple wisdom, and common sense. Indeed, over the 25 years of my association with this company, I have never received so many communications from readers, both educators and scientists, expressing their appreciation for Dr. Schneck's contributions.

Our association began under very sad circumstances. Our previous editorial writer, Dr. Gabor Levy, a perceptive individual who every month shared his insight into human nature with the readers of *American Laboratory*, passed away at the end of the year 2000. Dr. Schneck had been one of Dr. Levy's devoted readers, and on reading his obituary, he contacted me, offering to take over his role. I must confess that my willingness to take on Dr. Schneck was based primarily on his appreciation of Dr. Levy's work, and on reading his first contributions, I realized that I had been truly fortunate to have found such a thoughtful individual. From that time on, I have looked forward to reading his contributions, and our subscribers clearly are equally appreciative. Just a few of their comments are printed on the back cover of this book. I am delighted to be able to make this collection of Dr. Schneck's editorials available to the scientific community. I am sure we have many readers who will be pleased to review his work at their leisure. Moreover, we look forward to reading many more years of his editorials and the comments that they elicit from our subscribers.

Brian Howard, Ph.D.
Publisher and Editor in Chief

Author's Introduction

As stated in the Preface, this book is about being human. Being human is about being less than perfect. Being less than perfect is about making mistakes. Thus, it is an inevitable consequence of being human that errors will creep in here and there as one endeavors to document one's thoughts and opinions in a work such as this. Some are errors of *commission*; others, errors of *omission*. Some are simple typographical slipups; others are of a more serious nature, affecting actual content or meaning. Some mistakes can be overlooked, on the basis of one's appreciation for the "spirit of the law," rather than its strict enforcement based on a rigorous adherence to exact detail; others, one cannot just let go, unnoticed and not requiring attention/correction. In any case, I apologize right up front for the miscues in this book that were not caught and corrected before it went to press. I expect you will find several!

One thing is for sure, though, as I quickly discovered when I inadvertently referred to a light year as a unit of time in the essay, "On the Seven Elements of Knowledge": Discriminating readers *will* definitely let you know when you have really goofed! To date, that editorial still holds the record for having generated the most reader feedback—prompting me to write a follow-up editorial, "To Err Is Human, to Forgive Divine," that addressed a highly desirable human attribute—forgiveness!

The editorial, "There Is No Such Thing as a Learning Disability, Only Teaching Disabilities," generated the second most-numerous responses. These sparked a lively debate over the pros and cons of assigning specific individuals the responsibility of educating a child and assessing his or her ability to learn. For the record, three out of every four respondents generally agreed with the points made and the issues raised in that editorial—some offering various insightful qualifying remarks and observations that were much appreciated. There was, however, a unanimous consensus that the problems associated with assessing one's ability to "learn"—especially in our K–12 educational system—are exacerbated by: a) a very narrow-minded, myopic definition of "learning," b) a tendency to label—somewhat arbitrarily—without meaningful and accurate operational criteria and guidelines, c) a "one-size-fits-all" mentality to classroom teaching, d) pitifully (almost embarrassingly) low teacher salaries, e) equally low recognition of what constitutes "effective" teaching and "standards of learning," f) unreasonably large class sizes, and g) a *serious* lack of resources! School boards: Take note!

Periodically, die-hard perfectionists are intent on bringing to my attention "who/whom, he/him, I/me, she/her . . ." issues. Whatever! And then, there are those sticklers for accuracy who remind me that: a) Columbus was *not* en route to the *West* Indies because, in his time, all that were identified were the *Indies*, period! (see "Scaling 'Unreachable' Heights"); b) Michelson was an *experimentalist*, not a *theoretician* (see "Stay Teachable!"); c) Heisenberg was *Bavarian*, not *Prussian* (see "The Physiology of Relativity"); d) Lou Holtz was *not* at Notre Dame for 27 years—he was there for only 11 years (amassing a win-lose-tie record of 100-30-2), having also spent time at Minnesota and Arkansas (see "Attitude!"); e) it's redundant to say, "two-wheeled bicycle," since, by definition, a bicycle *is* a two-wheeled vehicle (see "Physiological Accommodation") . . . and so on. Okay! Okay! I'm only human!

But, far from being offended by having these errors brought to my attention, I welcome it! First of all, it tells me that my editorials are actually being *read*, which is very satisfying. I would hate to think that all of this work is going for naught because nobody is reading it. Second, it further points out that readers are not just casually glancing at these pieces, somewhat superficially, without *digesting* the material beyond a mere scan. To catch the kinds of errors that are being singled out for comment requires some attention to detail, which I also find comforting. Third, I really appreciate one's taking the time and making the effort to educate *me*, because I always attempt to "Stay Teachable!" And, finally, such feedback gives me the opportunity to *correct* this material for future reference, which, for the sake of precision, is definitely a plus.

I also appreciate the positive feedback that compliments me on my work. It is quite gratifying when somebody thinks enough of any given editorial to take time out of a busy schedule to say nice things about something that I have written—perhaps even expressing approval of the points I make and/or thanking me for influencing him or her in a helpful way. That type of recognition, too, makes it all worth it . . . so keep those cards and letters (and e-mails and phone calls) coming!

Part I: Searching for Knowledge and Truth—The "Out There"

On the Seven Elements of Knowledge
American Laboratory News, July 2001

The word "know" has come to mean what it does today via a rather devious route, whereby the absorption of food was equated to the absorption of information. Back in ancient Aryan times (perhaps 3500 years ago), words beginning with kn- or gn- were used to describe a swelling or biting. The reference to swelling is obvious in such derived words as "knot," "knee," and "knuckle," while the reference to biting shows up in words like "gnawing" and "gnashing." Corresponding to the idea of biting and swelling were the related concepts of eating (chewing food), followed by the associated distension of the stomach (bloating) and the absorption of food therefrom. Thus, by extrapolation, if one "eats" facts (as opposed to food), the brain (as opposed to the stomach) will swell, and, if one then absorbs these facts and attaches some meaning to them, one becomes aware of whatever information was contained in those facts—nourishing the mind just as food nourishes the body. So, we have the Greek *gnōstikos* followed by the Latin *gnoscere*, which evolved into the Anglo-Saxon *cnāwan*, which later became "knawen," then "knowen," and, finally, the shortened version, "know," which has survived to date.

Therefore, to "know" is to have absorbed information that endows us with an intellectual awareness of the meaning inherent in facts, figures, and sensory inputs. For purposes of discussion, such meaning can be considered to derive from seven basic elements—pillars, if you will—that are the foundation for all we call "knowledge." These seven elements of knowledge are: frame of reference, scale of perception, resolution, structure, order, relation, and synthesis.

As was formalized by Einstein in his Theory of Relativity, no observation or measurement is absolute and totally objective. Indeed, Einstein recognized that two events that appear to be simultaneous to one observer may not appear to be so to another observer, or, in other words, that time passes at different rates in different reference frames. Stated still another way, one cannot separate the measurement from the measurer—the observer, and the frame of reference on which the observation is being made. A simple example that illustrates this point involves me being seated in a vehicle traveling northbound at 60 miles per hour, and you being seated in another vehicle traveling parallel to mine at exactly the same speed in exactly the same direction. To me, you look to be quite stationary and not moving at all, whereas to a pedestrian standing still on the side of the road, we both appear to be cruising by rather rapidly. That's the essence of frame of reference and relativity: All knowledge is, in fact, dependent on the observer to which it is referred and there is really no such thing as an absolute reality. In the words of the famous writer Anäis Nin (known for her poetic style), "We don't see things as they are, we see them as we are." In other words, we are the ultimate instrument of knowing, the ultimate frame of reference, and "All our knowledge has its origins in our perceptions" (Leonardo da Vinci). Diane Ackerman, in her 1990 book entitled, *A Natural History of the Senses* (Random House, New York), explains it this way: "When scientists, philosophers, and other commentators speak of the real world, they're talking about a myth, a convenient fiction. The world is a construct the brain builds based on the sensory information it's given, and the information is only a small part of all that's available.... Evolution didn't overload us with unnecessary abilities . . .. We're given only the sensory information crucial to our survival—although . . . we can modify our sense and broaden that sensory horizon with technological amplifying devices."

Going one step further, what we see in our space/time continuum depends entirely on the level at which we are looking, the scale of perception. That scale can range in space from subnuclear dimensions hypothetically approaching zero length to supercosmic expanses hypothetically reaching out to infinite lengths and, in time, from miniscule fractions of a nanosecond approaching zero duration to huge time scales approaching light years* and on out to infinity. In turn, at each level of perception, we can only narrow down our observations—fine-tune them—to whatever extent we can discriminate as being separate, two adequate stimuli that are experienced very close to one another in space and/or in time. This fact is embedded in the concept of resolution—the ability that an anatomical sense organ or technological transducer has to distinguish as two individual pieces of information inputs that arrive extremely close to one another, either spatially or temporally.

Structure deals with the attributes that characterize a particular manifestation of reality that we want to know about. One may think of these attributes as the individual pieces of a jigsaw puzzle or the ingredients of a cake (flour, water, yeast, eggs, milk, and so on). The process of knowing—within the constraints imposed by frame of reference, scale of perception, and resolution—generally begins by impregnating (swelling) the brain with pieces of information that presumably define the individual elements that make up the whole of

*Recognizing that it was an error to refer to light years as a unit of time rather than distance, this issue was addressed in the editorial on page 186.

anything we want to know about. From this plethora of information, one then attempts to derive, usually by inductive reasoning, some order to what has been absorbed. The process is not unlike putting the individual pieces of a jigsaw puzzle together properly to form the entire picture. Order deals with the sequencing and arranging of structure (information) in time and space so that we may eventually, for example, extract meaning from words put together to form a sentence, sentences put together to form a paragraph, paragraphs put together to form chapters, and chapters put together to create a book.

The extraction of meaning is what relation deals with, and the process follows specific Gestalt Laws that govern the perceptual organization and management of sensory information. In a nutshell, these laws define our instinct to minimize confusion; make order out of chaos; and create the most stable, consistent, and meaningful interpretation of sensory stimuli, so that we can react most effectively in response to those stimuli. Thus, individual elements of an adequate stimulus that are spatially or temporally close to one another—even if we can resolve them as two separate inputs—are perceived to belong to a single unit or figure, i.e., to form conjugate clusters (this is known as sensory grouping); such grouping is further justified if the adequate stimuli share common features or are otherwise comparable in the attributes that define them. Going one step further, if consecutive individual elements of an adequate stimulus are perceived to follow one another in the same direction, they tend also to be grouped together, i.e., to form vectored clusters (this has to do with sensory tracking), and, when a physical space or region is enclosed by, or otherwise bounded by, a continuous closed curve, it tends to be perceived as a self-contained figure (this is known as the Law of Closure). The bottom line is that relation deals with how well we can extract similarities, connections, and/or affiliations from among the ordered pieces of information so that, once assembled, we can tell what our jigsaw puzzle is all about. This element of knowledge also deals with coordinating structure and synchronizing the ordered elements so that their ability to perform the functions for which they were intended is clear to us, and we are able to define those functions uniquely.

Finally, having gone through the cognitive processes of structuring, ordering, and extracting relations, as constrained by our frame of reference, scale of perception, and ability to resolve sensory inputs, the final step in knowing is synthesis, derived from the Greek *syn*, which means "alike, together with," and *thesis*, which means "a proposition." Thus, synthesis deals with our ability to combine into a whole everything we know in bits and pieces; how well we can organize and assemble into a self-consistent, meaningful, reproducible, logical entity the entire body of information that relates to whatever it is we want to know about; how well we understand this body of information; how well we can, by deductive reasoning, derive meaningful conclusions from this body of information; and how well the body of information, and the conclusions drawn from it, stand up to the test of time. If there is a coherency and consistency to the information, then we can truly call it a "body of knowledge."

The Seven Rudimentary Axioms of Reality

American Laboratory, December 2001

In William Shakespeare's *Hamlet*, Act III, Scene I, the Prince of Denmark exclaims, "To be, or not to be? That is the question." Interpreting broadly those ten short words, one could infer that the Bard of Avon was thereby summing up our eternal quest to understand the most elusive of all the mysteries of "Science"—namely, where did all of this come from? How does (or how can) something become manifest as reality? Even more basic than that, in the beginning, how could something have presumably been manufactured from nothing? From where do concepts such as "time," "space," and "matter" derive? By what magic, process, or miracle was reality created? For many, the answer to these questions of creation is, simply, "God." Others are not satisfied by this answer, adding further, "Where did he/she or it (God) come from?" What was it that originally produced a transcendence from "nothing" to "something?"—for in the very beginning, wasn't there, indeed, nothing? And do we not now have, in fact, something?

The issues raised above are addressed by a branch of philosophy known as ontology. From the Greek *onto-*, meaning "being," and the suffix "-ology," derived from *logos*, which means, "a discourse" (referring to a complete single treatment of the entire body of knowledge associated with the corresponding prefix to which it is attached), the field of ontology concerns itself with the study of being, as a process, such as the process of creating something out of nothing. Indeed, this process has fascinated, challenged, and even frustrated scientists since the "beginning" of "time" (since we have yet to formulate any promising definitive and comprehensive theories to explain it all). "Reality" (or "being") is defined as a state of actual existence (or occurrence), rather than merely apparent, imaginary, fictitious, ideal, or hypothetical. Taking this definition one step further, "existing in fact (actual)" means, "capable of being perceived and/or measured by stimulating some anatomic sense organ (not necessarily human) or technological transducer; and/or, capable of being ultimately conceived by the self-excitation of some intuitive sense." But these definitions are not very satisfying because if you study them closely, you will note that they are less definitive of reality than they are descriptive of this phenomenon—just paraphrasing the concept; using different ways to say the same thing. Such attempts to give verbal expression to vague sensory experiences illustrate how inadequate language is as a means for communicating what is basically unknown. Invariably, something gets lost in the less-than-rigorous translation.

For example, what does "state of actual existence" really mean? What do we mean by "perceptible," "measurable," or "conceivable?" And to whom, or to what, is this "state of actual existence" apparent? To what frame of reference is this state being related, and at what scale of perception? In other words, does it necessarily follow that the concept of reality must be attached to an observer? I'm sure we have all been asked at one time or another, "If a tree falls in the forest, and if there is nobody around to hear it, does it actually make a crashing sound as it hits the ground?" And how about this one: "Can there be some type of reality 'out there,' independent of our innate ability to perceive or conceive of it, perhaps even beyond our ability to ever even know about or measure it (as is professed by agnostics)? Or, is reality just a construct of our imagination and cognitive resources, embedded entirely in the senses, the mind, and our own intuition (as is professed by solipsists: You are because I say you are.)? Or is reality all of the above?"

The bottom line is that there are no answers to the above questions because we have not been endowed—anatomically or physiologically—with the ability to know everything! As a result, in order to even begin talking about reality in any sense, we must first introduce at least seven axioms that must be accepted as given—self-evident premises that are taken to be true without formal proof in order that we may have a starting point from which to move forward. Indeed, the very word "axiom" derives from the Greek *axioma*, which means "worthy, valuable, divine, admirable, beyond human"; it thus connotes well-established tenets that remain hitherto unviolated, even though they are accepted purely on that basis, i.e., that no "exceptions to the rule" have ever been identified—despite the fact that the "rule" (axiom) persists with no rigorous deductive proof or confirmation—it just works.

Keeping that in mind, I propose the following seven rudimentary axioms as essential to our understanding of the concept of reality; axioms that basically address the fundamental issues of who, what, where, why, when, and how, but use "p's" more than they do "w's" (purely for convenience):

1. The axiom of *potential* defines energy as an inherent property of anything that endows it with the ability to be "realized" in the sense defined earlier. Note that "energy" is a concept invented by human minds to explain the world as we experience it in various forms. We don't have a clue as to what it is (hence the need for this axiom), except that it is responsible for everything we are capable of perceiving at various scales of perception.

2. The axiom of *perpetualness* asserts that energy can neither be created nor destroyed; it can only be converted from one form into another. This conservation principle was not derived based on rigorous physical or mathematical theories (hence, again, the need for this axiom); it is a human-made conceptualization that allows us to solve problems that would otherwise be intractable, and it is a unifying concept that brings some sense of order to our existence—an order that, to date, remains unviolated.

3. The axiom of *provenance* admits that the source of the energy from which all of reality derives is indeterminate. In one sense, this axiom actually forms the basis for all religions, wherein faith—acceptance without proof—prevails over fact (as Anna so aptly explains to the King of Siam in the musical *The King and I*).

4. The axiom of *process* further confirms that how the energy from which all of reality derives was created from nothing is indefinable. This axiom takes axiom 3 one step further by saying, "Not only do we not know where this energy came from, but we also don't know how it was derived from something that did not exist in the first place—nada, zilch, total emptiness!"

5. The axiom of *perception* implies that we cannot measure directly the potential state in which exists the energy source from which all of reality derives; we can only experience kinetic states that derive

from potential states. This axiom has caused numerous confrontations between me and my physics colleagues, and may be the subject of a future editorial, but for now, I stick to my basic assertion that we can only perceive and/or measure movement, i.e., kinetic energy. We can work backwards to figure out and quantify the potential energy from which the kinetic energy was derived, but we cannot measure the former directly.

6. The axiom of *periodicity* claims that energy is cyclic, both large scale and small, in its regular manifestations from some indeterminate reservoir. "What goes around, comes around" is basically what this axiom says. We know it to be true for the fundamental vibrational states of numerous types of mechanical, chemical, and electromagnetic energy. This axiom goes one step further in claiming that periodicity is a fact of life for anything and everything, even though it may not appear to us to be so, if the period of the associated energy is quite large compared with time scales associated with the human experience.

7. And finally, the axiom of *purpose* declares that we are incapable of knowing absolutely what is the ultimate intent of all of the manifestations of the various forms of energy. This axiom, together with axioms 3 and 4, is actually the basis for the fundamental human drive for spiritual fulfillment, third only to the fundamental drives for survival of the self and survival of the species (the drive for sexual fulfillment).

So there you have it—my seven rudimentary axioms of reality and much food for thought, discussion, and future editorials.

The Seven Fundamental Laws of Reality

American Laboratory, June 2002

In Old English, the word *lagu* is derived from an earlier Scandinavian word that conveyed a sense of order—a layering of sorts; everything in its place. Thus, especially in the realm of physics, we think of laws (from *lagu*) as immutable concepts from which one can derive rational explanations for everything that we experience in our universe (such experience being defined here as "reality"). Taken together, laws comprise a rigorous set of rules that enable us to order our observations; to layer them in some logical sequence from which one can then establish relationships, synthesize theories, and predict outcomes. It may be convenient to organize all of reality into a set of seven fundamental laws that form the basis for all that we are capable of experiencing—political, social, spiritual, economical, chemical, and so on. In other words, the seven laws discussed briefly below are not necessarily confined strictly to the realm of science, but, more generally, they allow us to develop a paradigm (even better, a more rigorous feedback/feedforward control model) that can be used to explain everything that's going on in our existence. (See "Equilibrium," *American Laboratory* Jan 2002; 34[1]:6–8.) With this in mind, consider the following seven Laws of Reality:

1. *The Law of Provocation.* This first law asserts that all of what we experience derives from the unbalanced disturbance of quasi-equilibrated states of existence. Examples of disturbances include wars and revolutions (in history); resultant force-couple systems (in mechanics); plagues, epidemics, and disease processes (in medicine); and new inventions or discoveries in any discipline. In the arts, we define various periods (Middle Ages, Renaissance, Baroque, Classical, Romantic, Contemporary, and so on), the transition from one to the next being characterized by an innovative concept, a novel idea, an updated, groundbreaking technology, a more progressive approach, a modernized technique—some disturbance to the then-existing state of the art. In the economy, we speak of earnings reports, interest rates, corporate profits, productivity, gross domestic product, and unemployment rates, all of which fluctuate and thereby disturb existing states of affair. In government, we hold elections to change administrations and redistribute power; in meteorology, we speak of winter and summer storms, blizzards, earthquakes, tornadoes, and hurricanes. In our own personal lives, we demarcate and subsequently reminisce about milestones that are really disturbances—graduations, job changes, marriage, parenting, deaths in the family, geographic relocations, and so on. Indeed, in every aspect of our existence, one is always able to define some prevailing quasi-equilibrated state, some current, but not permanent situation (the *controlled system* in our feedback/feedforward control model) that gets somehow provoked to change to a newly equilibrated state. The ability of this system to respond to that provocation (which, in the language of anatomical sense organs, is called an adequate stimulus) is addressed by the second fundamental Law of Reality.

2. *The Law of Potential.* This second law states that the ability to become real derives, in turn, from an attribute with which quasi-equilibrated states are endowed: namely, potential energy, or if you will, "implicit reality," *capable* of being. Potential energy is what allows a quasi-equilibrated state to respond to any given disturbance. That is to say, for each type of disturbance that we can identify in our realm of existence, there is a corresponding potential energy function; if a controlled system is endowed with that particular type of potential energy, then it will be capable of responding to the corresponding disturbance (or adequate stimulus), thereby making us aware of it. Moreover, we become aware of it because the potential energy gets converted into kinetic energy, which is the only type of energy we can perceive, as formalized by the third Law of Reality.

3. *The Law of Propagation.* This law states that our ability to perceive reality—to experience (through stimulation of an anatomical sense organ or excitation of a technological transducer) the fact that a quasi-equilibrated state has been disturbed and is in some sense transitioning to a newly equilibrated state—derives from the movement created by such disturbance. Thus, this law defines kinetic energy as a property of what might be called "explicit reality," or "being." In our generic feedback/feedforward control model of reality, kinetic energy would actually represent the output signal of the controlled system, which we experience as primary dimensions of perception (such as electric charge and temperature), depending on the corresponding scale of observation. (See "On the Seven Elements of Knowledge," *American Laboratory News* Jul 2001; 33[15]:4.) Moreover, by extrapolation, one may further conclude from this law that, because of the movement associated with kinetic energy, disturbances to quasi-equilibrated states of existence do not tend to remain self-contained and localized, but rather, they radiate outward, away from the source of the disturbance—thus establishing the concept of space, and the primary dimension of perception, length, by which we define and quantify it. But is the conversion of potential energy into kinetic energy instantaneous? The fourth Law of Reality addresses this issue.

4. *The Law of Perseverance.* This law answers "no" to the above question by stipulating that the conversion of imperceptible potential energy into perceptible kinetic energy (and vice versa) always meets with a resistance to such change—a desire to maintain the status quo—such that the response is neither spontaneous nor instantaneous. This law

essentially defines *inertia* as a property of quasi-equilibrated states of existence, such that the response of the controlled system to an unbalanced disturbance is momentarily delayed, thus establishing the concept of time as a primary dimension of perception. The momentary pause corresponds to an imperceptible metastable state of equilibrium (an "acceleration" phase of the system response), during which potential energy is converted into kinetic energy, leading to an eventual, perceptible velocity phase of the response that will result in the controlled system transitioning (the perceptible "displacement" phase of the response) to a new state of quasi-equilibrium. Laws of Reality 5 and 6 address two fundamental principles that govern the transition process.

5. *The Law of Purgation.* This law states that in a generic, global sense, the conversion of potential energy into kinetic energy is essentially irreversible. Two factors contribute to this irreversibility: a gradual increase (due to disorganized randomness) in the number of possible paths available for the system to transition from one state to another (in the limit, approaching an infinite number of options, leading to ultimate gridlock); and a gradual decrease (due to dissipation) in the amount of kinetic energy that is available to be converted back into potential energy (in the limit, approaching zero, thereby making a return trip impossible). The randomness of the former increases the likelihood that the system will not be able to find its way back to wherever it came from; the wastefulness of the latter leads to ultimate decay—the universe is winding down, attenuating, moving farther and farther away from its original, purely potential state (wherein everything was totally organized and at least hypothetically possible), and closer and closer to a final, purely random kinematic state (wherein all possibilities have been exhausted and coexist, but which is totally disorganized). However, the *rate* at which this movement toward ultimate dissipation is occurring is *not* random, as suggested in the next law.

6. *The Law of Prudence.* This law constrains the Law of Purgation by requiring that the rate at which the universe is winding down be minimized. In other words, all conversions of energy will tend to follow a path of least resistance, thereby dissipating as little energy as is necessary to get from point A to point B. This law essentially establishes optimization and economization schemes as properties of energy conversion. In terms of our generic feedback/feedforward control model, one can envision that these schemes are embedded as the *controlling system* of the model, which uses minimum-energy

criteria (reference set points) to govern how an existing quasi-equilibrated state of reality will transition to a newly equilibrated state in response to a net disturbance. Thus, although the end is inevitable, the means to that end is limited by an attempt to minimize the randomness and dissipation of the in-between processes—to delay the inevitable!

7. *The Law of Periodicity*. This law asserts that the universe (not necessarily as we know it) will eventually be wound up again, reestablishing its order, making all of the kinetic energy once again potential, and making all things once again possible. That we do not know the "who-what-when-where-why-and-how" of it makes this law somewhat axiomatic, but as a principle of reality, it seems to fit our understanding that energy can neither be created nor destroyed, and that cyclic phenomena are inherent to all of our experiences with various forms of energy. (See "The Seven Rudimentary Axioms of Reality," *American Laboratory* Dec 2001; 33[24]:6–8.) In fact, this law takes us right back to the first law, the Law of Provocation, which then sends us once again through the whole sequence of laws in infinite periodic repetitions. So, indeed, everything old is new again, and what goes around comes around.

Seven Axiomatic Foundations of Analysis

American Laboratory, July 2004

In our perpetual quest to know all, there are certain givens that have to be accepted at face value. These are self-evident axioms, principles taken to be true without formal proof or hard evidence to answer questions like What?, Why?, and How? Indeed, if the validity of axioms is challenged, the standard rebuttal is: Since the truisms have yet to fail, and accepting them is prerequisite to moving off of square one in our efforts to formulate solutions to problems, why not accept them and move forward from there? Sounds good to me.

In a previous editorial (*American Laboratory* Dec 2001; 33[24]:6–8) I drafted seven rudimentary axioms that I consider to be essential for our being able to understand the concept of reality as it relates to the various forms of energy by which we experience it. It now seems appropriate to introduce seven more axioms, to provide an essential basis for our being able to analyze that reality. Such analyses require that we consider three things (from which the axioms are derived): First, we need to develop formulations that are consistent with the space–time environment in which our reality is experienced; second, these formulations must be as objective as possible, within the constraints imposed by the first three elements of knowledge: frame of reference, scale of perception, and resolution (see *American Laboratory News* Jul 2001; 33[15]:4); and third, the formulations must not violate any fundamental laws of nature, such that the solutions that derive from them are physically realizable. In other words, they can actually (as opposed to theoretically or hypothetically) be experienced through stimulation of an anatomical sense organ and/or excitation of some technological transducer.

Thus, as it relates to time, the axiom of causality asserts that a) there is no effect without a cause (an unbalanced disturbance of a quasi-equilibrated state of existence), and b) the cause always precedes (in time) the effect (i.e., the subsequent conversion of imperceptible potential energy into perceived kinetic energy). This axiom ties the past to the present, and introduces the associated principle of determinism. Determinism professes the doctrine that all of perceived reality (including human behavior) is the inevitable result of antecedant causes. Nothing happens spontaneously or instantaneously, although the identifiable cause is often elusive. Current actions are influenced by past deeds and every phenomenon is invariably determined by a history or sequence of events that led up to it. The attributes of a current state of affairs are not independent of incidents experienced previously; cause and effect are conjugate pairs. The axiom of causality is the basis for the Buddhist and Hindu notion of karma (from the Sanskrit word for "deed"), which asserts that the fate (destiny or kismet) of a person in a current state of existence is predetermined by acts, words, thoughts, and deeds that date back to that person's existence in a previous life, from which his or her soul has been reincarnated.

Speaking of fate takes us to the other extreme in time: the future, and to the corresponding axiom of predestination. This axiom asserts that, although causes precede effects in time, the causes themselves are influenced by events that have yet to transpire but are inevitable (predestined). Thus, both the future (a differential response) and the past (an integral response) determine the present. At first, this axiom seems difficult to defend because, whereas we have an inherent sense for the concept of cause and effect, the idea of not being in total control of our own destiny is intuitively hard to swallow. Upon further reflection, however, this idea may not be as remote as it initially appears.

For example, think back over your own life and note that many of the things you did, at what was then the present, were, in retrospect, actually done in anticipation of what you expected the future to hold in store for you. Whether you realized it or not, the "future" was, indeed, affecting the present. Whether or not you were conscious of it at the time, hindsight has since revealed that it was a future over which you had less control than you might have thought, or liked. Things like parental pressure, social pressure, unforeseen (to you) circumstances, surprise forks in the road, coincidences, unanticipated consequences of key decisions you thought you were making independently of any outside influences, and so on, all allowed "destiny" to strike when you least suspected it. But destiny may be just another way of saying that the future is governed by the laws of chance, which, in turn, reflect the number of degrees of freedom that are available for a disturbed system to transition from one quasi-equilibrated state A to some newly equilibrated state B. The most probable destination B of such a transition will invariably be the one that can be arrived at by the greatest number of possible paths. If we were smart enough to uniquely define all states of A and B, all possible routes between them, and all potential obstacles to be encountered along these paths, we could then apply the laws of chance (assuming we knew them!) properly, so that, to a reasonable degree of probability, we could predict that inevitable future.

Consider further that nature is full of examples of materials whose very response characteristics allow them to anticipate what is going to happen to them and, based on that "premonition," gives them the ability to be proactive rather than reactive to that anticipated event. For instance, automobile shock absorbers, responding to their rate of deformation (a differential response), are able to generate a resisting force before (proactive) the bump in the road causes the vehicle to bounce (a reaction). Thus, what we commonly call foresight averts an impending problem, which also introduces the associated principle of prescience. This principle postulates a knowledge of things before they happen or come into existence, again, perhaps, because they are governed by predictable laws of chance or by differential material response characteristics.

Could it be that those prophets who profess the ability to see into the future (such as psychic mediums) somehow have this physiologic ability to be proactive (i.e., respond to rates of change) rather than reactive? Your guess is as good as mine. But even as credible a scientific theory as the *transactional interpretation* of quantum mechanics predicts that the future communicates with the present. This is similar to the upstream reflection of waves propagating back in time to "warn" the oncoming fluid that it is about to encounter downstream geometric discontinuities in branching tube configurations, or the ability of a bat to respond to reflections received from its sonar-perceived environment. It seems that a quantum state, too, has the ability to respond to corresponding quantum waves that propagate forward from the present into the future and reflect backward from the future to the present to affect that quantum state. In fact, this transactional interpretation has allowed quantum scientists to explain several paradoxical results that could not be otherwise reconciled. Apparently, quantum states, too, can "see into the future."

Finally, some rather interesting studies have suggested that, due to a time delay in cerebral processing of sensory input, a person is actually subconsciously aware of a physical sensation (i.e., has already reacted to it) a full 500 msec before the brain is able to bring that information to consciousness, a phenomenon known as delay and antedating. In other words, the brain, too, can see into the future, recognizing that you will *think* something is happening to you now, when, in fact, the event has already transpired, and your body has already, subconsciously, responded to it! Thus, the brain knows that you will consciously perceive an event in the future of that event, and so it backdates that consciousness to a point 500 msec earlier. Result: You think that you are experiencing the sensory stimulation and reacting to it all at the same time, a form of the future (the conscious response) affecting the present (subconscious response). Delay and antedating introduces more generally the concept of processing, storing, and recalling information, which brings us to axiom number three, involving the time domain.

In a practical sense, it is difficult if not impossible to be all-inclusive in trying to formulate analyses that take into account the distant past and/or the distant future. Thus, analytical investigations, especially in continuum mechanics, frequently invoke the axiom of memory to constrain the first two time axioms, such that only the recent past and the immediate future are accounted for. This axiom is based on the assertion that we have, at best, only a limited ability to see into the future (i.e., most responses are indeed reactive, not proactive), and we can, realistically, only recall accurately the recent past (the so-called Principle of Fading Memory). Thus, the axiom of memory reduces the doubly infinite time domain into a smaller neighborhood around "now," arbitrarily defined on the basis of a number of considerations that are beyond the scope of this editorial. A word of caution is in order, however: If the axiom of memory is applied indiscriminately, as it often is in establishing physical and physiologic cause–effect relationships (the old Latin *post hoc, ergo propter hoc* pitfall: "after this, therefore, as a result of this"), serious misleading non sequiturs can often result.

The axiom of memory, as it relates to time, goes hand-in-hand with a corresponding axiom of neighborhood, as it relates to space. That is to say, the axiom of neighborhood allows one to distinguish between at-a-distance field forces and at-a-point contact forces. The stipulation is, however, that except in the case of field forces, most interactions among things (humans included) are influenced mostly by what is going on in an arbitrarily small neighborhood immediately around them (a sphere of influence, which also has associated with it a corresponding principle of local action). In physics, whether or not an interaction is long range or short range, in the sense of the axiom of neighborhood, has to do also with the related concept of the inertial mass, m, associated with that interaction. If m is relatively small, then from Einstein's $E = mc^2$ (the speed of light, c, being constant and frame-indifferent in a vacuum), so is energy, E. Furthermore, from the principle of Planck, $E\tau = h$ = constant, if E is relatively small, the corresponding time period, τ, of the interaction (the time it has to be "influential") must therefore be relatively large (or, equivalently, the frequency of the energy must be very small). But, since wavelength, $\lambda = c\tau$, for τ large and c constant, the effective region of influence, λ, of the interaction is also large (it has more time to spread out further), and so the influence is said to act "at a distance." In the limit, for m approaching zero, l approaches infinity, and we are left with field forces such as gravity and electromagnetism that, with effectively zero inertial mass and little inherent energy, can be experienced at great distances from their originating source. Going the other way, as m approaches infinity, λ approaches zero, and we are left with extremely high-frequency energy (like nuclear strong forces) that dissipates rapidly ("fading memory") over very short distances. Various forms of contact stresses, whose sphere of influence is appreciable only when distances involved are on the order of the separation of molecules (the so-called mean-free path), also act in conformity with the principle of local action and thus, too, obey the axiom of neighborhood.

To the above four space–time axioms we add three more, addressing objectivity, admissibility, and realizability. Quite simply, the axiom of objectivity formalizes the fact that, if I hit you over the head with a sledgehammer, the response of your skull to that blow is an absolute event. Thus, if witnesses are to describe that event accurately, their account of what you experienced must be purely objective, not dependent on who observed it, their respective frame of reference, or their particular vantage point. Your head reacted the way it did, period! A change of observer, frame of reference, and/or scale of perception will not alter the outcome; it must leave the event itself unaffected. Indeed, coordinate systems are human-made inventions that offer convenient ways to quantify our space–time domain of existence, but in so doing, they must not change the physics of what happened, which is what the axiom of objectivity demands. Real physical events are not "aware" of (and do not care) what particular coordinate system happens to be employed to describe those events. Thus, to ensure that the physics and the math are self-consistent, any equations that are formulated to quantify absolute physical phenomena or material behavior must also satisfy the associated principle of frame-indifference, i.e., they must take the same form and predict the same outcome, regardless of the coordinate system in which they are defined.

Taking this reasoning one step further, and allowing for a wide diversity of mathematical formulations, the axiom of admissibility requires that such formulations a) be dimensionally homogeneous (i.e., apples = apples and oranges = oranges), and b) not violate any known and accepted laws of nature, such as conservation of mass, energy, linear- and-angular momentum, and so on. While this stipulation might seem obvious, the fact is that in the esoteric world of abstract mathematics, there do arise occasions when the math can be inconsistent with the physics or, theoretically at least, can predict events (such as violations of the Second Law of Thermodynamics or discontinuous behavior of terms like $1/r$ as r goes to zero) that are not in conformity with accepted laws of nature. The axiom of admissibility suggests that such inconsistencies be discarded as being unrealistic, which leads us to the last of these seven axioms: the axiom of just setting. This axiom requires that, when all is said and done, mathematical formulations of physical events must yield well-posed, physically realizable solutions, uniquely consistent with the given boundary, initial, and compatibility conditions that constrain them. In other words, what is predicted must be capable of being physically realized in some sense, not just "hypothetical." Believe it or not, this axiom has only been satisfied in the very simplest of limiting cases. Mathematically, we scientists are good at dealing with "perfect" gases, Hookean-elastic (linear) solids, Newtonian (linear) fluids, perfectly elastic collisions among "hard" particles, extremes of variables such as temperature and pressure, situations that are clearly black and white and fundamentally quite routine, and we claim a modest degree of success in those that represent slight perturbations around the norm. Experimentally, we do somewhat better, but in the in-between gray areas, we have a huge way to go, especially when it comes to applying these axioms to the study of humans (physiology, behavior, medicine, etc.) and the variables that affect them. More on the latter in a future piece.

Pro or Con or . . . Neither?
American Laboratory News, February 2003

In my consulting career, I have been called upon several times to provide expert biomechanical testimony in litigation involving carpal tunnel syndrome. In each hand, the carpal tunnel is formed by the eight wrist bones (carpals) curled along the bottom and sides of the wrist (with the joint in supination, or palm up) and a ligament (the flexor retinaculum) that spans across the remaining top (palm) side of the wrist. Among the anatomical structures passing through the region thus enclosed (the "tunnel") are the median nerve, some muscle tendons that flex the wrist and fingers, and a few blood vessels that serve the hand. Compression of the median nerve produces tingling and numbness in the fingers, non-specific aches and pains in the hand, and a variety of other symptoms (such as weakened grip strength), all grouped into the clinical condition known as carpal tunnel syndrome. Right up front, I will tell you that the specific etiology of this syndrome is unknown. That being the case, the often-insinuated possibility that it is a work-related "cumulative strain" disorder is entirely ill-defined, a fact complicated still further by the virtually endless list of confounding factors that are associated with both the development and progression of this affliction of the wrist.

But that's exactly the point: When we really don't know a whole lot about something, many speculative theories abound. Everybody has an opinion about what might be happening; unsubstantiated misconceptions and non sequiturs (tantamount to old wives' tales) often prevail, and the peer-reviewed literature on the subject turns into a cluttered mess of voluminous material that is more confusing than conclusive.

For example, the last time I did a Web search on carpal tunnel syndrome, I got 646,028 hits. When I narrowed the search considerably by going to the National Library of Medicine's *PubMed* Web site, I managed to reduce that number to 4709 "recent" citations, some advocating the work-relatedness of carpal tunnel syndrome, others poohpoohing the idea, and most of them admitting that we really don't know for sure.

This situation, like so many others involving things we are not sure of, reminds me of a relevant scene from the musical comedy, *Fiddler on the Roof* (1964, based on the book by Joseph Stein). The show's central character, Tevye, finds himself discussing with a group of his townsfolk the pros and cons of knowing what is going on in the world outside of their little village of Anatevka. "Why should I break my head about the outside world? Let the outside world break its own head!" declares one of Tevye's colleagues. "He's right," says our hero to those gathered around him. But the young student and aspiring social reformer, Perchik, violently disagrees, exclaiming, "You can't close your eyes to what's happening in the world!" Tevye pauses for a moment, looks around at his audience, then concurs: "He's right, too." Hearing this, a disgruntled onlooker protests. "*He's* right," says the challenger, pointing to the first commentator, "and *he's* right" (pointing to Perchik). "They can't *both* be right!" Tevye, appearing very contemplative, looks directly at the protestor and proclaims, "You know . . . you are also right!" So much for differing opinions.

In one of my cases, I was presented with an impressive, 180-page review of the scientific literature, in which 425 publications were offered to substantiate the allegation that there are specific biomechanical "risk factors" associated with corresponding activities in particular occupations—work-related risk factors that place an individual in jeopardy of developing carpal tunnel syndrome. Proponents of this concept argue that activities that involve repetitive wrist flexion, with the wrist in chronic pronation and deviated toward the ulna (i.e., "awkward" postures), where "forceful" gripping (i.e., "excessive exertion") may be required, under possibly extreme environmental conditions (such as cold), if engaged in for significant periods of time will definitely place the worker at risk for developing the syndrome. Also implicated are exposure of the wrist to chronic low-frequency vibration and activities involving extensional "pinching" motions and/or fine finger movements, like operating typewriter and computer keyboards.

The list of industries that place workers at risk in the above-defined sense is rather exhaustive, including automotive, garment, major appliance manufacturing, music, aircraft, fishing, meat packing, electronics, forest, domestic/cleaning, railroad (by implication in the cited review, not specifically referenced), heavy equipment, bearing manufacturing, supermarket, foundries, medical . . . have I left any out? (In fact, few industries were spared.) Equally impressive was the list of "risky" activities, numbering over 30 and including everything from drilling rocks to laying bricks, knitting, operating staple guns, typing, working on an assembly line, and making shoes. You name it—it was listed as an occupational risk. But risk of what?

Well, again, we're not entirely sure. One theory says that the risk involves cumulative microtrauma to delicate muscle tissue, with consequent swelling and inflammation of the tendons that pass through the carpal tunnel, such that they might ultimately compress the nerves that pass through it. Sounds plausible enough (Tevye's first commentator), but another says, "No, that's not it. The real problem lies in using tools (like traditional scissor handles) that directly compress the nerves in the hand." Okay, we might be tempted to buy that argument until still another one asserts that it is not a problem of nerve compression at all; it's not even a neurological issue—in fact, it's a vascular problem. Citing how often "carpal tunnel release" surgery fails to resolve this pathologic condition, some observers claim that this is because the condition is one in which bulging muscles induce extravascular compression that obstructs the free flow of blood through the vasculature that supplies the wrist. Such impedance to flow leads to an ischemia that eventually damages the nerves and tendons coursing through the carpal tunnel. Whatever the real pathological mechanism might be, at this point in the deliberations, Tevye would be inclined to say of the proponents of the work-relatedness of carpal tunnel syndrome, "You know, they're right, and they seem to have the evidence to prove it."

But wait: Chances are, one in every five of you reading this editorial right now is suffering (or has suffered) from carpal tunnel syndrome, regardless of what you do for a living. Moreover, there is no definitive evidence that this 20% incidence rate in the general population as a whole is significantly exceeded in the workforce of any given occupation, which is to say, if you're gonna get it, you're gonna get it, no matter what. Sixty-three percent of you will be afflicted in only your dominant hand, 20% will experience the problem only in your other hand, and only 17% of you will have both hands affected. The probability is also very high that, of those of you who are encumbered with this unfortunate condition, two out of every three to as many as 10 out of every 11 are middle-aged, postmenopausal women, and odds are that it most likely runs in your family.

All of these observations explain why another review that I came across, of comparable length with an equal number of literature citations, made the point that evidence for the work-relatedness of carpal tunnel syndrome was meager, at best, and not at all conclusive in a rigorous, scientific method sense (see Schneck DJ. "Koch's Postulates." *American Laboratory News* Feb 2002; 34[4]:4). The authors of this second review argue that those afflicted with this syndrome actually had an anatomical predisposition to develop it, perhaps due to an abnormal presence of too many muscle fibers within the carpal tunnel, and/or to an enlarged median nerve, and/or to carpal tunnel stenosis, and/or to a very high carpal-tunnel-contents-volume to carpal-tunnel-volume ratio (i.e., a very small canal compared with its contents), and/or to vascular perfusion problems in the region of the carpal tunnel, and so on (another long list). Additional confounding factors (contributing variables that cloud the issue of causation) include such things as sex (the increased incidence in postmenopausal women suggesting a possible hormonal connection), age (in those with a predisposition to the condition, the natural aging process makes it inevitable), a history of gynecological surgery (hysterectomy and oophorectomy), psychosocial factors (including anxiety/depression), a history of wrist fracture and/or bone dislocation, systemic conditions that result in edema (fluid retention), diseases such as diabetes, weight (obesity), manual dexterity, and family history (genetics). Again, the list goes on and on, which is why carpal tunnel syndrome is described clinically as being idiopathic, which means "a disease of unknown cause."

So, to those who do not believe that carpal tunnel syndrome is a work-related issue, Tevye would say, as he did to Perchik, "You are right, too, and you seem to have the evidence to prove it." To those out there who would question how one group could be right when they expressed views on this subject that are diametrically opposed to those expressed by another group declared to be right, Tevye would say to them, "You know, you're right, too." And in all three cases, he would be right, because when it comes to issues about which we know little, "You pay your money, and you take your choice." There are plenty of studies out there to support whatever position you choose to take. Those of us who have been around long enough to know that statistically based investigations can be judiciously manipulated (shall we say) to make whatever point one is trying to make also know enough not to accept the results of such investigations at face value. By the same token, inherent assumptions embedded in most mathematical analyses often greatly limit their practical usefulness, and experimental studies, too, are not without their own technological limitations. That's not to say that we should stop doing research. That is not at all the point of this editorial. All I am saying is that when it comes to issues, like carpal tunnel syndrome, that we aren't quite sure about, let's at least be up-front enough to admit it. Let's stop preaching, as if they are gospel, theories about these still-controversial issues (such as the etiology of the disease, especially its work-relatedness). Like Tevye, let's admit that, so far as we now know, "everybody might be right" (or, conversely, everybody might be wrong). The proof of our ignorance lies in the very volume of literature that is out there on this and other subjects. If we really knew what we were talking about, that volume of literature could be reduced to one, short, definitive paper.

Can We ... Should We ... Measure Everything in a Purely Objective Way?

American Laboratory News, June 2005

About 10 years ago, I came across an interesting editorial entitled, "Science, It Seems, Is Not An Exact Science." Writing in the March 6, 1995, edition of the *Roanoke Times & World-News*, Justin Askins, then an Associate Professor of English at Radford University (Radford, VA), declared that we should not give science an "unmerited reverence," but, rather, see it for the "mythology of wild ideas" that it is. Furthermore, scientists, contends Askins, should be viewed as "little more than entertainers"!

By coincidence, this editorial was perfectly timed, because the topic Mr. Askins was addressing was particularly germane to what we were then covering in an Honors Colloquium that I was teaching that semester at Virginia Tech (Blacksburg, VA) entitled, "Omniology: An Integrated Approach to the Study of Everything!" So, one day I decided to challenge the class with the following question: "Is it conceivably possible for us (humans) to measure everything in a totally exact, purely objective, free-of-bias, investigator-independent way ... and ... if so, *should* we?" In other words, assuming we can even define what is meant by "exact and purely objective" (relative to "absolute" standards of right and wrong), is it possible for us to devise ways to measure uniquely such things as disturbances to quasi-equilibrated states, perception, resistance, domains of influence, reactions, Shakespeare's effect on 20th-century writers, human intelligence, emotions, "fundamental" particles, the physiologic effects of

– 23 –

watching a sunset, the Mozart effect, and so on? Perhaps even more importantly, if we *could* devise such ways, *should* we pursue them to their logical conclusion?

Needless to say, these considerations led to a lively class discussion. In keeping with a common practice, which is to write down on a flip chart recorder (so all can readily see them) key points raised in such discussions (the originator[s] of those points, of course, remaining totally anonymous), we assigned a scribe to take notes. Recently, while cleaning out an old file drawer, I came across those notes and thought it would be fun to share some of them with you.

First of all, it did not take us very long to unanimously agree that the first question ("Can we?") is fundamentally a moot point. We *can't*, because, among other things: a) Anatomically, we are not endowed with the hardware (sensory architecture) required to perceive energy in all of the infinite variety of forms in which it can become manifest, which is to say, in a very basic sense, we don't even know *what* to measure! b) Assuming we *could* know what to measure—as it relates, for example, to asking the right questions—then, still, *technologically*, we can only achieve very limited success, in the measurement process itself, the accuracy of that process, its precision, ability to resolve to an absolute level of exactness, and so on. In fact, the Heisenberg Uncertainty Principle basically says that, "What you see is *not* what you get!" The measu*ring* affects the measure*ment*. c) Moreover, the measu*rer*, too, affects the measure*ment*. It is literally impossible, from a purely *physiologic* point of view, to avoid systemic errors in the objective interpretation of results, i.e., *bias*, derived mainly from one's (intentional or unintentional) inclination to gather certain types of evidence and information to the exclusion (and often at the expense) of others, and one's inherent tendency to assume things not in evidence. The general inability of investigators to keep their studies truly *random* and *absolutely objective* creates a situation wherein the results are unavoidably skewed toward a predetermined conclusion, or self-fulfilling prophecy. "If a man's only tool is a key, he will envision every problem to be a lock," tells Abraham Maslow.

This last consideration brought back memories of one of my professors in medical school, who made the same point when we discussed how radiologists tend to view (read) and interpret X-rays. "The way they were brought up!" said he, and then went on to make two salient points regarding bias: The first involved what is called a false negative. The radiologist is likely to miss something that *is* there because he or she, subconsciously, is not *looking* for it—most likely due to the particular training that the individual received, from a particular mentor, who subscribed to a particular school of thought regarding what to look for in radiographs. The second point was related to false positives. In this case, the radiologist *reads into* the X-ray something that might, in reality, *not* be there (or, might be an artifact), simply because he or she *is* looking for it and has (subconsciously) already decided ahead of time that it was going to be there and he or she was going to find it! "It's just a fact of life," concluded the instructor, "reading radiographs is a subjective process because the bottom line is that we are all human!"

Not to belabor the point, suffice it to say here that due to human frailties, implicit assumptions (conscious or subconscious), anatomical deficiencies, observational uncertainty, transduction imperfections, cognitive constraints, creative inhibitions (including societal pressures), interface errors, technological limitations, issues of scale (e.g., boundary-layer theory, particle/wave duality, etc.), incomplete observations, the natural tendency to skew and bias experimental results, difficulties in interpreting those results, perceptual flaws, arrogance, and just plain downright errors (to cite but 16 items from the long list we came up with) . . . it is *impossible* (we all agreed) for humans to measure *anything* (much less *everything*) in a totally exact, purely objective, free-of-bias, investigator-independent way. Furthermore, the class also agreed that the inherent problems related to how science is perceived (as is the case, too, with medicine), have more to do with scientists and the general public, than with *science, per se*. Scientists (like physicians) *want* the public to believe that they have, or can get—using the "scientific method"—all of the answers. "It's just a matter of time and patience," they say. And the general public *wants* to believe that that is, indeed, the case—we all need a hero! Thus, the symbiotic relationship that exists between what scientists *want* the public (including themselves!) to believe and what the public *wants* to believe creates the myth that puts science on the pedestal that Askins talks about in his editorial.

Bottom line: Basically, one sees what one is looking for (as in the radiology example), hears what one is listening for, and justifies whatever it is that occupies a position of priority in that individual's efforts—rationalizing as necessary. That's one of the reasons that history is replete with examples of major scientific breakthroughs that were discovered by accident, not by design (or intent). And that's also why science really *isn't* an exact science but, rather, a work-in-progress, a perpetual search for truth. One must realize that the scientific method is a means to an end, not an end in itself—a *method* (as the name clearly points out), not a *result*. Thus, nothing is really held sacred, for, as the philosopher Karl Popper so aptly observed (and history again confirms), any scientific theory is vulnerable to being proven wrong at any time.

So when all was said and done, the class concluded, *for sure*, that: a) because there are questions that will *never* be asked (we don't know what we don't know), and b) most of those that *are* asked can never be answered with total, absolute accuracy (due to the long list of limitations mentioned), then c) knowledge will forever be incomplete and subjective. Moreover, it is more than likely that, over the course of time (and again, verified by history), even what we think we *do* know will eventually be proven to be wrong!

That having been said, the discussion quickly turned to the second question, "Should we?" (i.e., be able to measure anything and everything in a purely objective way). Now the fun began and the debate livened up.

On the one hand, there is the point of view that says, "Yes... we should at least *strive* to measure everything objectively, because that might ultimately allow us to know everything—the truth, the whole truth, and nothing but the truth!" Among the advantages of such knowledge are the ability to predict and control the future; cure all diseases and other physiological problems; eliminate all bigotry, racism, and prejudice (by eliminating ignorance); move toward world peace and a Utopian existence; and do all kinds of other wonderful things.

On the other hand, opponents argue that we *shouldn't be* able to measure everything objectively because we might find out things we don't want to know, like: when (and of what) we will die; or, maybe there really *is* a connection between certain types of physiologic limitations and intelligence; or, maybe the objective criteria by which we "measure" how much somebody loves us actually winds up proving that, in fact, this individual really *doesn't*; or, maybe the world really *is* going to end during our lifetime; or, in fact, maybe there is *no* God... and... going one step further... maybe *all* religions are all wet; or, the information obtained by "objective" means might be used in a destructive rather than a constructive way... and so on.

There were, of course, suggestions and considerations raised by the class that fell somewhere in between these two extremes. One that I really liked addressed the issue of "the splendor of mystery and the magic of the imagination." If we could measure and "know" everything in a purely objective way, "we wouldn't be much more than super-efficient machines." The wisdom, as always, is in knowing where to draw the line, where to compromise in order to keep life exciting and full of mystique. "We should be open-minded, but our minds shouldn't be so open that our brains fall out!" Another student, in keeping with our earlier conclusion, suggested that, "to postulate that people are *capable* of measuring everything is more of an *extrapolation* based on history, or wishful thinking, than a *fact* based on realistic expectations." However, "to assert that something is *impossible* rules out a great portion of the unknown, which is a dangerous path to follow. History is also replete with examples of the impossible being achieved. So we must be careful to keep our expectations *realistic*, without compromising *possibilities*."

Here's a thought to ponder, as raised by yet another student: "There is no such thing as harmful information. Instead, there are harmful *interpretations* and *uses* of that information. *That's* what causes the problems that derive from scientific achievements. So the key is to keep seeking truth, but carry a big stick!" And yet another: "If it is possible for 'something' to be able to know 'everything,' that 'something' would have to be outside of the universe, in order to know everything about it. It's like a (hypothetical) brain having to be more intelligent than the brain it is trying to understand. But since, as far as we know, our universe is doubly infinite, that 'something' would have to exist on a different plane of reality . . . or . . . in some other (not-yet-defined) way, be able to exist beyond the extent of our universe, which is probably impossible?"

And one last one (for now): "Everything *perceptible* is *real*, even if only in one's imagination; but everything *real* is not necessarily *measurable*, or *quantifiable*, in a totally objective way, if at all (as discussed earlier). Thus, we must accept imaginary constructions, whether or not they can be quantified, as part of our reality, because to exclude them would require excluding all other mental processes as well—even the perceived patterns of order upon which the 'sciences' are based."

By now, you have no doubt guessed that these students have very bright young minds. Over the years that I spent in the classroom, they taught me much more than I ever taught them! In the interest of time and space, I will close this editorial with what, in the end, I found to be the most interesting aspect of this little exercise . . . and that is: how, what began as a classroom discussion of knowledge and truth (i.e., science), quickly turned into a discussion of power (politics and religion) . . . which evolved into a discussion of good and evil (ethics and morality) . . . which ended in the reaffirmation of the third most powerful of all fundamental human drives: the need for *spiritual fulfillment!*

Units of Measurement: The Glass and the Spoon

American Biotechnology Laboratory, October 2004

My mother was a great cook. Even though our family's menus were limited, our appetites were always deliciously appeased. What she lacked in repertoire, my mother more than made up for in mastery. She also never worked from cookbooks (I don't recall that she even owned one) or books that began with, "The Idiot's Guide To . . .." She was among the last of a breed of old-school *balebostehs*—the Yiddish word for capable homemakers—women who operate entirely on instinct and intuition; "doin' what comes natur'lly" (to steal a line from an Irving Berlin song). None of her recipes were written down anywhere. Thus, after Judi and I were married, the process of passing these precious family recipes down the line by word of mouth became a real challenge, especially considering the fact that a year and a half after our wedding, we moved to Cleveland, OH, a long way from Brooklyn, NY.

I recall one specific instance when Judi wrote to Mom asking her to send us instructions for making two dishes for which she was famous—gefilte fish (ground, stuffed fish formed into balls and cooked in salt water) and a type of traditional bagel made especially for the Jewish holiday of Passover. Here's what my mother sent back as a list of required ingredients:

For the Passover bagels: "You will need 2 glasses of matzo meal. Make sure they are small juice glasses, not the big ones like you use for milk. Then add some salt, probably a little bit like fits into the palm of your hand, maybe about half of a regular soupspoon. Add 'to taste' as much sugar as you and Danny like, but no more than 3 big soupspoons or the bagels will taste too sweet. The same for potato starch—just enough that the mixture should hold together nicely (you will be able to tell how it feels), maybe about 3 soupspoons, more or less. Add a half-glass of oil, one-and-a-half glasses cold water (use the same juice glass each time), and six whole eggs, but not very big ones."

For the gefilte fish and stuffing: "Early in the morning is the best time to shop because everything is fresh, everybody is still in a good mood, and the lady in the live fish store will be very helpful. You will need mostly carp (it's cheaper), some Michigan whitefish (the more you use, the whiter will be the result), and some mullet. After the fish is cleaned from the scales and the bones taken out, add a few soupspoons of salt, wrap it in saran wrap, and refrigerate overnight. To make the filling for the fish, you will need also some peeled onions, ground horseradish (about a soupspoon and a half, more or less), pepper and sugar (again, 'to taste'), two soupspoons of oil, four 'jumbo' eggs (bigger than the ones you used for the Passover bagels), a half juice glass of water (same glass you used for the bagels), a couple carrots; and this is important: more-or-less two glasses of matzo meal, *no more*! If you use too much matzo meal, the fish balls come out too hard. I don't know to tell you exactly how much is enough, but you are an intelligent girl so you should understand what I mean and you can 'feel' when the amount is just right."

There you have it: measuring units called the juice glass, the standard soupspoon, and the palm of her hand. These, and a lot of experience, were all my mother needed to satisfy all of her culinary requirements—just as a 6000-foot-long line of rope, an hourglass filled with sand, and a hand log were all that sailors needed long ago to measure the speed of their ships. They would attach one end of the rope to the log and then tie 120 knots, spaced 50 feet apart, along the log line. The log was then thrown overboard so that it floated, remaining essentially stationary with respect to the ship, which was now moving away from it at a certain speed. This speed was determined by the number of knots that went overboard in a time measured by the hourglass. For example, if a length of rope from the log to just the first knot went overboard in a 30-second time interval, the ship was known to be traveling at the rate of 50 feet per 30 seconds, or 100 feet per minute, or 6000 feet per hour, which is approximately one nautical mile (6076.11549 feet)* per hour, so one knot became the equivalent of one nautical mile per hour, a unit of speed that prevails even in today's modern world.

The fact of the matter is that, dating back over 300 years, units of measurement were rather primitive, not universally standardized, and like my mother's "juice glass and soupspoon," quite arbitrary. Moreover, the earliest units that *did* exist (at least for the measurement of length) quite understandably used the human body as a reference, like my mother's "palm of the hand." Thus, the *cubit* of Noah's time was based on the length of the forearm from the elbow to the tip of the middle finger, and could vary anywhere from 18 to 22 inches, the inch being the width of a man's thumb (or the length of the forefinger from its tip to the first joint). Twelve inches ("more or less," by my mother's standards) defined a foot, which, in Greek culture, was supposedly the actual length of the foot of Hercules. In reality, the foot could vary by as much as 3 or 4 inches, as could the yard (from the Saxon word *gird*, meaning

---

*Taken from the definition of a "standard" nautical mile as given in *Webster's Third New International Dictionary*, Unabridged, published by G & C Merriam Co., Springfield, MA, 1969.

the circumference of a person's waist), which was determined by the distance between the chin (or the tip of one's nose) and the end of the outstretched arm. This was the furthest distance one could pull a piece of cloth, which was just about long enough to use as a sash tied around the waist, hence the name. The yard was approximately equivalent to some three feet. Twice that amount, roughly equal to the span between the tips of the middle fingers with the arms fully outstretched to the sides of the body, became a fathom (from a word root meaning "to grasp," in the sense of "hugging," from a position of outstretched arms).

The Romans figured out that the average pace-step was about 2.5 feet, doubled that to 5 feet, and then multiplied by 1000 (hence the use of the word root "mil") to define the statute (land, as opposed to nautical) mile—5000 feet (today, 5280 feet). More than a mile became a league, ranging anywhere from 2.4 to 4.6 statute miles (3.452 statute miles in England), and less than a mile became a furlong (0.125 statute miles, or 40 rods, where a rod = 16.5 feet = 5.5 yards). Since mass production and high-tech industry did not yet exist, accuracy was not really an issue back in those early days of mensuration, nor was standardization or universality. These considerations were first addressed by the French in 1790 when, in the midst of a major revolution, they apparently saw fit to create a standard decimal system of weights and measures called the metric system. Go figure! (Excuse the pun.)

Although the metric system does attend to matters of standardization, accuracy, and universal consensus, it is still somewhat arbitrary in the way that the "standard" units of measurement are defined (see, for example, "Space," *American Laboratory* Nov 2002; 34[22]:6–8; "Time Revisited," *American Laboratory* Nov 2003; 35[22]:6–10; and "Space Revisited," *American Laboratory News* Aug 2004; 36[17]:4–6). That is to say, the units are not derived from fundamental principles; they are *assigned*, based on uniform subdivisions of arbitrarily defined numerical ranges in the dimensions of human perception. Dimensions of perception, such as length, time, mass, electric charge, and temperature, were conceptualized to describe, qualitatively, the human experience at various scales of perception.

In reality, there is only one dimension of perception—kinetic energy— and only one reality variable—velocity. That is because the only thing that stimulates anatomical sense organs and technological transducers is the movement that results from the conversion of potential energy into kinetic energy as disturbed systems undergo a transition from one quasi-equilibrated state to another (see "Energy," *American Laboratory*

News Aug 2003; 35[17]:4–6). However, since the sensing of movement can occur at various scales of perception (subnuclear, nuclear, atomic, molecular, continuum, cosmic, supercosmic, etc.), one can identify a separate primary dimension of perception for each such scale.

Units of measurement (from which, parenthetically, the word "dimension" is actually derived) have been invented to *quantify* the human experience that is qualitatively described by dimensions of perception. It seems reasonable to expect that such quantification should be based, in a very fundamental way, on our ability to discriminate—through sophisticated technological enhancement of our natural senses—between two adequate stimuli that are perceived very close to one another in space and/or in time, in other words, on our ability to *resolve* sensory inputs down to very fine levels, i.e., to perceive as being separate two signals that are received almost simultaneously in time and/or superimposed in space. That expectation should become even clearer as our understanding of measurement matures. That is to say, as we come to realize that the concept of units of measurement is intimately tied to, and should be based on, the corresponding concept of resolution, the establishment of proper units of measurement becomes more than just a matter of systematically subdividing into smaller pieces some arbitrary larger range of a dimension of perception.

The field of quantum mechanics has helped to formalize this notion that units of measurement should correspond to the lowest limit to which we can resolve change at any particular scale of perception. It has done so by postulating that change occurs not continuously, but in discrete small steps, wherein in each such transaction, finite amounts (quanta) of potential energy need to be converted into kinetic energy before any discernible (resolution) effect can become manifest. Thus, not unlike the parallel phenomenon in nerve conduction physics, which requires a minimum receptor depolarization potential to be prerequisite to the generation of an action potential (i.e., for the nerve to fire), various threshold levels can be defined in quantum mechanics according to the formula, $E = nhf$, where h is Planck's constant (6.626×10^{-34} Joule-sec); f is the corresponding frequency of oscillation, in cycles per second, of the energy driving the transition from one state to another; and $n = 1,2,3 \ldots$ represents whole number multiples of the quantum amount of energy, hf, exchanged in the transaction. (Note: At the quantum-mechanics scale of perception, physical events are most appropriately described in terms of the reciprocal of time [one of the primary dimensions of perception], which is frequency, scaled by

Planck's constant. Thus, although Joules and seconds are, themselves, arbitrarily defined units of measurement, the scaling factor that is Planck's constant "fixes" them, in some sense, to establish a more appropriate [based on considerations of resolution] fundamental unit of measurement, which is hf at this level of perception.)

A similar formula, at a different (molecular) scale of perception—where absolute temperature, T (another primary dimension of perception), in degrees Kelvin (another arbitrary unit), is the more appropriate dimension for describing physical events—utilizes Boltzmann's constant, k (1.3805×10^{-23} Joules per degree Kelvin) in the energy (E) equation, $E = nkT$. Again, the latter is used to quantify discrete energy transactions, this time, in the kinetic theory of gases, and again, Boltzmann's constant "fixes" (scales) T to yield a more appropriate unit of measurement, kT, based on considerations of resolution.

One could postulate the same idea at still another scale of perception, where unit mass, m (in arbitrary kilogram units), is the more appropriate dimension of perception, and thereby suggest that Einstein's energy equation, $E = nmc^2$, follows this same line of reasoning. This time, the constant speed of light, c, in a vacuum (3.00×10^8 meters per sec), squared, assumes the role of scaling factor, and mc^2 becomes the appropriate unit of measurement at this scale of perception.

Indeed, one could go on to generalize this whole discussion by proposing a universal formula that would read something like this:

> Perceived energy converted from potential to kinetic = (whole number multiples, n, of quantum states) × (appropriate universal constant) × (appropriate primary dimension of perception)

Where "appropriate" means "characteristic of the scale of perception under investigation," and the product "universal constant" × "primary dimension of perception" defines the "appropriate" quantum unit of measurement for that scale of perception. The obvious question(s) that then arise are: Are these "constants" *really* constant or do they, in fact, merely identify the limitations in our ability to measure? In other words, is change really continuous, but we just don't perceive it that way because of the limitations in our ability to resolve? Are there "fundamental" units of measurement, like "primary" dimensions of perception, that are what we really mean when we say, "universal constants"? Do at least some "universal constants," in reality, simply quantify the concept of "resolution," being the lowest limit to which we can perceive "change"? Unfortunately, at this point in my thinking, I have more questions than answers, but I am fascinated by the possibilities and what they might mean in terms of a more thorough understanding of the physical principles of measurement.

Energy

American Laboratory News, August 2003

Let's talk about this thing we call "energy." Notice that I did not say, "Let's define this thing we call 'energy,'" because, truth be told, we can't define it; we can only describe it. We do not know for sure (universally speaking) what energy is, where it came from, or when or why it exists. We do know that "things" endowed with energy (whatever it is) can make things happen (i.e., can perform work) because we can experience the expression of that work. In fact, the very word "energy" derives from such experiences because, etymologically, it comes from the Greek *en-*, meaning "in," and *ergon*, meaning "work." Thus, early investigators recognized that energy was some inherent property that seemed to be required to drive processes capable of accomplishing purposeful activities—i.e., a property prerequisite to doing work. How's that for a backdoor approach to labeling something based solely on one's ability to experience its effects (i.e., to know it is there) rather than being able to define exactly what caused those effects (i.e., to know what preceded and was responsible for the event you experienced, like knowing exactly who made the violin you are playing, and how it produces the beautiful sounds you are hearing)? Just label the cause "energy" and accept on faith (not unlike a religion) that it is somehow related to its effect—useful work. All of which would be fine, were it not for the fact that we tend to equate putting a label on something with knowing what it is, i.e., we think of *labeling* and *defining* as synonyms. We tend to further pigeonhole our observations in an inductive sense, failing all too often to extract more fundamental principles, in a deductive sense, from our specific experiences and observations.

For example, we now know that work derived from energy is but one form of this omnifarious (available in all varieties) property that indeed can manifest in an infinite number of ways, and not all of them are necessarily perceptible to us. Thus, we identify many types of energy that can be experienced (e.g., ultrasonic, thermodynamic, electromagnetic, chemical, nuclear, atomic, cosmic, mechanical, etc.).

It is further useful to presume that energy is an indestructible attribute; it can be converted from one perceptible form to another, but neither created *de novo* nor destroyed.[1] Therefore, in the broadest sense, energy is a universal, all powerful (omnipotent), ubiquitous (omnipresent), and everlasting property that is both the source (potential energy) and the realization (kinetic energy) of all that can be experienced. Whatever it is, energy is the inherent attribute from which all of reality derives, and although attempts to define it are at best abstract and at worst wrong (or at least naive), we can say for certain that anything endowed with energy is capable of producing actions or effects in perceivable forms. By "perceivable forms," I mean, specifically, actions that are capable of stimulating some anatomic sense organ (not necessarily ours), or exciting some technological transducer responsive to those actions.

We see, then, that energy is a convenient concept; it is a label we devised to explain and quantify events in our Universe as we experience them in various frames of reference, at different scales of perception. Establishing the concept of energy allows us to get off of square one—i.e., to avoid getting bogged down by things we may never fully comprehend (mostly because of our inherent anatomical-physiological-sensory/cognitive-technological limitations) in favor of things that lie within the scope of our ability to perceive and understand. Energy in hand, we can now move forward in our perpetual quest to seek the truth, our insatiable desire to know. In this respect, I am reminded of Edwin Powel Hubble's observation that, "Equipped with five senses, man explores the universe around him and calls the adventure science." (Aside: Replace "energy" with "God," and "science" with "religion," and I think you would have to agree that the two concepts are not as far apart as they might appear at first glance. In both cases, faith plays a major role.)

Going one step further, with due respect to its omnifarious modes of perceptibility, I maintain that energy is of only two types: that which is capable of being (potential energy), and that which is in evidence, i.e., is capable of being perceived (kinetic energy of motion). I claim further that kinetic energy derives from potential energy when quasi-equilibrated states are disturbed, and are responsive to such disturbances.[2] Finally, I can reasonably justify the allegation that only kinetic energy can actually be measured directly; it is impossible to measure potential energy directly because, as its name implies, this form of energy is *capable* of being—an abstract conceptualization that explains why a quasi-equilibrated state is responsive to a threshold disturbance—but is not yet actually realized, absent such a disturbance.

So how can one measure what is not yet real? This is where the arguments begin with my colleagues, although I do have physiology on my side: Anatomical sense organs do respond only to movement (kinetic energy). In refuting my contentions, my colleagues direct me to the scores of mathematical potential energy functions that are defined in numerous literature references. These formulas, they claim, clearly exemplify how potential energy can be measured; they conclude by saying, "How absurd to think otherwise!"

But a closer examination of how these potential energy formulas were historically derived reveals that they evolved using the same backdoor, inductive approach we used to define energy in the first place—that is, not really knowing what it is, but knowing what it does (i.e., work). In other words, these "potential energy functions" were arbitrarily invented by working backwards. First, we perceived various forms of kinetic energy—the effect, specific measurements taken following the disturbance of quasi-equilibrated states. Then, we labeled the physical phenomenon presumed to have caused those effects—the intensive potential properties that allowed such quasi-equilibrated states to respond to corresponding disturbances, the "potential energy" from which the measured "kinetic energy" derived. Last, we invented mathematical formulas to quantify those measurements, calling those formulas potential energy functions. The process is not unlike that used to develop so-called "phenomenological constitutive models" in viscoelastic theory; we know that springs and dashpots have nothing to do with the "real" make-up of the material being modeled, but they suffice and are effective for analytical and design purposes, so we use them anyway.

Let us illustrate this working-backwards process with a simple example: the potential energy function, $U = mgy$, associated with the force of gravity between the earth and a mass (m) located some distance (y) above the earth (g is the gravitational acceleration constant). My colleagues argue that U is a measure of gravitational potential energy; I argue that it is not. How can it be? We do not even know what gravity is, much less from where it derives, so how can we measure it *per se*? How can you measure something directly if you don't even know what it is you are trying to measure? The only thing you can do to quantify it is to work backwards, indirectly and inductively, from what you observe, experience, and measure to be its effects. Recall that the Greeks coined the word "energy" by observing that things endowed with "it" can do work.

Likewise, we only experience the effects of gravity—or more precisely, the effects of something we call gravity, a word that derives from the

Latin *gravis*, meaning "heavy." One such effect is that a mass (m) released from some height (y) above an arbitrary reference point will fall, under what we attribute to be the influence of gravity—the attractive force between the earth and m, proportional to it through g (Newton's Second Law of Motion)—to some lower height (i.e., heaviness), achieving in the process some energy of motion, kinetic energy that can be perceived and measured (the effect). Working backwards from what we experience as a manifestation of the earth's attractive force (gravity), we can arrive at a convenient way of quantifying that experience from our empirical observations. Thus, U = mgy does not *measure* the potential energy of gravity, it quantifies our experiencing of the *effects* of gravity—two entirely different concepts.

"So what?" you might say, "That's a subtle distinction. You are merely playing with semantics!" To which I would respond, "Maybe I am, maybe I'm not." But to my way of thinking, it's an important distinction, most especially for students, because it forces you to: 1) stay constantly aware of what we really don't know, even if we have a label for it; 2) maintain the proper perspective in distinguishing what it is we can measure from what we can't, especially as it relates to knowing the difference between inductive and deductive reasoning; 3) avoid getting lulled into a false sense of security that could lead us astray in objectively interpreting what it is we are "measuring"; and 4) recognize that what we said above using gravitational potential energy as an example applies as well to our descriptions (in the form of derived potential energy functions) of electromagnetism, radioactivity, nuclear "strong" forces, and so on. We describe/quantify them (not define/measure them directly) by working backwards from their perceived and experienced manifestations.

And what are those perceived and experienced manifestations? We call them Dimensions of Perception, which in reality are the various forms by which we can experience kinetic energy. In other words, what we claim to be the infinite ways in which potential energy can become manifest are actually empirical observations and "measurements" that we carry out in different frames of reference (perhaps by different observers) at different scales of perception. Thus, for example, when we speak of electromagnetic energy, identifying electric charge as its primary dimension of perception, we are really talking about events as we measure them at the atomic scale of perception. Similarly, chemical, thermodynamic, or sonic forms of energy identified with temperature as the primary dimension of perception actually reflect events as we measure them at the molecular scale of perception, while various mechanical forms of energy identified with mass as the primary inertial dimension of perception are really associated with events as we measure them at the continuum scale of perception, and so on.

Finally, I envision "disturbances to equilibrated states" as creating situations wherein the potential energy at a given point in space has been altered relative to another, leading to a nonuniform distribution of this energy. Such potential energy gradients cause energy to flow (i.e., be converted to kinetic energy, which we can perceive) from the region at the higher energy level to the region at the lower energy level (reversibly in conservative systems) in an effort to "level the playing field." In that sense, the concept of "opposites attracting" might perhaps be more accurately described as the physical phenomenon wherein energy gradients seeking neutralization cause energy to flow (be attracted) to a less concentrated region, from one where it is more concentrated. If there is no such gradient (likes), then there is no natural driving force for the flow of energy. Indeed, trying to force energy to flow under these circumstances, one encounters strong resistance (repulsion). So, opposites attract, likes repel, and positive charge in electrical theory actually refers to a region of lower potential energy (strange, isn't it?), while negative charge identifies a region of higher potential energy, because it is presumed that electricity "flows" from negative to positive (although, historically, the exact opposite was thought to prevail, which in retrospect may actually have been correct). But, then again, maybe there are no electrons, or protons, or elementary particles, or whatever ... just energy! Make any sense?

References

1. Schneck D. *The seven rudimentary axioms of reality.* Am Lab 2001; 33(24):6–8.
2. Schneck D. *Equilibrium.* Am Lab 2002; 34(1):6–8.

Equilibrium

American Laboratory, January 2002

From the Latin *aequus*, meaning "equal," and *libra*, meaning "balance," the word "equilibrium" implies some equally balanced state of affairs— a purely potential state in which something is capable of happening, but isn't happening. Something is not happening because the balanced state of affairs remains undisturbed. Something is *capable* of happening because the balanced state of affairs is endowed with certain types of potential energy (characteristic intensive potentials) that enable it to respond to corresponding types of specific disturbances. A boulder sits precariously balanced at the very edge of a cliff, endowed with gravitational potential energy, but remaining perfectly motionless. Nothing is happening. Suddenly the ground trembles, or a strong gust of wind hits the boulder, disturbing it, and something *does* happen: The boulder is displaced ever so slightly from its delicately equilibrated state. This disturbance causes its gravitational potential energy to be converted into kinetic energy as it tumbles to the ground below.

But the boulder is also endowed with adhesive and cohesive intensive potentials—nuclear, atomic, and/or molecular forms of energy that combine to give it its characteristic size, shape, mass, and consistency. Properly disturbed (like being subjected to the shock of tumbling down a rough terrain), some of these potentials may not be strong enough to hold the mass together—to resist the disturbance—and so as the boulder plummets to the ground below, parts or all of it might simultaneously break apart into smaller pieces, each careening off in a different direction. Some pieces might land in a pool of cold water (still a third disturbance), dissipating the thermal energy with which the boulder might have been endowed as it absorbed and was heated by the sun while it sat at the top of the cliff. Such energy, too, has a corresponding intensive potential associated with it.

And so the list goes on—the point being that there are many types of potential energy functions (characteristic intensive, per-unit-mass potentials) that we are aware of because of the way systems endowed with such intensive potentials respond when they are disturbed from an equilibrated state. Indeed, one may further theorize that intensive potentials define the very properties of a system that endow it with the ability to become physically realized in a variety of perceptible states—that realization resulting, in fact, from the system's response to a corresponding disturbance. In turn, our perception of that realization results from our awareness (through anatomic/sensory or technological transduction) of the kinetic energy that derives from the corresponding potential energy. What I am suggesting, then, is that potential energy, *per se*, cannot be measured directly—a principle that I have formalized into an "Axiom of Perception" which is based on the following reasoning.

We know that the human body's anatomical sense organs respond only to movement—to spatial gradients in potential energy functions (i.e., accelerations) and the motion that results therefrom, rather than to the potential energy functions themselves. Through physiologic processes such as sensory adaptation, our bodies "tune out" steady-state disturbances that are not perceived to be threatening. That's why you are not consciously aware of the clothes on your body shortly after you get dressed in the morning: Your tactile senses have equilibrated with the pressure exerted on them by the clothing. Neither are you cognizant of the temperature of the bathwater after your thermal senses equilibrate with the water temperature (unless you agitate the water, causing it to move against these senses); nor do you smell perfume anymore after you have inhaled it continuously for some time. All of these examples illustrate how our body's sense organs, in an effort to avoid suffering from sensory overload, are designed to respond only to changes (that could signal impending danger) in corresponding adequate stimuli (disturbances such as heat, light, sound, and so on), not to the stimuli themselves, if they do not change in time or space. Thus, we are not aware that intensive potentials exist for any particular type of energy, i.e., they don't become manifest until equilibrated states are disturbed, converting potential energy into perceptible kinetic energy. It is the latter that stimulates anatomical sense organs, or excites technological transducers designed to respond to that particular type of energy. In other words, reality derives from movement, which results from disturbed equilibrated states.

It follows from the reasoning above that we therefore cannot measure potential energy directly; we can only work *backwards* from the measurement of different forms of kinetic energy to *define* potential energy functions from which that kinetic energy was presumably derived. In other words, we perceive reality as the process by which one equilibrated state transitions to another. That process has a corresponding type of kinetic energy associated with it that we call a "dimension"—a measure of what is taking place, with different dimensions corresponding to different scales of perception. *Being*, then—a perceptible, kinetic, transitional state—derives from *equilibrium*—an imperceptible potential ("capable of being") state—because certain properties (intensive potentials) of the latter are disturbed beyond their ability to resist such disturbance. Our awareness of the transitions that take place derives from our ability to measure specific attributes (dimensions) of kinetic states.

Equilibrium can thus be defined more precisely as "the state of a system wherein some (relative equilibrium) or all (absolute equilibrium) of the intensive potentials that define the properties and physical state of the system remain undisturbed, either from within or from the surroundings of the system." Intensive potentials that are uniformly distributed and unchanging in space and time, such that the system is not in the process of transitioning from one state to another, are what characterize an equilibrated state. Moreover, when an equilibrated system is disturbed passively, beyond its ability to resist, it has a natural tendency to transition from an unstable state of higher intensive potential (the boulder sitting at the top of the cliff) to a more stable state of lower intensive potential (the boulder coming to rest at the bottom of the cliff). The transition process itself is governed by minimum-energy principles that constrain it to proceed at least cost. Finally, one may define the special case of "neutral" equilibrium as corresponding to a multiplicity of equilibrated states that share equally the same set of intensive potentials, such as is the case when one simply moves the boulder to different positions along a perfectly flat surface; it has no particular preference for any one of them, and is perfectly happy to come to rest anywhere along the surface.

Defined as above, absolute equilibrium in a global sense is actually a hypothetical (asymptotic) state, because if the entire universe were to be in this state, absolutely nothing would ever be happening and reality as we experience it would have no way of being brought into existence. In fact, some have suggested that the formal definition of death should be, "the physiologic state corresponding to absolutely equilibrated organ systems and biochemical processes, wherein no form of metabolism is in evidence." In fact, all real systems are actually in various states of quasi-equilibrium, always transitioning in some sense (on various time and space scales) from one state into another—which brings up a very important point with which I will close: A system may *appear* to be in equilibrium when viewed at one scale of perception, when, in fact, it is not in equilibrium when viewed at another scale of perception. For example, a chair sitting in the middle of a room may appear to an observer looking at it on a continuum scale to be perfectly still, doing nothing, equilibrated. We know, however, that within that chair, electrons are flying madly about; and we further realize that we couldn't even see that chair if not for the fact that light traveled to and from it (movement); our eyes were, in fact, imperceptibly and rapidly scanning it (movement); and all the mechanisms by which the image was processed by the retina and brought to realization in our visual cortex involved movement at the molecular and atomic scales of perception. Equilibrium may indeed be more of a hypothetical conceptualization (as is potential energy) than a matter of fact!

Time

American Biotechnology Laboratory, December 2002

The word "time" has an interesting origin: It derives from a Medieval Latin root, *ti*, which means "to stretch" (as in, also, stretching the last note of the musical scale so that it leads into, or *resolves* to its dominant mode, do). But what is it that is being stretched? If we equate "stretch" with "expand," one can reasonably suggest that time is the mechanism that allows us to expand (stretch) our awareness. But of what are we aware? We might glean a clue as to what our ancestors were particularly aware of by noting that the early Old English (Anglo-Saxon) word for everyday time was *tid*, which later became "tide," as in Yuletide, eventide, springtide, good tidings, and so on. This suggests that among our earliest forms of conscious awareness was the roughly 12-hr cyclical rise and fall "stretching" of the ocean, responding to the varying gravitational attractions of the moon and the sun as the Earth rotates about its axis. Perhaps this is the origin of the English proverb, "Time and tide wait for no man."

In any case, our rather limited awareness of the shifting waters of the ocean—tide, the earliest meaning of time—evolved into the more generic concept of time, which came to mean a generalized, expanded awareness of anything. We now know that that awareness derives from our brain's unique ability to sequence (tag) incoming physiologic cues that originate from the stimulation of specific anatomical sense organs by various forms of kinetic energy (adequate stimuli, see *American Laboratory* 2002; 34[1]:6–8). In other words, time is the primary dimension of physiologic consciousness. The physiologic sequencing of sensory information (which gives birth to the concept of time and the consciousness derived therefrom) is that quantifiable attribute of our brain that gives us the ability to perceive that:

1. Cause (disturbance of a quasi-equilibrated state) and effect (resulting conversion of potential energy into kinetic energy) do not (indeed, cannot) occur simultaneously. That is to say, the response of a system to some form of excitation is delayed (metastable state of acceleration) for two reasons: first, because of the inherent inertia of the system (i.e., its desire, or natural tendency, to maintain the status quo, as Newton observed in formulating his First Law of Motion), and second, because energy conversions (in this case, potential into kinetic) cannot occur instantaneously. Our perception of that delay, embedded in our brain's

ability to sequence, store, and retrieve information, makes us conscious of time as a primary dimension of reality.

2. There is an inherent periodicity that characterizes events in our universe; this periodicity is also a fundamental property of the various forms of energy that we are capable of experiencing (see *American Laboratory* Oct 2000; 32[20]:6). As was mentioned in addressing the very origin of the word "time," our perception of that periodicity (and thank you, also, Mr. Fourier, for allowing us to quantify it), embedded in our brain's further ability to recognize a particular type of incoming cue as being one that it has experienced before, also makes us conscious of time as a primary dimension of perception.

3. There is some duration (again perceived by identifying, sequencing, and recalling incoming sensory cues) that defines a system's eventual transition (involving velocity and displacement phases) from one quasi-equilibrated state to another. Thus, we can track the passage of time and, by retrieving from memory sensory cues stored in some logical sequence, can further identify events as a) having already taken place (a consciousness derived from medium-term secondary and permanent tertiary memory that give us a sense of past); b) taking place even as we are experiencing them (a consciousness derived from short-term primary or working memory that gives us a sense of present); or c) not yet having taken place at all (i.e., no memory, which gives us a sense of future).

The exact anatomical pathways and physiological mechanisms by which the above information-processing operations are accomplished have not yet been entirely identified and/or described, but there are some interesting theories that are worthy of mention. First of all, we know that the means by which our brain identifies an adequate stimulus and its intensity is by recognizing which nerve (or neural network) is firing (i.e., which sensory modality is providing the input), at what rate (digital frequency), and with what type of bar-code-like or Morse-code-like pattern. Different nerves respond to different forms of energy (adequate stimuli) at different threshold intensities, at different frequencies, in different combinations (networks), and with differing patterns. The brain deciphers this incoming information to determine if it is threatening (real or imagined)—in which case it tracks through the fear center (amygdala) to elicit downstream fight-or-flight (911) responses—or, if it is benign—in which case it is diverted to the hippocampus for further cognitive processing. Either way, the incoming information is now tagged (by the amygdala in the case of emotional responses, or the hippocampus in the case of cognitive responses) to give it temporal (sequencing) significance. Current theories suggest that the tagging may be accomplished in one or more of the following ways.

The brain might have temporary memory slots or mailboxes that are filled in a particular sequence so that, for example, box A is filled first, followed by box B, then box C, and so on. In recalling the stored information from its anatomical location, the brain then knows that the material retrieved from location A came in before the material stored in location B, which preceded the material that can now be found in location C. Alternatively, the tagging centers of the brain might actually code the incoming information stereochemically by endowing it (or the neurotransmitter associated with it) with a biochemical label, in much the same way that a clothing-check person tags items for subsequent retrieval. Thus, for example, an item coming through first might receive a triangular biochemical tag, the next one a circular biochemical tag, and the next one a square biochemical tag. In recalling the stored information, the brain then knows that the material carrying the triangular tag came in before (i.e., preceded in time) the material carrying the circular tag, which took place in time prior to that material carrying the square tag, and so on.

There may be other yet-to-be-identified ways in which information is tagged by the brain to give it temporal significance, but the point is that such tagging and storing in working memory for later identification is what gives us a sense of sequencing and, as a result, a sense of time. Those individuals in whom temporal tagging/storing of sensory information has gone awry (such as some on the autistic spectrum, others who suffer from Alzheimer's disease, have experienced a stroke, brain damage, etc.) have an impaired sense of time, poor recall ability (especially short-term), and/or experience difficulty in making sense out of the adequate stimuli that they perceive. To them, the world is confusing, which may explain much of their behavior.

The rate at which the brain can receive, tag, store, and retrieve sensory information from within (interoception) or from without (exteroception) is called its cerebral information processing rate (IPR). This rate constrains, among other things, our ability to distinguish as being two separate pieces of information sensory inputs that arrive spaced very close to one another in time (i.e., the resolution capability of our information-processing circuitry), and it is unique to any given individual. As an illustration, consider that the human sense of vision (because of the ways in which optic neurons fire when stimulated, and the resolution characteristics of the visual system) is capable of processing images at the maximum rate of about 50–60 per sec—a fact exploited by cinematographers in making motion pictures. That is to say, digitizing real-life continuous motion into a series of still frames that are cast upon the retina of the eye at rates on the order of 50–60 per sec will make the motion appear, to the observer, to be continuous, even though in reality it (i.e., the motion) is being projected onto the retina in discrete, sequential time steps. The lower limit of this discretization is around 24 frames per sec—the so-called flicker speed, below which the processed images are, indeed, actually seen as the individual, discrete frames (i.e., distinct still shots) that they are. Thus, below the flicker speed, one observes movement in a jerky, rather than continuous, fashion. This jerky movement is also observed at very fast speeds, because when the recorded images are projected onto the retina faster than it can process them, this sense organ loses the in-between frames that it cannot catch as they quickly fly by, and so, again, the motion is envisioned to be discontinuous as it changes from one configuration to another.

The bottom line is that each of us is endowed with characteristic nature- and nurture-derived capabilities to process information at specific rates—and these will vary from individual to individual. One might then think of "real time" as the situation wherein the brain is processing information in a one-to-one correspondence with the rate at which it is coming into the central nervous system—which, in some sense, might be representative of perceived events as they are actually taking place. Any deviation, which is more likely the rule rather than the exception, from this one-to-one correspondence makes "biological" time quite an individual-specific experience, a type of subjective physiologic relativity (see *American Laboratory* Dec 2000; 32[24]:6).

Finally, in speaking about biological clocks, it should also be mentioned that all tagged time cues received through sensory extero- and interoception converge eventually on the suprachiasmatic nuclei (SCN) of the hypothalamus, which establishes the biorhythm that we associate with most (probably all) physiologic processes. Thus, just as the sino-atrial node acts as a natural cardiac pacemaker for the heart, the SCN, located near the preoptic area of the anterior ventral hypothalamus, seems to act as a natural cerebral pacemaker. The SCN, responding to time cues, synchronizes the body's internal processes with the daily (circadian), monthly (menstrual), and yearly (circannian) cycles of our environment. Thus, our expanded awareness (perception of time) is also linked to our consciousness of the biorhythms that characterize all physiologic processes, e.g., the cyclic beating of the heart, periodic firing rates in neurons, rhythmic breathing patterns, oscillating peristaltic movements in the gastrointestinal system, diurnal variations in body temperature, timed release of urine (bladder function) and fecal wastes (rectal function), timed release of endocrine hormones to correspond with their role in metabolic processes, sleep/wake cycles, periodic 90-min sleep stage cycles, female menstrual cycles, patterns of gait, and the 4- to 6-hr cravings for food (hunger cycles), to mention just a few—which reminds me: It's time to go have some lunch.

All God's Creations Got Rhythm!

American Laboratory, October 2000

Almost two years ago, I read an article in *Inc.* magazine (Jan 1999; 21[1]:56–67) in which the author, David Shenk, bemoaned the "tsunami of information that is pounding away at us, making all of us more anxious, less effective, and sometimes even sick." His concern was that the recent information explosion and the enormous proliferation of new knowledge pose significant challenges to our educational system (how do we effectively incorporate such a rapid output of new material into our classrooms and curriculums?) and further threaten our physiologic well-being (how do we manage to cope when the information is streaming in faster than we can handle it?). In response to Mr. Shenk's anxiety, I wrote a letter to the editor (which was not published) explaining that the author had failed to carry the subject through to its logical conclusion, hence his misgivings about the eventual outcome. You see, the key to understanding what is happening is to recognize that ours is a history of cyclical events, both large scale and small. These events derive from disturbances of equilibrated states—disturbances that spiral us up (progress) to a new plateau or down (decay) to a more stable state, or neither (a conservative retreat to the previous status quo).

Viewed in terms of the issue at hand, which is to say, the information explosion to which we are currently being subjected, one notes that our heritage is, in fact, replete with such disequilibrating periods of information *explosions*. Unless we recognize that these unstable times are historically followed by equilibrating periods of information *implosions*, with these two states undulating back and forth like the tides of the sea, we have missed the whole point! That is, every time we begin to suffer the consequences of information overload (explosion, the state we are in now), there invariably follows a natural progression of events that lead us to seek common denominators from among the plethora of information. Extraction of such common denominators further allows us to distinguish the signal from the noise in the information. Eventually, from such inductive reasoning, new fundamental principles emerge. In turn, these fresh new ideas bring insights by which the enormous volume of fragmented information can be effectively condensed into much smaller groups (implosion, the direction we are heading). These groups are recognized by the likes of Newton, Maxwell, Einstein, and others to be special cases that derive by deductive reasoning from more general laws, and the entire cyclic process starts all over again.

Recognizing the periodicity of the human experience is the essence of understanding everything. Have you ever wondered, for example, why we sleep daily or eat meals several times a day or have a pulse or use the bathroom on a rather regular basis? The answer is really quite obvious: Our bodies are not equipped with the huge resources they would need to carry out the process of living, in one step, from birth to death. Imagine the size of the stomach that would be required to accumulate, all at once, at the very instant we are born, all of the food we will ever need throughout our lifetime. So, we have instead a "gas tank" that we periodically fill and empty several times a day, every day, throughout our lives to provide for our nutritional needs.

Similarly, your heart cannot pump blood throughout your entire body for a lifetime with one single continuous contraction. Because of its limited size, this small organ must cyclically fill and empty on average approx. 60–80 times each minute for as long as you live. Likewise, in the absence of a bladder that too periodically fills and empties, we would all need diapers on a full-time basis, which would make our lives considerably more complicated than they are already! It is physically impossible for you to drink an entire glass of water in a single gulp, or take a long enough stride to get across a room in a single step, or inhale in one breath enough air to last a lifetime.

Our limited physiologic resources and constrained anatomical storage capacity make it necessary for us to do whatever it takes to get only partway toward a goal, then repeat the same thing over again to advance a bit further, then do it still again, having replenished our provisions, and so on, going through a spiraling iterative process to eventually arrive at our destination. Inherent to the very way in which our bodies work, then, are biorhythms, the rhythms of life, the ebb and flow of recurrent physiologic events that march along at a cadence consistent with the maintenance of both individual life (survival of the self) and that of the species. And, we are not alone. Energy, in all forms, likes to vibrate (the frequency of vibration determining how that energy is perceived).

If energy vibrates too fast (beyond ultraviolet at approx. 750 million-million cycles per second or 750 terahertz), humans cannot perceive it at all without technological help in the form of transducers. Slow it down to the 400–750 terahertz range, and we can "see" it in a visible spectrum that ranges from violet at the high end to red at the low end. Slow it down further into the 1–400 terahertz range, and we can "feel" it as heat energy in the infrared range. Reducing the frequency further allows us to "hear" energy that vibrates in the 20–20,000 cycle per second range, and to "feel" it again, this time as mechanical vibrations up to approx. 2000 Hz through our tactile senses. These senses also allow us to "touch" energy that has slowed down so much that it congeals into forms we associate with mass: stuff!

Elastic restoring forces drive disturbed systems back to their previously equilibrated state, but inertia causes them to overshoot, and voila, we have periodic motion again, which decays with time. The earth rotates around its axis; the planets revolve around the sun; birds flap their wings; dogs wag their tails; tides come in and out . . . rhythm . . . it's everywhere! So much so that one can accept as an axiom the fact that all forms of reality are cyclic in their regular manifestations, such cycles being of large and small scale. So what is all of this concern about the information explosion? I see it as but one more cycle in the open-ended quest for knowledge. I see it as an impending opportunity to formulate still another basic principle in math, physics, or some other of the natural, social, and applied sciences. I see it as a means for moving one step closer toward, for example, world peace and prosperity, a unified field theory in physics, or an understanding of physiologic processes as they relate to disease and disability in medicine. I see it, Mr. Shenk, not as "data smog" and cause for alarm, not as a sign that "we may be on the verge of an attention-deficit-disorder epidemic," not as a dilemma that prevents us from "coming to conclusions," but rather as exactly the opposite: something to look forward to, because around the next corner may be lurking the next great advancement in human history. That's the way it's always been and that's the way it will always be because all God's creations got rhythm!

Time Revisited

American Laboratory, November 2003

Further to my epistle on time (*American Biotechnology Laboratory* Dec 2002; 20[13]:4–6), consider that one of the most fundamental axioms of natural physics is that—in whatever forms it becomes realized—energy is periodic in its regular manifestations from whatever source(s) it derives (see also *American Laboratory* Oct 2000; 32[20]:6–8). Thus, our perception of time seems to have evolved, at least in part, from our awareness of that very periodicity in our own experience. For instance, we receive visual cues that stem from the inherent cycles of our universe, such as the circadian diurnal (day)/nocturnal (night) alternating light/dark cycles associated with the earth's rotation about its own axis relative to the position of the sun at any given time. We call each such cycle a day in our life. We are also aware that each day, the amount of daylight varies in circannian cycles, corresponding to how long it takes for the earth to complete one full trajectory around the sun; we call each such cycle a year of our life. We observe further that the earth has a heavenly body (the moon) that revolves around it in regular menstrual cycles, from which derives the corresponding concept of a month, and so on.

Going one step further, timed biological responses (biorhythms) have become conditioned reflexes that represent genetically coded adaptations to these inherent cycles of our universe. The bilateral suprachiasmatic nuclei near the preoptic area of the anterior ventral hypothalamus thus assume the role of biological clock, to time physiologic processes so that they are synchronized with the corresponding time of day—a kind of cerebral pacemaker. Our perception of time, then, is also linked to our awareness of these biorhythms that are associated with physiologic processes, and while the actual ambient cues with which these biorhythms were originally made to coincide are no longer absolutely necessary in order to elicit a response, it is important to note that if they are not there, the timed sequence of important physiologic processes with which they are correlated—such as sleep/wake patterns, eating habits, and menstrual cycles—are significantly affected. Absent these regular cues, the body gets thrown off schedule.

It is also important to realize that time, as a fundamental dimension of perception, is a qualitative concept that expresses our awareness of such things as past, present, future, and periodicity. To quantify time requires that we develop a system of units that can be used to scale this perception according to a mutually agreed-upon set of standards. Such quantification forms a branch of the science of horology, from the Greek *hora*, meaning "time" (the same root from which the word "hour" is derived), and *logos*, which means "telling." Thus, any device that tells time is called a horologe. One of the earliest horologes was based on our qualitative awareness of the alternating periods of lightness and darkness that coincide with the periodic rising and setting of the sun. The sundial came into existence around 1500 BCE in ancient Egypt to track the shadow cast by the sun upon a graduated disk as the earth revolved around its own axis. The Anglo-Saxon *daeg* later became "day" to designate the total duration of sunlight; and because of the direction in which the sun's shadow moved across the sundial as the earth rotated (as tracked in the Northern hemisphere, when the long stem of the dial was oriented in an east-west direction, with its elevated cross-bar positioned on the east side until noon, after which the device was rotated 180° in the afternoon), we now have the designation "clockwise" to correspond to that direction of movement. Eventually, an entire day came to include daylight plus darkness, the total time for the earth to complete one full revolution around its axis.

The Egyptians arbitrarily divided the major portion of the sunlit day into 10 parts (perhaps because we can count on 10 fingers), each part being called an hour. They then added another fifth of that (two parts) to account for the twilight time at dawn, and two more hours to account for the dusk twilight. Finally, although there was no way to measure the passage of time at night (because sundials do not work in the dark), it nevertheless seemed appropriate to divide the period between the end of dusk and the beginning of dawn into 10 parts as well—which is one theory of how the day came to be divided into 24 equal units, each called an hour. (Can we assume that such division was accomplished at one of the two times in the year when the sun crosses the equator, and day and night are of approximately equal length, i.e., around September 23, the autumnal equinox, or March 21, the vernal equinox?)

Another theory that attempts to explain why there are 24 hours in a day is based on the sexagesimal number system that prevailed at the time of the Babylonian (now Iraq) Sumerians, later adopted by the Egyptians. The sexagesimal number system uses 60 as its base and requires that all numbers be divisible by six (as in 12 hours of daylight; 12 hours of darkness; 24 hours in a day; and, perhaps as well, 12 inches in a foot; 36 inches in a yard, etc.). Why it is 60, as opposed to the now more popular decimal system that is based on the number 10, is not really known for sure. It may have been some magic number that was used to unify the then-existing systems of measurement, or maybe it was a good way to divide into smaller units the 360 day/night cycles that were thought at the time to be a measure of how long it took the earth to complete one full orbit around the sun ($360 = 60 \times 6$, i.e., all sixes). Indeed, that is why the circle (also the Egyptian hieroglyph for the sun) is divided into 360°. Then, too, the number 60 also has many divisors: 1, 2, 3, 4, 5, 6, 10, 12, 15, 20, 30—it's a nice number, so much so that it was even assigned its own unit, the cycle (as in Alfred Lord Tennyson's, "Better fifty years of Europe than a cycle of Cathay," in his poem, *Locksley Hall*).

Moreover, the use of a sexagesimal number system also explains why the hour and the degree are further divided into 60 units, each called a minute (from the Latin *minus*, meaning "less"), and why each hour is divided a "second" time, breaking the minute into 60 subunits called, appropriately enough, seconds. Today, we further subdivide the second—this time using the decimal system—into hundredths of a second, thousandths (milliseconds), millionths (microseconds), billionths (nanoseconds), trillionths (picoseconds), quadrillionths (femtoseconds), and so on. We even think we can narrow down to 10^{-43} seconds following the Big Bang, our understanding of when the universe was born, prior to which time the four fundamental forces of nature were unified (i.e., there was only one such force).

Going in the other direction, seven days became a week (from the Greek *wechsel*, for "change") because of the astrological belief in ancient civilizations that planet earth was influenced by each of the then-known-to-exist seven heavenly bodies, in regularly repeating patterns that assigned a specific day to a specific body. Thus, the Sun's Day became Sunday; the Moon's Day became Monday; the Day of Tiu (the Teutonic god of war, identified with the Norse god Tyr and the Roman Mars, hence the planet) became Tuesday; the Day of Woden (the most important Anglo-Saxon god, identified with the Scandinavian god Odin and the Roman Mercury, hence the corresponding planet) became Wednesday; the Day of Thor (the old Scandinavian god of thunder, identified with the Roman ruler of all gods, Jove, or Jupiter, hence the planet) became Thursday; the Day of Frigga (highest goddess of the ancient Scandinavians, often associated with Freya, the goddess of love and beauty, hence the Roman goddess and corresponding planet Venus) became Friday; and, finally, the Day of Saturn became Saturday. We then start the week all over again (Middle English *weke*, for a "turning").

About four weeks (29.5 days) became a month, the approximate time it takes the moon (hence the corresponding name) to make one complete revolution around the earth; just over 52 weeks, some 365.25 days, became a year (possibly derived from the word stem "ir," which connotes "to go more"), the approximate time it takes for the earth to complete one full orbit around the sun. The Romans originally divided this year into just 10 months; hence, month 10 was December, 9 was November, 8 was October, 7 was September, and so on. These names were kept for months 12, 11, 10, and 9, respectively, when the year was extended to a full 12 months, adding August (to honor the first Roman Emperor Augustus Caesar), July (to honor Julius Caesar because he was born in this month), June (one theory suggests that this month was named to commemorate the *juniors*, the youth taken to be soldiers of the state), May (the month of the greater magnus god, Jupiter), April (the month of flowers, from the Latin *aperio*, "to open"), March (the month of Mars, when fair weather allows wars to start up again), February (the month of the feast of cleansing, from the Latin *februa*, the Roman festival of purification), and January (the doorway of the year, from the Latin *janua*, for "door").

At this point, we switch back to the more popular decimal system to go beyond years to tens of years (decades), hundreds (centuries), thousands (millennia), millions (mega-eras), and billions (eons). Current thinking is that our own universe may be as old as 20 billion years (the Hubble Age), or as young as 12 billion. Planet earth came along some 4.5 billion years ago, and the first forms of life appeared on it about a billion years later. To put things into perspective, if we started to time events from the Big Bang ($t = 0$) and scale them so that today is just 24 hours later, then what would eventually evolve to become us came along just nine seconds ago. For 23 hours, 59 minutes, 51 seconds of the 24 hours from $t = 0$ up to today, life that was to become Homo sapiens did not even exist!

While you think about that, ponder this: We have noted that our qualitative perception of time is intimately linked to our awareness of the periodicities inherent in our universe, but our ambient environment is not our only source of sensory stimulation; much of that stimulation derives from interpersonal dynamics. We get constant perceptual cues from one another—through body language, facial expressions, tone of voice, etc. Those cues, in turn, can bring out the best in us, or the worst. Approach someone in an intimidating manner, and do not be surprised to be greeted by a defensive, even hostile, response. Approach that same person in a nonthreatening way, with an attitude of goodwill, and you can expect a much more agreeable, friendly response. People naturally tend to react in kind to their perception of how they are being approached; they take their cues from you (and vice versa), even though they might be misinterpreting those cues (how often have you heard the expression, "I didn't mean it that way; you misread my intent"?). Regardless of your intent, if it is perceived in a menacing way—especially by children—you will get an apprehensive fear response (i.e., the body goes into 911 survival mode); if it is perceived to be harmless, you will get a confident all-clear response (i.e., the body relaxes into a warm comfort zone). So, the next time you get something less than a positive response from another person, think about the cues you may have been sending, and look in the mirror to find the possible cause for that response. Having said that, it is now "time" for me to go look in the mirror.

Space

American Laboratory, November 2002

Despite numerous attempts over several years, I have been unable to draft a satisfying etymological basis for the word "space." To date, I have discovered that the word apparently originated sometime around 1300 A.D., and derives from the Latin *spatium*, a word of unknown origin that refers to a "room, area, distance" or "stretch of time." *Spatium* evolved into the Old French *espace*, the "e" gradually disappearing with usage over time in a process called apheresis (from the Greek prefix *apo-*, meaning "away," and *haireîn*, meaning "take").

Personally, I have my own theory about space, which correlates with its being associated with a stretch of time and with distance. In my theory, everything that can be experienced—all of reality—derives from the unbalanced disturbance (e.g., the Big Bang?) of a quasi-equilibrated state of existence.[1] Such disturbance leads to a delayed conversion of potential energy into kinetic energy, various forms of which are part of a set of dimensions of perception that allow us, through our senses, to experience the world around us. One of these perceptual dimensions is length, L, by which we become aware of, define, and eventually quantify the fact that disturbances to quasi-equilibrated states do not remain localized and self-contained. Rather, because realized energy is, by nature, energy of movement, such disturbances propagate radially outward in all directions away from the source of the disturbance (a kind of domino effect).

Our awareness of this propagating outward in every direction that becomes manifest over a stretch of time, during which the disturbance traverses distances, L, of varying magnitude, gives rise to the concept of "space." In other words, our consciousness of propagating disturbances is what gives reality the attribute of having some perceptible expanse, which may be what the ancients were referring to when they coined the word *spatium* to connote the region that extends in all directions away from an arbitrary point of reference. Whether or not they actually realized this connotation in a cognitive sense, we will probably never know.

The fact that space is defined to be three-dimensional is peculiar to the mathematics that we use to locate uniquely any point in this domain of reality, and to the methods we use to quantify its associated dimension of perception, length. That is to say, first we establish a mutually agreed-upon and fixed point of reference from which we will measure length (or distance). This might be the actual location from which the propagating disturbance originated, or the position of an observer, or some fixed star in our spatial galaxy, or any other arbitrary point of reference that we deem to be appropriate for whatever reason we all find to be mutually acceptable. Having thus chosen this origin from which to measure length, we then find that it takes three such measurements—each independent of the other two—to locate uniquely any point in space relative to our point of reference. The three measurements that unambiguously locate any point in space relative to any other are called the spatial coordinates of the respective point; thus, the entire family of such spatial coordinates that can be independently and uniquely defined maps out the three-dimensional domain of our reality—the domain we call space.

Hypothetically, space can extend out to infinity from any arbitrary point of reference, but for practical purposes, our space (i.e., the domain within which we experience reality) consists of our entire universe. Estimates suggest that the universe within which we live—the observable expanse that encompasses, quite simply, everything within our experience thus far—is composed of at least 100 billion galaxies that span a region of some 10–15 billion light years in extent. One light year is some 5.87867 trillion miles, or about 1013 kilometers, so we are talking here about a big domain! In fact, the radius of the observable universe is called the Hubble Length, 1.18×10^{26} m.

Within this cosmic region, our disk-shaped galaxy (the Milky Way) was formed within the first million years or so following time, $t = 0$ (the Big Bang?), and it, too, is a big place—consisting of 100 (or more) billion stars spanning a region about 100 thousand or more light years (10^{18} km) across by about 6000 light years thick. Beyond that, we speak of intergalactic space. Focusing in still further within the Milky Way, our own 5.5-billion-year-old star, the sun, maintains a rather huge (10^{10} miles across, beyond which we speak of interstellar space) solar system, which includes billions of smaller stars, asteroids, comets, meteors, aggregates of cosmic dust and gas, and nine planets (from outside in, Pluto, Neptune, Uranus, Saturn, Jupiter, Mars, Earth, Venus, and Mercury), some with orbiting moons or satellites. All revolve around the sun, and are held to specific trajectories around this big star by balancing dynamic forces of motion against gravitational forces of attraction. (Note: The origin and exact nature of gravity remains one of the great mysteries of science, along with the strong forces that hold nuclei together, the weak forces associated with radioactive decay, and electromagnetism.)

So, we have the more generic *World Book Dictionary* definition of "space" as "the unlimited room or place extending in all directions and in which all things exist." Our own earth—one of the nine planets listed previously—moves through this space, which is more specifically divided into four subspaces: interplanetary space consists of that region inside of 10^{10} miles from earth (i.e., lying within the solar system), but moving radially inward only to about 10^6 miles from earth. It is the space within which dwell all eight of the other planets except earth. Translunar space continues on inward about another order of magnitude to 10^5 miles from earth, engulfing the region within which lies the earth's moon, which revolves around the planet on a trajectory of mean radius 239,000 miles. Continuing inward, we enter the cislunar space (the prefix "cis-" refers to the fact that we are now on the earth's side of the moon, as opposed to "trans-," which connotes the interplanetary side of earth's satellite) and this space takes us to the outer limits of the earth's exosphere at about 1000 miles up (1.61×10^6 m). The final subspace takes us through the exosphere down to about 300 miles above the earth's surface, i.e., the outer limit of its atmosphere, which, too, is divided into four general subspaces.

Subspace 1, the thermosphere, ranges down from about 300 miles above the earth's surface to 50 miles (264,000 ft or 80.5 km), and is so-named because temperature increases with altitude within this region. Subspace 2, the mesosphere, continues on down to 30 miles (158,400 ft or 48.3 km), and is so-called because it lies in-between the stratosphere below and the thermosphere above. In this subspace, most of the earth's ozone layer is created in a virtually isothermal environment. The mesosphere and thermosphere are also frequently referred to collectively as the ionosphere because, in this space, solar ultraviolet radiation ionizes what little air is present. Subspace 3, the stratosphere, continues down to 10 miles (52,800 ft or 16.1 km) above the earth's surface; its name derives from the Latin *stratus*, which means "a spreading out," referring to the fact that air spreads out (becomes rarefied) at these altitudes. Subspace 4, the troposphere, takes us the rest of the way down to the earth's surface, and is the atmospheric layer within which we live, and within which there is a steady fall in temperature with increasing altitude.

Our space thus lies within about a 10,000-ft boundary layer of air that surrounds a 5.98×10^{24} kg, somewhat spherical (6.38×10^{6}-m-radius or 7926-mile-diam at the equator) mass located about 28,000 light years from the center of our galaxy and 92.9 million (on average) miles from the sun, a mass that we call home. To us, home is planet earth—estimated to be about 4.5 billion years old in its present form, an offspring having less than one-millionth the total mass of its parent sun, and being only 1/100th its physical size. Like the planets that orbit around the sun and the moon that orbits around the earth, we, too, in our own space, gravitate toward and travel in orbits around those who influence us the most. For any given individual, one can define an abstract sphere of influence—a physical space within which are contained friends and family, professional acquaintances and fellow workers, role models that we strive to emulate, and so on. To the extent that we connect with these folks, follow them, impersonate them (at least in our mind and to some extent in our actions), and otherwise allow them to impact our lives in very significant ways, one can liken our own movements within our physical space to those of celestial bodies in outer space.

Taking this reasoning one step further, it would be nice if the role models toward which we gravitate also provided a stabilizing influence that kept us traveling in the proper orbits. Perhaps the absence of such role models at all, much less appropriate ones, might be one of the missing ingredients that results in some individuals losing the stabilizing influence of a positive "gravitational pull" that causes them to go astray into "bad orbits" that lead to bad things. It's a thought worth considering, but not now, and not here. Rather, I will close with one final observation about space—less literal than figurative.

There are times when we choose to isolate ourselves from those around us, from our activities of daily living, and from the concerns of the moment. We request that we be given some space, by which we really mean "time"—time to be able to think, to get away from environmental influences that may cloud our judgment. We say, "Give me some space," meaning, "Leave me alone. Give me 'room to roam'—both mentally and physically. Let me break orbit enough to establish some identity, to 'find' myself. I need time to be introspective, to sort things out, to get 'in tune' with myself, to expand my horizons." Thus, "space" can mean not only a physical expanse, but also, as mentioned at the beginning of this editorial, a "stretch of time," a duration, a "while" for contemplating . . . which implies that in some sense, "space" and "time" might be interchangeable concepts. Indeed, perhaps they are. I leave you with that thought.

Reference

1. Schneck DJ. The seven fundamental laws of existence. *Am Lab* Jun 2002; 34(12):6.

Space Revisited

American Laboratory News, August 2004

Further to my epistle on space (*American Laboratory* Nov 2002; 34[22]:6–8), consider that a fundamental law of reality is that disturbances to quasi-equilibrated states do not remain self-contained and localized, but rather propagate radially outward, away from the source of the disturbance (*American Laboratory* Jun 2002; 34[12]:6–8). Our awareness of this spreading out establishes the concept of space and the primary dimension of perception, length (L), by which we describe and quantify it. One way to measure how fast the disturbance is scattering away from its source, and hence the resulting region of influence ("space") being progressively created by it, is to quantify the rate ($\partial/\partial t$) at which the closed surface area (A, measured in some sense by the square of a characteristic length) is growing, where A totally encompasses both the source (S) of the disturbance and the volume (V, measured in some sense by a characteristic length, cubed) of the neighborhood around S that has thus far been affected by it. Mathematically, the time rate of change of this bounding surface can be functionally correlated with the corresponding change in V using the divergence theorem, which allows double integrals over a surface (i.e., area integrals) of any time-varying vector function to be reversibly converted into triple integrals (i.e., volume integrals) over the corresponding region enclosed by the surface.

Physically, the dimensions (L^2/t) of the time rate of change of A define a kinematic transport coefficient (α). The latter is a measure of both the mobility of the propagating disturbance, i.e., the inherent ease with which it can move away from its source (related to its original strength, as in, for example, the Big Bang) and how much resistance it encounters as it propagates away from its source, i.e., the permeability of the space that it creates. Examples of kinematic transport coefficients include thermal diffusivities, mass diffusion coefficients, fluid kinematic viscosities, turbulent eddy diffusion coefficients, and electromagnetic diffusivities. The product of the extensive property, mass (m), with an intensive kinematic transport coefficient (α), defines a transition parameter known as action, of which the quantum of action, h = Planck's constant, is a prominent example. It is important to realize that the generic dimensions (L^2/t) can also be derived from 1) the product of an intensive linear momentum (i.e., velocity, having dimensions L/t) with a characteristic space dimension (length, L); 2) an intensive energy function having dimensions $(L/t)^2$, with a characteristic time dimension (t); or 3) an intensive moment of inertia (having the dimensions L^2 of the square of a radius of gyration) with a characteristic circular ($2\pi \times$ linear) frequency (having dimensions 1/t of reciprocal time). These products are called conjugate pairs, which will be discussed later in further detail.

But first, I want to mention that in the previous "Space" editorial, our discussion of "the unlimited room or place extending in all directions, and in which all things exist," was limited only to the macroscopic region extending from the outermost reaches of our universe down to planet earth. We stopped short of getting into the microscopic molecular, atomic, nuclear, and subnuclear regions of space, partly because we did not formally establish a length scale for measuring "space" at these levels of perception. That is to say, realizing that space, and its corresponding dimension of perception, length (L), are (like time) qualitative concepts, by which we think of something as having a certain physical "size," we now need to quantify L by introducing arbitrary units of measurement for this perceptual dimension of space. Furthermore, since we have been talking about planet earth, let's start by taking the distance along a great circle on this planet, from the North Pole to the Equator, traveling along a meridian (longitude) that passes through Paris (why not?), and dividing that distance into 10 million equal pieces, calling each a meter (from the Latin *metrum*, meaning "measure"). Indeed, this is precisely how the meter was originally defined. It was subsequently refined to a more accurate definition involving the exact length of a bar of platinum-iridium. Then, in 1960, we got really fancy, defining the meter to be exactly 1,650,763.73 vacuum wavelengths of the orange-red light emitted from the isotope krypton-86 (note the accuracy to two decimal places), which is approximately 39.37 in. (the word "inch" being derived from the Latin *uncia*, meaning "a twelfth part," in this case, of a foot). Having thus defined the basic unit of length, the meter, we can further subdivide it into tenths of a meter (decimeters), hundredths (centimeters, 2.54 cm = 1 in.), thousandths (millimeters), millionths (micrometers = microns), billionths (nanometers), etc., and, going the other way, 10 m = 1 decameter, 100 m = 1 hectometer, 1000 m = 1 kilometer (just over 0.62 miles), and so on.

Keeping in mind the above units of length measurement, we now define a continuum scale of perception, which, in our experience, takes us down to about 10^{-4} meters, and within which realm *mass* is the basic dimension of perception. The continuum-space scale was invented for convenience. That is, in many aspects of applied mathematics, science, and engineering, we seek the simplest approach that yields practical (and practicable) solutions for whatever purpose these solutions are to be used—approximations that suffice to solve whatever problem we are dealing with and whatever need we are seeking to meet. Oftentimes, those needs can be met by considering that a particular material under investigation uniformly fills all of the space it occupies; the entire region is assumed to consist everywhere of that material even though, based on atomic and molecular theories, we know better. Those theories tell us that most of space is empty, that matter, *per se*, occupies but a tiny fraction of this vast expanse at any level of perception, and that it has a discrete microstructure that demands careful attention to detail. All well and good, we say, but there *are* situations in which we can get away with ignoring that detail in favor of statistical averaging. We can effectively neglect discrete microstructure in favor of the statistical manifestation of the whole, and that's what the field of continuum mechanics deals with: the statistical behavior of the whole. Of course, once you start talking statistics, you have to guarantee a significant-enough sample size to justify that approach. In the case of continuum mechanics, such justification comes in the form of a Knudsen number (Kn), which is the ratio of the molecular mean-free path, λ (or, in the case of turbulent flow, the mixing length), to the smallest length scale (L) that characterizes the particular problem you are dealing with. Generally speaking, if Kn = λ/L << 1.00 (typically, of order 0.01 or less), the continuum hypothesis is valid, meaning that enough molecules occupy a given infinitesimally small region of space such that, for our purposes, emphasis may be placed on features (properties) that describe whatever is under scrutiny in a "holistic," statistical, macroscopic sense, as opposed to a molecular, discrete, microscopic sense.

Consider that at typical temperatures and pressures near the surface of the earth there are some 3×10^{10} molecules of air packed into 10^{-9} cubic centimeters of space, such that, usually, Kn << 1.00 for all intents and purposes. Even getting into the earth's exosphere, at about 500 km up, there are still about 7×10^{7} molecules of air in every cubic centimeter of space, and Kn < 1. In both cases, these are numbers large enough for an average taken over the molecules to be independent of their number, for all practical purposes, and the numbers get even better when one is dealing with liquids and solids. Thus, the continuum formulation should give (and generally does give) fairly reasonable results if applied in the region from about 10^5 m above the earth's surface (the base of the thermosphere, where λ is of order 10 cm) down to 10^{-4} m (the Knudsen length, which is 1000 times the typical mean-free path for air at sea level, at normal atmospheric pressure). On the other hand, if $\lambda \to L$ (e.g., rarefied gas dynamics) or if $L \to \lambda$ (e.g., "creeping" flows), then all bets are off: The continuum assumption breaks down and the mean-free path of molecules requires specific attention. The continuum formulation also fails in other situations, such as when the density of a material is so high that intermolecular collisions determine its dependence on previous history for present response, or at very high Mach numbers in gas dynamics and very low Reynolds numbers in viscous flows. There are also intermediate regimes, called slip flow ($0.01 \leq$ Kn ≤ 0.10) and transition flow ($0.10 \leq$ Kn ≤ 1.00) regions, where the continuum hypothesis has to be evaluated on an individual, case-by-case basis. In those cases where its validity is in question, and certainly if Kn > 1.00, one enters the next smaller region of space, at the molecular scale of perception.

In the molecular realm of statistical mechanics, kinetic theory, chemical/heat/sound energy, and thermodynamics, temperature is added to mass as primary dimensions of perception, and our spatial experience in this domain goes down to 1.0584×10^{-10} m (about an angstrom unit): the Bohr length, which is the atomic diameter of the ground state of a hydrogen atom. Below that, we get into the atomic realm of quantum mechanics, electromagnetism, and radioactive decay, where electric charge now joins in as a primary dimension of perception, and the smallest length of any significance is the so-called Compton wavelength of the proton, which is its approximate nuclear diameter, 1.32×10^{-15} m. Then we enter the mysterious, exotic realm of high-energy nuclear physics and its elementary particles, where gluons, gravitons, leptons, and "tasty, colorful, honest (truth, top), beautiful (bottom), charming, yet strange, up and down" quarks create a bizarre wonderland of imaginative fantasy, down to the hypothetical microscopic Planck length of 4.05083×10^{-35} m, where, it is believed, the quantized nature of gravity first becomes evident, and below which the common laws of physics as we accept them break down.

The Planck length is purely theoretical, being calculated from three fundamental constants: the universal gravitational constant, $G = 6.67259 \times 10^{-11}$ N–m^2/kg^2; Planck's constant, $h = 6.6260755 \times 10^{-34}$ J/sec; and the speed of light in a vaccuum, $c = 2.997925 \times 10^8$ m/sec. Thus, $\lambda_{Planck} = [Gh/c^3]^{1/2} = 4.05083 \times 10^{-35}$ m. This number is sometimes calculated by an alternate method that yields a somewhat smaller value on the same order of magnitude, 1.6160×10^{-35} m, but regardless, there is no way that we can measure or even relate to lengths anywhere near that small, which leads to the very legitimate question: Does "space" (or "time" for that matter) really have any experiential significance at or below the molecular/atomic scales of perception? Remember, our awareness (ability to experience) of space is what makes it real to us, so on that basis, the answer to the question posed has to be probably not, since we have no particular awareness of space and/or time, *per se*, in such tiny denominations. That brings us back to the concept of conjugate pairs introduced earlier.

Recall that velocity and length, energy and time, and radius of gyration squared and frequency are all conjugate pairs in that, in each case, their product defines a kinematic transport coefficient. Could it be then that, depending on one's scale of perception and degree of resolution, *one* of the pair of conjugates is a more appropriate dimension of perception than the other? For example, length and time may be appropriate dimensions of perception on a *macroscopic* scale of perception (say, from mid-way through the molecular domain out to infinity), where *coarse* resolution capabilities (say, down to the electron microscope at around 0.2–0.5 nm, or perhaps even as small as one angstrom unit) suffice to solve most problems of practical interest. But it may very well be that L and t need to be replaced by their respective conjugate pair, intensive linear momentum and energy, on a microscopic scale of perception (say, from mid-way through the molecular domain down to zero, passing through the atomic, nuclear, and subnuclear regions) where a greater capability for fine-tuning (resolution) is definitely required. Certainly, we can measure momentum and energy at these smaller scales more easily than we can length and time, and we can also experience the former two more readily at these incredibly small scales than we can the latter two, for which we have no "feel" at nuclear and subnuclear levels of perception.

Taking this reasoning one step further, I would also like to suggest that the concepts of conjugate pairing, scale of perception, and corresponding resolution may offer a plausible approach for providing some insight into the phenomenon of the particle-wave duality. That is to say, whereas mass moment of inertia and its corresponding intensive property, radius of gyration squared (i.e., variables normally associated with particles) may suffice to describe physical attributes in a macroscopic, coarse domain, these need to be replaced on a finer, microscopic level of perception, requiring greater resolution, by radius-of-gyration-squared's corresponding conjugate pair: frequency, which is a property associated with waves. I will leave this thought to be pondered, for now, as one deserving further consideration at another time.

Space–Time Reality Variables
American Laboratory News, March 2005

In my editorials on energy[1] and equilibrium,[2] I emphasized that our perception of reality is predicated on the existence of *movement*—which is to say, we can only perceive *kinetic* energy, which is derived from implicit *potential* energy. It follows, then, that embedded in the primary dimensions of perception that define our sense of "reality" are corresponding measures of movement. These measures include such things as physical displacement (which is associated with the primary dimension, L, of space), velocity (which introduces the primary dimension, t, of time, through the rate-of-change of L), and acceleration (which is the time-rate-of-change of velocity). Furthermore, focusing one's attention on the movement of specific quantities of material establishes the corresponding scale at which that reality is being perceived.[3]

For example, if one wishes to examine, specifically, the behavior of tiny bits of material, like atoms (or smaller), the study of the movement of such quantities defines events that are taking place at the electromagnetic scale of perception, which is associated with the corresponding primary dimension, Q, of electric charge. On the other hand, if one's intent is to describe, specifically, the behavior of larger pieces of material, like molecules, the study of the motion of such quantities defines events that are taking place at the thermodynamic scale of perception, which is associated with the corresponding primary dimension, T, of temperature. Focusing one's attention on the movement of still larger quantities of material brings us into the continuum scale of perception, where events are governed less by the microscopic atomic/molecular structure of matter than they are by the macroscopic inertial properties of the specific material whose behavior is being examined, which material can thus be considered to be a continuously distributed quantity of mass, M, the primary dimension associated with this scale of perception. And so it goes—into the nuclear and subnuclear scales at the low end of the material-size spectrum, and the cosmic and supercosmic scales at the high end. All such scales are defined according to the specific unit quantity of material whose behavior is of interest.

At *any* scale of perception, however, "reality" derives from movement, and movement, in turn, is defined by combinations of the space–time variables, L and t, respectively. Indeed, when the behavior of materials is defined independently of the scale of perception (or, equivalently, "per unit mass"), such behavior is termed "intensive"—as opposed to *extensive* properties that do depend on the extent (amount) of the system under observation. In previous editorials, I have written separately about space[4,5] (and the qualitative dimension, L, by which we perceive and describe it) and time.[6–9] It now seems appropriate to combine them in order to illustrate how the generic concept of movement translates dimensionally into combinations of L and t that define for us the intrinsic concept of "reality." To do so, define a generic reality parameter, R, which is equal to some numerical constant, C, multiplied by a space–time reality variable, V, where V is defined to be the space–time combination, $L^j t^k$, j,k = 0, ±1, ±2, ±3 ... ±n, and n = the number of degrees-of-freedom (independent dimensions) that are characteristic of the domain of interest. Thus, $R = CV = CL^j t^k$, and the mass-dependent (extensive) counterpart of R is $R^* = MCV = MCL^j t^k$, where M is the particular quantity of material associated with the corresponding scale of perception.[3] For j and k ranging from zero to plus or minus n, and arbitrary C, R can obviously take on many values (49, for example, just for C = 1 and n = a three-dimensional space/time domain)—way too many to consider all of them here, so let's examine just a few special cases to see how this works:

Suppose C = ½, j = +2, and k = –2. Then $R = \frac{1}{2}(L/t)^2$ defines the basic reality variable associated with specific (intensive) energy, which comes in two forms: potential and kinetic.[1] In potential form, this value of R defines intensive potentials, or "charges," φ, which are the source of everything "real." The corresponding extensive quantity, $R^* = \frac{1}{2}(M)(L/t)^2$, defines the perceptible form of R, which is the kinetic energy of M. Note: For C = 1, the corresponding extensive quantity, $R^* = M(L/t)^2$, defines the "moment" of a force, $F = ML/t^2$, having a lever-arm of length, L, about a given point; or, in the case of a pure couple, its corresponding "torque"; or, as it relates to the conversion of energy into work, an "effort" function, FL. Conversion of imperceptible intensive potentials into perceptible kinetic energy (reality) takes place when a quasi-equilibrated state is disturbed.[2] We perceive that disturbance as a force, F, which, according to the extensive form of Newton's Second Law of Motion, is given (for constant M) by Ma. The quantity "a" is the space–time reality variable called linear acceleration (intensive force), defined by $C = 1$, $j = +1$, and $k = -2$, i.e., $R = L/t^2 = a$, and $F = Ma$. (Note: for $j = 0$, $R = 1/t^2$ defines "angular acceleration," such as radians per second^2. Note, also, that a disturbance results from a spatial gradient in intensive potential, i.e., $a = \blacktriangledown\varphi$, so that a disequilibrated state corresponds to one in which φ is not uniformly distributed, thus generating a disturbing force, F, usually proportional to $-\blacktriangledown\varphi$.)

If we think of intensive potentials, φ, as representing "capable of being" (potentially realizable), and intensive forces, a, as "causing to be" (changing "potential" to "kinetic," disturbing, accelerating), then the next space–time reality variable of interest is "being" itself, which is defined by the variable associated with movement, i.e., speed! Intensive speed is defined by $C = 1$, $j = +1$, and $k = -1$ (reciprocal time), which yields $R = (L/t) = v$. (Note: The corresponding extensive quantity, $R^* = Mv$, defines the linear momentum of M, which we observe to be the derivative with respect to "reality variable," v, of kinetic energy, $\frac{1}{2} Mv^2$. In turn, the derivative with respect to v of linear momentum is the extensive quantity, mass, M. Note, also, for these values of C and k, that $j = 0$ yields such quantities as frequency, angular velocity, and shear rate, all with dimensions $1/t$.)

Going one step further, if we think of time, t ($C = 1$, $j = 0$, $k = +1$), as "resistance to being" (representing the perceived inertial delay between cause, $F = Ma$, and effect, Mv),[8] then space may be thought of in terms of the cascading "propagation" of a disturbance (transport of "being") away from its source, once the effect of F has become manifest.[4] There are actually two aspects to the concept of propagation: the specific process of the "spreading out" itself, and the resulting region created ("space") by this process. The process is defined by the basic intensive reality variable given by $C = 1$, $j = +2$, and $k = -1$, i.e., $R = L^2/t$, which we recognize to be the dimensions of kinematic transport coefficients, α (such as mass diffusion coefficients, thermal and electromagnetic diffusivities, kinematic viscosity, and intensive forms of Planck's constant and angular momentum). (Note: The corresponding extensive quantity, $R^* = M\alpha$, defines a quantity called "action," which has the same dimensions as the extensive angular momentum of M.) Among other things, kinematic transport coefficients allow one to quantify the transition of one quasi-equilibrated state into another (i.e., the reality that we "perceive"), as a result of the former having been disturbed.

The actual region created as a disturbance propagates away from its source is defined by setting $k = 0$ ($t^0 = 1$), and $C = 1$. That is to say, we see in this case that R, for $j = +1$, $+2$, and $+3$, respectively, defines for us the corresponding geometric (extensive) properties of spatial length ($j = +1$ for distance, wavelength, radius of gyration, centroid, etc.), spatial expanse ($j = +2$ for surface area, radius-of-gyration-squared, which is *intensive* moment of inertia, etc.), and spatial bulk ($j = +3$ for volume). (Note: $j = -1$ in this case defines the reciprocal of wavelength, which is wave number.)

And so it continues—with every kinematic space–time combination, $CL^j t^k$, and corresponding kinetic counterpart, $MCL^j t^k$, representing some perceptible physical aspect of "reality," in a domain having "n" generalized degrees-of-freedom (independent dimensions). For example, the case $C = 1$, $k = -1$, and $j = +3$ defines a volumetric flow rate, such as milliliters per minute (L^3/t); switching j to -1 in this case (i.e., $R = 1/Lt$) defines an intensive impedance; and $j = -2$ (i.e., $R = 1/L^2 t$), an intensive mass flux (unit quantity of material, per unit time, per unit area). Skipping ahead to $k = -3$, we have, for $C = 1$, such things as specific intensity for $j = 0$; "jerk" for $j = +1$; and specific power (or "fluxion") for $j = +2$. Then, for $k = +1$, and $C = 1$, one encounters, again, the basic dimension of time ($j = 0$, which also includes the period of vibration), and for $k = +2$, $C = 1$, and $j = +1$, a quantity called "compliance."

Without belaboring the point, what is quite conspicuous, as one develops these exercises and compares them to the human experience, is the fact that, in real life, most of the kinematic and kinetic quantities encountered are described in terms of the *reciprocal* of time (i.e., $k = -1$, -2, -3...). This observation strongly suggests the possibility that in actuality, time, as it relates to our awareness of it, takes on greater importance as a measure of *rate* than of *duration*; it serves effectively as a yardstick for assessing our consciousness of how fast a system is reacting to, responding, and recovering from having been disturbed. What helps to reinforce this suggestion is the further observation that most anatomical sense organs are phasic-type transducers rather than tonic type. That is to say, they respond most effectively, in an integral and differential sense, to rate-sensitive changes in stimulus than they do in a proportional sense to the magnitude of the stimulus, and its duration, *per se*. For the most part, the magnitude of any given adequate stimulus determines only *if* a particular sensory nerve fiber will respond—i.e., different fibers are responsive to different adequate stimuli, and have different (biased) threshold response potentials to those stimuli, but the response itself is stimulus-rate-dependent. Moreover, those sensory receptors, like Pacinian corpuscles, that have the ability to adapt (recover) most rapidly, are, correspondingly, the ones that are most rate-sensitive (for example, to vibratory inputs). Those sensory transducers, like Ruffini corpuscles, that adapt least rapidly, are, not surprisingly, more suitable for detecting the slowest-varying inputs; while those, like Golgi tendon organs, that adapt somewhere in between very fast and very slow, cover the intermediate range of variable sensory inputs.

If all of the above is, in fact, true, then in the realm of physics, in order to determine the response characteristics of physical systems, it may be of less importance to know "how long" (k positive) than it is to know "at what pace, or tempo" (k negative). Certainly, this is the case for fluids and viscoelastic materials, where most of the quantities in which time does appear in the numerator (such as intensive fluidity, Lt) are, in practice, defined more commonly in terms of the reciprocals of those quantities (such as intensive dynamic viscosity, having dimensions 1/Lt). These reciprocals are those variables with which the physics of the corresponding quantity (in this case, flow resistance) is more readily associated, suggesting that the reciprocal quantity is the more natural one in terms of the human experience—the other being more of an abstract derived concept. Finally, then, one can add to our definition of "time"[7,8] its being "the dimension of (or a measure of) rates-of-change"—which is to say, "our ability to sense changes that occur at a certain rate, and that derive from kinetic energy of motion, which, in turn, results from the disturbance of a quasi-equilibrated state that is endowed with the intensive potential that allows it to respond to that disturbance." Perhaps a bit long?

References

1. Schneck D. *Am Lab News* Aug 2003; 35(17):4–6.
2. Schneck D. *Am Lab* Jan 2003; 34(1):6–8.
3. Schneck D. *J Prof Iss Eng Edu Prac* Jul 2002; 128(3):100–6.
4. Schneck D. *Am Lab* Nov 2002; 34(22):6–8.
5. Schneck D. *Am Lab News* Aug 2004; 36(17):4–6.
6. Schneck D. *Am Lab* Oct 2000; 32(20):6–8.
7. Schneck D. *Am Lab* Nov 2003; 35(22):6–10.
8. Schneck D. *Am Biotech Lab* Dec 2002; 20(13):4–6.
9. Schneck D. *Am Biotech Lab* Jan 2003; 21(1):4.

Entropy

American Laboratory News, December 2003

In thermodynamics, it has always been observed that, although it is possible to convert mechanical work completely into heat, it is not possible to convert heat completely into work, i.e., as is formalized by the Second Law of Thermodynamics—the work-to-heat transition is not completely reversible, since there always remains a quantity of heat energy that is not available to do useful work. It turns out that this unavailable energy results from the disorderly activity (or the state of disorder) of the molecules involved at this (the thermodynamic) scale of perception. That is to say, *useful* thermodynamic work can only be derived from directed, orderly, synchronized molecular motion (kinetic energy).

To illustrate this concept, consider a simple tug-of-war. One or more individuals pull on one side of a rope against the resistance offered by one or more individuals pulling in the opposite direction on the other side of the rope. All of the individuals involved are working very hard, huffing and puffing and sweating, their muscles straining, exerting as much force as they can possibly develop in an effort to get the other side to yield. If the opposing sides are of equal strength, however, absolutely nothing happens. Despite all the exertion and all the effort, the rope remains stationary—motionless—no useful work is accomplished. On the other hand, think of how much more effective this arrangement would be, and how much of this elbow grease could be harnessed for useful purposes, if all of these same individuals got on the same side of the same rope and exerted the same maximum effort. Clearly, by working together, pulling simultaneously in the same direction, complementing and supplementing each other's power, these individuals could accomplish much more than they could previously, when they were working against one another. (The moral of the story is not a bad one to be learned in the study of life, in general, is it?)

Moreover, by reducing from two to one the number of different directions (degrees of freedom) in which these individuals are at liberty to pull on the rope, we have improved the effectiveness of the pull. Thus, it is in the thermodynamic sense that *random* molecular motion is wasted in that, statistically speaking, for a very large conglomeration of particles having many degrees of freedom, it is most probable that for every molecule moving one way, another is moving in exactly the opposite direction with comparable speed, so that the two cancel out one another (just like the tug-of-war example) as far as any meaningful coordinated effort is concerned. That's what the concept of entropy is all about—the net ability that systems have to do useful work or, more accurately, the *lack* of such ability, which is exactly what the word means.

"Entropy" derives from the Greek prefix *en-* meaning "in," and *tropē* meaning "a turning (toward)"; hence, entropy connotes "a turning (of energy) toward the inside," a form of energy that cannot be "turned outward" (released) to do useful work. Such uselessness derives from the random, disordered internal architecture of physical systems that possess many degrees of freedom, a haphazard arrangement that impedes from being mobilized (harnessed) into a focused effort ("useful" work) the movement of each individual element of the system. Therefore, entropy is a measure of such internal disarray. It is a property of the system in the sense that its value indicates what proportion of the total energy contained in that system is in a form that is not available to be perceived in any meaningful way (useful work) by an outside observer.

Stated another way, entropy is a measure of the number of possible configurations in which a system having a given total energy (closed and isolated) can be perceived. Furthermore, that configuration corresponding to the most disordered state of affairs (i.e., maximum entropy) represents a state of equilibrium at that respective scale of perception, wherein the total (thermodynamic) energy is entirely, randomly kinetic, such that no work can be done (see related editorials in *American Laboratory* Jan 2002; 34[1]:6–8 and *American Laboratory News* Aug 2003; 35[17]:4–6). The capacity of a thermodynamic system to perform useful work is zero at equilibrium because it exists in a state of maximum molecular randomness, which precludes the probability that any organized, synchronized, directed motion can take place at this scale of perception. Thus, absent a potential source of energy from within, no further change in the state of the system can occur spontaneously.

The only way to affect this status quo is to supply additional energy from outside the system (disturb the equilibrated state) through an exchange with the environment of mass (e.g., fuel and food, as in an open system) and/or energy (e.g., derived from a nonisolated system subjected to an unbalanced force couple network)—an exchange that is often labeled flow work. To put it more succinctly, a closed (i.e., cannot exchange mass with its environment), isolated (cannot exchange energy with its environment), thermodynamic system in equilibrium has minimum free energy (that which can potentially be mobilized to do useful work), maximum entropy (lots of disorganized kinetic energy), and is in its most probable spontaneous state corresponding to total chaos. Any external disturbance to this state upsets the random balance of kinetic energy by establishing new gradients in intensive potentials. These gradients, in turn, drive the system toward a newly equilibrated state, by a process we call transport, and in accordance with a minimum energy principle (i.e., via a path of least resistance). The actual transition is what we perceive to be reality, at the corresponding molecular scale of perception.

A rather straightforward line of reasoning allows one to extrapolate the thermodynamic concept of entropy derived for the molecular scale of perception to a more generic concept that applies at *any* scale of perception. Thus, I modestly and humbly offer for your consideration the idea that the more choices (degrees of freedom) a system has in which to configure itself (become manifest), the more likely it is to eventually equilibrate at the one configuration that is most random (i.e., has the greatest entropy), wherein the only thing that prevails is total confusion and corresponding gridlock. Let's consider a few examples of how this principle manifests itself in the many choices we face daily to make the very simplest of decisions that were once so easy and straightforward.

When I was a child, banking was easy. I went to the Williamsburg Savings Bank in Brooklyn, NY, opened a passbook savings account, and watched my money grow at 3% interest. Not so today: Today we have account options—statement savings with or without service charges (depending on minimum balances); basic checking with or without unlimited "free" check writing; interest-earning NOW (negotiable order of withdrawal) checking accounts; "classic" checking; PRIMEline checking for senior citizens (50+); certificates of deposit (CDs) with varying yields depending on their term, which can range from six months to ten years; Jumbo CDs (in excess of $50,000); brokered CDs; callable CDs; money market accounts; premium savings accounts (having tiered interest rates tied to higher balances)—the list goes on and on, and with it, the confusion as to which account is the right choice for me.

As a youngster, when my family and I went to a shoe store to buy me a pair of sneakers, I had basically two decisions to make: Did I want regular or high-top style, and did I prefer them in black or white? Today, I need to decide if I am in the market for a running shoe, a walking shoe, a basketball shoe, a tennis shoe, an athletic shoe, a casual shoe, or a cross-training shoe (whatever that is). There is a rainbow of colors to choose from, a variety of different styles, and an incredible range of prices. Now I have shifted the responsibility to my kids, who buy me sneakers for my birthday.

Although we were the last family in our neighborhood to own a television set, deciding which channel to watch was easy. There were only three basic networks: ABC, NBC, and CBS. Today, if you have a satellite dish, there are hundreds of choices. My family still has cable, but even then, we can surf more than 50 channels, so deciding what to watch (and who makes that decision) can lead to lively debates!

Similarly, I was the first member in the history of my entire family to get a driver's license, but once I did, the choice of what vehicle to purchase was relatively straightforward. There were essentially the big three major manufacturers of automobiles: Ford, General Motors, and Chrysler, and each had no more than five basic models to choose from, ranging from simple to luxurious. Have you purchased a car lately? If so, you know what I am talking about. Today, the choices of manufacturer, model, type of engine, body style, type of transmission, braking system, suspension system, color, interior, available accessories, price, and financing options seem endless. One practically needs a professional consultant just to be advised of what's out there, not to mention making an intelligent decision about what to buy!

Without belaboring the point, I think you get the message. In today's world, the number of degrees of freedom that we have available to us for making decisions that relate to just about every aspect of our activities of daily living—from choosing a career, to buying a house, to shopping for groceries, to planning for retirement, to investing our money, to raising our children, to choosing (and financing) a health plan, to something even as simple as deciding which cell phone plan to subscribe to—is increasing at an exponential rate, and it promises to get worse. As these degrees of freedom increase, and with them, the corresponding number of choices we have at our disposal, it is increasingly difficult to make *any* decision at all, much less the *right* one, to the point where we become gridlocked. We don't know what to do and we are confused; thus, we often decide to do nothing—that's society's version of entropy.

Generalizing still further, each time another choice or possibility presents itself, it offers yet another potential realization of the myriad of possibilities that are inherent in implicit reality—all that is capable of being (as perceived by some frame of reference, at some scale of perception, to some degree of resolution). But this is not a bottomless pit of possibilities, so I modestly and humbly offer yet another concept for you to consider: In a global sense, when we (generically) run out of the available pool of flow work (choices), we will have reached a state of what I call *grand entropy*. In other words, reality is winding down, like a clock, running out of available free energy, asymptotically drifting away. The entropy of the universe is, indeed, gradually increasing toward a limit where nothing further will ever be capable of happening. There will be no more potential energy; we will have used it all up. In a state of grand entropy, all forms of energy (everything possible) will be (or have been) manifest—in purely kinetic, totally random, entirely disordered form—and total chaos, with its associated gridlock, will prevail, however briefly, universally. Nothing new will be lurking just around the corner; there will be nothing to look forward to—no more future. This will, indeed, be the end—grand entropy, absolute equilibrium, *finis*, the demise of all creation.

But wait! Before we get all depressed about this, let's remember that a) we *know* that our universe will not exist forever—that's a given, and b) the end (hopefully) will not come in our lifetime, nor (in all likelihood) in that of many, many generations yet to come (millions, in fact). Also consider the possibility that when we do reach the final state of grand entropy, something might be around to rewind us—to bring us back to the beginning, to the original state of pure potential energy (zero entropy), when everything was inherently possible and a grand unification energy, also however briefly, prevailed. If this possibility is feasible, then there is a bright side to all of this entropy stuff and, indeed, out of chaos there will once again come order. Can it happen? Did it happen? Will it happen? Your guess is as good as mine!

Beware of Medical (and Scientific) Fads
American Biotechnology Laboratory, January 2005

Claudius Galenus of Pergamon (131–201 A.D.), a Greek physician to the Roman emperor Marcus Aurelius, developed his Ebb and Flow Theory of the human cardiovascular system around the middle of the second century. It took over 1500 years to discover that he was wrong! In 1913, riding the wave of Louis Pasteur's (1822–1895) Germ Theory of Disease, the Thompson-McFadden Commission of the United States Public Health Service issued a "definitive" report that came to the following unequivocal scientific conclusion: "Pellagra is in all probability a specific infectious disease communicable from person to person by means at present unknown." It only took about a decade for Joseph Goldberger (1874–1929) to show that, in fact, pellagra is not caused by an infection, but rather by a dietary deficiency of niacin (nicotinic acid), part of the vitamin B complex. It seems we are getting better… or are we?

One would think that the above two examples, and many others like them (e.g., the caloric and ether theories in physics), amply illustrate the dangers of group dynamics in forcing skeptics to conform to mostly speculative scientific fads. But, alas, this tends not to be the case, at least not when it comes to the current craze that thrives under the umbrella term "work-related musculoskeletal disorders (WMSDs)." The use of this moniker dates back to the work of Bernardino Ramazzini (1633–1714), who, in 1700, published his observations of the relationship of disease to employment activities in a book entitled *De Morbis Artificum Diatriba* [Diseases of Workers]. More than 300 years later—with but a mere smattering of hard scientific evidence to verify suggested cause/effect relationships, and being presumably smart enough to know better—we nevertheless still cling to Ramazzini's original assertion, i.e., that work-related ergonomic risk factors contribute in a first-order sense to compromising musculoskeletal health. This is yet another example of how we humans tend to be superficial in assessing any given situation (it takes on the order of just 7 seconds to form a first impression of somebody), opting instead to take the easy way out: jumping to conclusions based on unsubstantiated circumstantial evidence. Writers of detective novels make a great deal of money exploiting this affectation. Quite regrettably, even in real life, all too many innocent victims are falsely accused, sentenced to prison terms, even executed, based on scanty evidence that is subsequently (too late, for some) found to be flawed.

According to Ramazzini (and a concept that is still in vogue today), exposure to certain work-related "risk factors" is qualitatively associated with (not rigorously, scientifically proven to be a cause of) musculoskeletal diseases. The major risk factors are 1) "excessive" force of exertion (biomechanical overload, especially in weight lifting), 2) repetition of movements, 3) "unnatural" or awkward body postures (especially working with the arms overhead, and kneeling), 4) duration of exposure to the suspected risk, 5) excessive vibration, 6) environmental extremes (such as working in "unusually" hot or cold conditions or being exposed to hygienic "dangers"), 7) working continuously, without taking adequate periodic breaks, and 8) being subjected to mechanical "stress concentrations" (disproportionately greater loading of one region of the musculoskeletal system relative to another).

The operative words above are "qualitative" and "associated." Indeed, to date, there are no strict, individual-specific, dose-response criteria that quantify what exactly constitutes, for that person, excessive, overload, repetitive, unnatural, awkward, long duration exposure, extreme, unusual, dangerous, or disproportionate, in a sense that threatens that individual's health and well-being. The very few attempts to develop such criteria tend to be anecdotal, rather than based on rigorous, carefully controlled, randomized, double-blind investigations, or strict, statistically meaningful, unbiased, longitudinal (prospective) studies. Moreover, there are no universally accepted operational definitions for what, exactly, one means when one talks about repetitive strain injury, cumulative trauma disorders, wear-and-tear afflictions, overuse damage, or degenerative conditions. Indeed, these are not scientific terms, and when used in relation to issues of causation, provide little or nothing in the way of understanding. They are neither injury/disorder-specific enough, nor rigorously/precisely/operationally defined enough to provide any meaningful insight into cause/effect relationships. That is why the word "association" is often used, rather than "causation." Association may or may not have anything to do with causation.

Still, as we continue to cling tenaciously to the notion that there are these work-related risk factors, the literature on the subject is proliferating at an incredible rate, helped along by two significant and often-quoted government reports: the 1997 NIOSH Publication No. 97-141, "Musculoskeletal Disorders and Workplace Factors," and the 2001 NAS piece, "Musculoskeletal Disorders and the Workplace." Be that as it may, consider the following: The average day is 24 hours long, one-third of which we are (or should be) sleeping. That leaves 16 waking hours, half (or more) of which typical working adults spend on the job. Thus, since we are at work for better than 50% of our adult waking hours, is there not, statistically speaking, a better than 50–50 chance that any type of affliction, be it musculoskeletal, cardiovascular, psychological, infectious, etc., can, by a straightforward analysis, be shown to be positively correlated (i.e., associated) with work activities? Why, then, are we not all suing our employers for "work-related risk factors" that are, indeed, responsible for anything and everything that is wrong with us? (The fact is, many are, and are reaping huge financial settlements.)

The answer, of course, is that just because a degenerative type of musculoskeletal affliction (like carpal tunnel syndrome, herniated spinal disks, osteoarthritis, etc.) occurs on the job does not necessarily make it work-related. This is especially true if the "risk factor" deemed to have caused the affliction happens, also, to be among the things one does anyway as a routine activity that is just a part of everyday living, like climbing up and down stairs, using one's hands, walking, or lifting things (including sometimes-heavy grandchildren!). Indeed, following a logic identical to that developed above, one can very easily show that there is a better than 50–50 chance that the affliction is not work-related but, rather, is correlated with the natural aging process, other typical activities of daily living, hereditary issues, and lifestyle (especially alcohol, drug, and tobacco abuse, and obesity). I call aging, smoking, and obesity a nonwork-related primary trifecta of musculoskeletal risk factors, inherent dangers that might even have been mitigated by work activities, rather than exacerbated by them—exactly the opposite of what ergonomists claim, which, in fact, is the very basis of such healthy interventions as exercise physiology and rehabilitation medicine! There is a very interesting one-to-one correspondence between what, on the one hand, ergonomists cite as a "work-related risk factor" and what, on the other hand, exercise physiologists claim is a "healthy use of the body." I tend to side with the latter.

Speaking of 50–50 chances and medical fads, I am reminded of an editorial that is germane to this very topic. It appeared in the March 16, 2003, edition of *The New York Times Magazine* Desk section. Written by Lisa Sanders, M.D., the editorial was entitled, "Medicine's Progress, One Setback at a Time." In it, Dr. Sanders recalls entering medical school some 10 years earlier, and hearing the Dean declare in an opening white-coat ceremony, "Half of what we teach you here is wrong—unfortunately, we don't know which half!" Based on my own experiences in this profession, I am inclined to think that the Dean may have been somewhat conservative in his estimate, and that the actual percentage is considerably higher! This point of view is reinforced by Drs. Mark Hyman and Mark Liponis in their book, *Ultra-Prevention* (New York: Scribner, 2003). In discussing "The Myths of Modern Medicine," they start right out with "Myth 1: Your Doctor Knows Best" and "Myth 2: If You Have a Diagnosis, You Know What's Wrong With You." Without coming right out and saying so, they imply, and I agree, that there is a huge gap between the concepts of "reasonable degree of *medical* certainty," which goes to the issue of diagnosis and treatment, and "reasonable degree of *scientific* certainty," which gets to the heart of criteria that specifically define cause/effect relationships. Making a diagnosis and treating a patient, even if that treatment is effective, does not necessarily mean that one knows exactly what is wrong with a patient, much less what caused it. (I discuss this at some length in my books, *Engineering Principles of Physiologic Function*, New York: NYU Press, 1990, and *Biomedical Desk Reference* [with Dr. Alan Tempkin], New York: NYU Press, 1991.)

In and of itself, I am less concerned with the fact that 50% or more of what doctors learn in medical school is actually wrong than I am with the existence of an establishment that 1) believes otherwise, 2) refuses to recognize that uncertainty is the essence of the medical profession (as it is, to a great extent, the scientific profession as well), 3) declares its point of view to be unquestionable (especially in court!), 4) veils itself in a cloak of authenticity, and 5) quells (often violently) any attempt to challenge or refute its various positions (it was literally worth one's life to challenge Galen, and not much has changed since). Yet if scientific formulations are to withstand the test of time and prevail as viable theories, they, as the famed philosopher of science Sir Karl Popper (1904–1994) pointed out, must be expressed in a way that subjects them to the possibility of "falsification." They must be couched in a way that allows them to be challenged; indeed, such challenge should be encouraged! I might add to that, the theories must be quantified and terms rigorously defined. Especially in the case of WMSDs, it should be incumbent on the accuser to quantify his or her allegation that the "risk factors" to which he or she was exposed at work did, indeed, subject his or her musculoskeletal system to a biomechanical loading that exceeded its ability to tolerate such loading without consequence. Merely having a treating physician say so hardly meets the civil case criterion of guilt by a preponderance of the evidence, especially when that "evidence" is gleaned mainly from the accuser's qualitative description of what happened, and the physician's opinion is based "to a reasonable degree of medical certainty" on the *post hoc, ergo propter hoc* ("after this, therefore as a result of this") philosophy, which is lame at best!

But alas, we humans are a fad-oriented society, and science and medicine are no exceptions. We latch on to something that sparks our interest—a fashion, diet, style of music, type of art, movie star, clinical procedure (like what used to be a routine removal of tonsils), the prevailing scientific theory of the day (like global warming and the "Big Bang"), a catchy phrase (like work-related musculoskeletal disorders)—and it becomes the craze until something else comes along to usurp it, or prove it to be wrong. Again, this capriciousness, by itself, would be quite tolerable were we not guilty of refusing to recognize (or to admit) that "half of what we teach you here is wrong." That denial of our authenticity could, and often does, lead to trouble.

Thus, when the newly formulated germ theory of disease dominated the medical community (driven from around the middle of the 19th century through at least a quarter of the 20th century by the growing field of microbiology), any disease for which there was no known cause was automatically classified as "zymotic" (an early term for infectious disease, from the Greek word for the fermentation process believed to cause it). Today, we seem to be looking for a genetic basis for everything because the human genome project has established a new fad. So, too, any degenerative musculoskeletal disease whose etiology is not clearly defined, but that can, by whatever means, be shown to have some vague association with the labor force, is being automatically categorized as a work-related musculoskeletal disorder. And why not? After all, people do work. People spend half or more of their waking hours at work. We don't really know what causes these afflictions, and it's a very lucrative business. Is it for real? Perhaps, until the next fad comes along.

Part II: Searching for **Self and Identity**—The "In Here"

What Is This Thing Called "Me"? Part 1: Levels of Organization of the Human Body

American Laboratory, December 2004

With this editorial, I launch what I hope will be an intermittent series on the human body, looking at it from perspectives that may be somewhat different than those of standard textbooks on anatomy and physiology. The series is intended to give some insight into the question, "What is this thing called 'me'?" — both from a quantitative, nuts-and-bolts point of view, such as was expressed in my editorial, "A Biomedical Engineer Views the Human Body" (*American Laboratory* Feb 2003; 35[3]:6–8), and from a more qualitative, aesthetic viewpoint, such as was expressed in my editorial, "A Musician Views the Human Body" (*American Laboratory* Mar 2003; 35[5]:6–10). That having been said, let's begin at the very beginning: The human body is essentially organized into six anatomical levels, increasing in size from atoms to molecules, cells, tissues, organs, and systems.

In all, the "typical" adult organism of "average" build contains some 7000 trillion trillion (7×10^{27}) atoms of numerous kinds, but nearly 97% of one's body weight consists of just four of them: oxygen (63.1%), carbon (20.7%), hydrogen (10%), and nitrogen (2.8%). The remaining 3.4% includes at least 40 other elements, several of them (like copper, cobalt, magnesium, manganese, and zinc, totaling collectively less than 0.038% of body weight) appearing in hardly measurable trace amounts, even though they play critical roles in controlling metabolic (biochemical) processes.

Atoms, in turn, are organized into molecules, most of them (at least 60% of body weight) being in the form of water. Just over 34% (of the remaining 40%) is divided about equally between body fats (lipids, 17.1%) and proteins (17%). What is left, then, consists mostly of nonvolatile, incombustible residue (5% body "ash," including mainly inorganic minerals like calcium, the most abundant cation and fifth most abundant element in the body, essentially confined to the musculoskeletal system, and iron, 66% of which is found in blood hemoglobin), and 0.9% of various organic (carbon-containing) and inorganic "extractives," over half of which are in the form of carbohydrates. The balance includes such things as urea, carbon dioxide, coloring pigments, and anything else that does not fit into one of the other categories.

It is worth emphasizing that the numbers quoted above are approximations based on averages accumulated from a wide variety of sources. Specific values for any given individual will vary, but, statistically speaking, they should lie within a reasonable range of the means noted. Furthermore, anatomic data vary between adult men and women, between adults and children, and among adults of different ages, anthropometric build, hereditary lineage, diet, lifestyle, state of health, and so on. For example, women have about 15% less muscle mass than do men, whose muscle mass is usually 40% of body weight. However, the average female makes up for this difference with about 10% more adipose (fat) tissue than the 14–18% that is typical for men, larger breasts, and heavier reproductive organs. Moreover, even for a given individual, body composition goes through cyclical changes as often as daily, but certainly during the course of a lifetime. Thus, to speak of, for instance, body water as accounting for 60% of a person's body weight is not to suggest that this number is etched in stone for that particular individual, for all time, with no exceptions. Nor is it to suggest that all parts of that individual's body are 60% water. The brain may be as much as 84% water, the lungs 78%, the bones 22%, and the dentine of teeth only 10%. Sixty percent is just the average water content for the body, taken as a whole, for a "typical" person of "average" build.

Keeping the above in mind, we come to the next level of organization of the human body, which is the cell, its basic functional unit. Various estimates suggest that the adult body consists of some 100 trillion (10^{14} or more) cells, self-contained masses of protoplasm that can be classified into about 200 different types depending on: a) what they look like, b) what they do (which, in turn, is a function of the nature and quantity of biochemical substances that they contain and the various reactions in which these constituents participate), c) the rate at which they do what they do, d) where they are located, e) what stage of development they are in, and f) whether or not they are doing what they are designed to do (i.e., their state of health). All of these considerations are embedded into the prefix that identifies the cell, to which is attached the suffix "-cyte" (from the Greek *kytos*, meaning "hollow vessel"). Thus, a "hematocyte" is a blood cell, a "myocyte" is a muscle cell, and an "osteocyte" is a bone cell. One of my very favorites is a "polymorphonuclear leukogranulocyte of acidophilic type." This is a type of white (leuko-) blood cell (-cyte) that "loves" (-philic) to be made visible by a color reaction that uses an acid (acido-) chemical stain (usually eosin dyes, hence the alternative name, eosinophils: eosin-loving). Furthermore, when viewed under a microscope, the cell is further distinguished by its many (poly-) nuclei (-nuclear) of various forms (-morpho-), embedded in a granular-appearing (granulo-) protoplasmic matrix! Don't you just love it?

One may envision cells to be self-contained little villages surrounded by a "picket fence" (the plasma membrane), inside of which are contained all of the services that are necessary for these villages to function. Thus, they have their own a) governing body, housed in the nucleus of the cell, within which is contained its constitution and bylaws (the human genome) carefully stored away in a safety deposit box, the nucleolus; b) utility services to provide 1) energy: 100–2000 mitochondria per cell, which are tiny generating stations that supply its main operating fuel, the battery or ATP (adenosine triphosphate), and 2) sewage disposal: 300 or so lysosomes and 200 or so peroxisomes per cell, which take care of detoxification activities, destruction of unwanted material (such as foreign substances and cellular debris), and recycling; c) highway networks: the endoplasmic reticulum and cytoskeletal microtubules; d) industries that make all of the unique products for which the village is world famous, housed in ribosomes, the protein manufacturing plants of the cell; e) packaging and distribution centers: the cellular Golgi complex; f) storage facilities: glycogen granules, lipid droplets, vacuoles, and secretory vesicles; and whatever additional organelles ("little organs") individual cells might need to perform their assigned function. That assigned function is determined early on through a process known as differentiation. Differentiation is that process by which the single cell that was originally "me" became specialized, so that as I grew from one fertilized egg to a grown adult, the 100 trillion cells that are now "me" can perform all of the functions necessary to keep themselves, and therefore me, alive. For the vast majority of these cells (with the notable exception of red blood cells and some others), this also includes reproducing themselves via centrally located centrosomes, which contain centrioles surrounded by centrosphere protoplasm. Cells specialized to perform specific functions are assembled into four types of tissue. If one envisions atoms and molecules to be the chemical units of which the human body is comprised, and cells as its basic functional units, then tissues assume the role of primary structural units: the building blocks from which the body's organs and systems are constructed. Thus, we have epithelial, connective, muscular, and nervous tissue.

Epithelial tissue consists of cells arranged in continuous sheets, either to wrap around (encase or cover) surfaces, thereby providing a sheathing to protect body structures, or to line cavities and canals (in which case they are called endothelial cells, from the Greek *endon,* which means "inner"). Much of this tissue is flat and smooth (as in the skin), but some epithelial cells a) have fingerlike projections (microvilli) that increase the tissue surface area to maximize absorption (as in the small intestines); b) have contractile properties, as in the cilia of myoepithelium, from the Greek *mys*, for "muscle," to help propel things along (for example, in the lining of the small intestine, the respiratory tract, and the fallopian tubes); c) have the ability to manufacture and secrete certain chemical compounds, as in the glandular epithelium of the endocrine and exocrine organs; d) are excitable, meaning that they are capable of being stimulated, as in the neuroepithelium of the functional layers of the sense organs; or e) have phagocytic capabilities, i.e., they are "eating" cells (from the Greek *phagein*, which means "eat"). These cells can engulf things, either to transport them (like taxis, in a process called active transport) to places they would not go otherwise (or not get there fast enough), or to digest and destroy them (as in the reticuloendothelial system of the spleen) when their presence is undesirable.

Connective tissue (which also includes all body fluids and fat tissue), as the name implies, consists of cells arranged in configurations that support and connect body parts, either directly or through fluid transport. Thus, in addition to body fluids and fat, connective tissue includes a) the cartilage (gristle) and joint (synovial) fluid that allow bones to glide smoothly over one another; b) the 206 bones of the skeletal system, which forms a "scaffolding" to support body structures and provide them with mobility; c) the tendons that connect muscles to bones; d) the ligaments that maintain the alignment of bones where they articulate with one another; e) the interlacing networks of fibers that provide a structural framework for muscles, bone marrow, spleen, liver, lungs, kidney, and other body organs; and f) the bandlike coverings (fascia) that envelope the body beneath the skin (like plastic wrap) and that also separate layers of muscles nested within one another. Because of this impressive variety of functions, one finds an equally impressive variety of connective tissue types, including fibrous, areolar ("loose"), white, yellow, elastic, mucous ("jellylike"), and reticular ("netlike"). Together, epithelial and connective tissue make up about half of the total body mass, in roughly a 1:3 (epithelial:connective) ratio. The other half is basically muscle and nerve tissue, in about a 4- or 5-to-1 (muscle:nerve) ratio.

Along with myoepithelium and neuroepithelium, muscle and nerve tissue also have the property of being excitable, which means that they are capable of generating an electrochemical signal (action potential) when provoked by an adequate stimulus of sufficient strength. In the case of muscles, the action potential incites to a working state excitable cells that are concerned with generating movement, both internal and external. Internal movement is accomplished primarily by involuntary smooth muscle tissue, both of the vascular (blood vessel) and visceral (body organ) type, and cardiac (heart) muscle tissue. External movement is accomplished by the 639–656 (depending on how you count them) voluntary striated skeletal muscles, which transform chemical energy into mechanical work. The work appears as the effort required to maintain postural balance and/or to locomote parts or all of the animal body.

The fourth basic type of tissue, nerve tissue, provides the structural architecture for the human body's communications network. Nerves transmit information (encoded into action potentials) to (afferent, sensory) the central processing centers (CPU: brain and spinal cord) of the body, from (efferent, motor) these centers to "target" organs and tissues, and among (internuncial, interneuronal) themselves. Indeed, any given nerve can interact at various synaptic junctions with as many as 10,000 other nerves en route to or from the CPU, forming complex neural networks that wire the body like an elaborate telephone system. Armed with nearly 50 miles of "cable," nervous tissue can provide service to all of its "customers" (the cells of the body), directly or indirectly, ensuring that not one of them will be without service, and the lines are constantly buzzing with information about the state of the organism, and the need to intervene when that state is being disturbed or threatened.

At the next level, organs are combinations of any two or more tissues that are organized (integrated and coordinated) to perform a specific, well-defined task. That mission is determined by which of the organ's constituent tissues dominate(s) its structure, both in quantity and activity. For example: a) Some organs (like the lungs, kidneys, and spleen) might have the primary task of processing the materials they deal with (lungs oxygenate the blood that courses through it, while removing carbon dioxide; the kidneys cleanse the blood of the toxic waste products of metabolism; the spleen rids the blood of worn-out red blood cells at the incredible rate of 2–10 million per second, and so on). b) Other organs, such as the liver and certain glands, might have the primary task of manufacturing things, like making bile (liver), which is used in the small intestine to neutralize acids and emulsify fats for subsequent absorption, or producing hormones (endocrine glands) to affect or control the activity of other cells, tissues, and/or organs. c) Still other organs, like the body's senses, have the primary responsibility of transducing energy (the adequate stimulus to which they respond) from one form (such as heat, light, or sound) into another (electrochemical action potentials). d) Organs like the skin, and those included in the body's immune system, have the primary task of protecting the body from invasion, from "losing its insides," or from yielding to foreign organisms. e) Organs like the heart are primarily responsible for pumping things—moving them from one part of the organism to another.

f) The organs of reproduction (breasts, ovaries, prostate gland, testes, uterus, etc.) have the primary task of giving the human body the ability to procreate—to make other "me's" (but not exactly like me!).

All organ tasks are concerned ultimately with the maintenance of the life of the particular individual involved (survival of the self), and with perpetuation as a whole of the breed of animal to which that particular individual belongs (survival of the species). Note the conspicuous use of the word "primary" in the discussion of organ tasks. Virtually all of the organs of the body can (and do) perform more than one task (i.e., they are quite adept at multitasking), so classifying them as being purely regulatory, manipulative, secretory, productive, reproductive, etc., is somewhat simplistic, even misleading. Furthermore, many organs are able to assume each other's task(s) if any of them should "go down" or have to be removed for whatever reason; they are quite multifaceted as well in their talents and abilities. In that sense, there are many "backup" arrangements and a great deal of redundancy built into the structure and function of the human body.

A collection of organs assembled, like the instrumental sections of an orchestra, to work together toward the accomplishment of a common goal that could not be achieved by any one of the organs acting alone is referred to as a system of the body. Thus, we have the respiratory system, digestive system, cardiovascular system, musculoskeletal system, immune system, nervous system (with central, peripheral, sympathetic, and parasympathetic components), excretory system, lymphatic system, reproductive system, endocrine system, etc., systems that do for the entire organism what the organelles do for individual cells. Using the symphony orchestra analogy, one can easily appreciate the fact that the entire human organism, as an integrated functioning unit, must encompass the collective mission of all organ systems acting in concert. No one organ system is self-contained and independent of any other; no one of them could exist without the help of the others. It's a team effort: cooperative, controlled, integrated, coordinated, optimized, fine-tuned, holistic. The human body is, indeed, a symphony orchestra attempting to harmonize at its finest!

To be continued . . .

Each of Us Is a Minority of One

American Laboratory, January 2001

Have you heard the latest? Scientists have recently read the 3.3-billionth chemical letter (base pair) in human DNA. We now know the alphabet—the letters, in sequence, of the language that defines the entire human genome (the human genome actually contains twice that many letters—a duplicate set, 6.6×10^9 base pairs—because each human cell is diploid, containing two sets of chromosomes). Although we are still a long way off from using this alphabet to construct any words or sentences, the first major step in that direction has now been completed. I got to thinking about the astronomical numbers involved here and decided to do a little brainstorming with one of my classes.

I asked the students the following question: "What do you think the total population of the earth is today?" They seemed to agree that around six billion was a pretty good estimate. Then I asked them, "OK, how many people do you think have inhabited the earth, cumulatively to date, since the first Genus Homo (which was to become the human race as we know it today) was identified some two million years ago? For the purposes of this discussion, let's assume an evolutionist approach rather than a creationist approach, if nothing else, because it yields higher numbers." Following some further deliberation, we came up with the following estimate: Taking a generation to be the period of time spanning about 20 years, and assuming the human body is about two million years old in its current Homo sapiens form, some 100,000 generations have preceded ours. Moreover, since some two-thirds of all of the people who have ever reached the age of 65 are still alive today, let's be generous in assuming that every generation that has preceded ours had an average population of 500 million. That being the case, up to today's generation, about 50.006 trillion people have inhabited planet earth (a purposely high estimate).

Next, I asked the class to speculate further: "Taking into account the fact that planet earth will not be around forever, and that it can only sustain a finite amount of life, how many people do you think have yet to inhabit this planet until its ultimate demise?" Being again generous (on purpose), we agreed that one million more generations will likely follow ours, averaging 10 billion people in each, so that a total of 10 quadrillion humans have yet to follow us before it's all over. Putting all of this reasoning together, we concluded that, from beginning to end, some 10.050006 quadrillion (that's 10,050,006,000,000,000)—give or take a quadrillion—humans will have graced the surface of this planet throughout its lifetime (hopefully, not prematurely annihilated as a result of war). So, what was the point of this exercise?

In order to make my point, I now asked the class to shift gears and consider something else. "Suppose," I said, "somebody gave you a set of 400 beads, containing 20 each of 20 different colors. Suppose further that you were told to use each color as often as you liked, and sequence the colors at your discretion in stringing the beads together to form a chain necklace. Finally, you were constrained to use only 20 beads total in creating each chain. Question: How many different combinations could you possibly string together from this pool of beads? That is to say, if you were to make one chain necklace using 20 beads from this pool of 400, how many choices do you have in terms of what this necklace might look like?" Being mostly engineering students, the class was proud to declare that the strict mathematical answer to this question of permutations and combinations is 20 raised to the 20th power, or, written out, 20^{20} = about 104,857,599,992,000,000,000,000,000 different possibilities for any given necklace chain! OK, we conceded that some of these combinations might be duplicates (for example, mathematically, in the sequence ij, the possibility i = 1, j = 2 is considered to be different from that when i = 2, j = 1, even though if you physically turn the latter around, it looks identical to the former when one is considering colors in a necklace chain), but still (see later), we have a number that's roughly 105 billion quadrillion, compared to the 10-or-so quadrillion we arrived at earlier in estimating the cumulative population of the earth from beginning to end—the former number being ten and a half billion times higher than is the latter! So, again, the students ask, "What's the point?"

The point is that our body makes proteins—the "stuff" that is "us," the necklace chains that are strung together to form biochemical trademarks that characterize each and every one of our distinct features—from 20 different "beads" called amino acids. Each amino acid can be used as often as is necessary, and the beads are strung together in sequences that are defined by our very own, uniquely personalized DNA code. Thus, even a simple protein that might contain a string of as few as 20 amino acids (most proteins contain hundreds or even thousands of amino acids) can come in 105 billion quadrillion different styles or patterns. "But wait a minute," exclaim the skeptics in every crowd, "we just conceded that many combinations and permutations are actually duplicates of one another! And when you stop to think about it, still others, and the proteins associated with them, may not necessarily be compatible with our particular form of life." Recognizing the value in such reasoning, I yield to the skeptics' concerns, but get the class to agree that I am not being unreasonable when I dismiss a whopping 99.9% of the 105 billion quadrillion possibilities, thus allowing only 0.1% of them to be realistically viable. That still leaves us with better than 100 million quadrillion different combinations of amino acids that can appear as living proteins—still 10 million times more than the projected human population of the earth from its beginning to its demise. And, mind you, that doesn't even take into account the hundreds of thousands of proteins that comprise the entire human body! We are still looking at only one simple 20-amino-acid protein chain.

So here's the real point: Given the simplest, most statistically generous scenario of a grand total of 10 quadrillion people, among which are distributed as few as 100 million quadrillion possible combinations of proteins, what is the probability that any two of these people share the same combination, i.e., have exactly the same characteristic anatomical features and physiologic function? Even if one concedes further (as the genome scientists have claimed) that we share in common as much as 99.9% of the total base pair sequence in DNA, I submit to you that the chances of any two individuals winding up with exactly the same genetic code (nature), much less exactly the same expression of this code (nurture), is probably well below one in a million, less than 0.0001%. In other words, not too likely—and that's based on as liberal an estimate as one can imagine. The probability that anybody ever has, or ever will, be exactly like you is essentially zero, because there are so many more potential possibilities than there are humans that will ever inhabit this planet.

So what is all of this talk about ethnicity, race, religious preference, and so on? The fact of the matter is that each and every one of us is a minority of one. When they made you, they threw out the mold. In many ways, you are an improvement over older models; newer models yet to come may include still further refinements in design. So isn't it about time we stopped trying to generalize, systematize, and categorize our humaness in favor of appreciating, cultivating, and acclaiming its diversity without being threatened by it? Each one of us has such wonderfully unique anatomical traits and physiologic capabilities. Let's enjoy them! Exploit them! Cherish them! And then maybe, just maybe, we can start learning how to get along with one another without judging on the basis of ill-defined, arbitrary, meaningless criteria. If nothing else, maybe the Genome Project will have accomplished that!

A Biomedical Engineer Views the Human Body

American Laboratory, February 2003

During my 40 years as a biomedical engineer, I developed a convenient paradigm for systematically studying, analyzing, quantifying, and teaching physiologic function based on an engineering approach. The approach is formulated on the observation that the human body can be characterized by seven basic features that become manifest through six fundamental processes governed by five essential conservation laws, subject to four primary constraints, imposed at three rudimentary levels of organization, to satisfy two predominant physiologic perspectives and one *au fond* purpose. I call this paradigm my countdown approach (7-6-5-4-3-2-1-0) to the engineering analysis of physiologic systems. Space will not permit me to elaborate on the details, but I can share with you here, briefly, an outline of this countdown.

The seven basic features of physiologic function fit neatly into the canonical form of a standard feedback/feedforward control system diagram; to wit:

Feature 1: The entire human organism can be viewed as a controlled system, one that functions characteristically as a basic engine. That is to say, we have a controlled system that takes in fuel, converts part of it to usable energy to drive its metabolic processes (which is what further classifies it as a living engine), performs its function, and has a sophisticated subsystem to exhaust the waste products of its various activities.

Feature 2: The controlled system has a mechanical output, u_o. In other words, everything it does, at various levels of organization, whether it is voluntary locomotion of parts or all of the animal body (a specific feature of the animal kingdom), or involuntary mobility, etc., involves motion, kinetic energy, and dynamic activity. If metabolically induced movement ceases, so does life.

Feature 3: All of the controlled system's outputs, u_o, are monitored (primary feedback control signals, u_p) through sensory transduction (transduced feedback control signals, u_t), i.e., all of the body's operating systems are continuously audited for subsequent verification. The human engine has the ability to perceive and react to adequate stimuli—various forms of kinetic energy derived from both its internal (corporeal) and external (ambient) environments.

Feature 4: Verification and, when necessary, calls for responses to transduced signals, u_t, are accomplished through sensory integration, which takes place at a central command post. This command center compares u_t with desired operating setpoints, u_r (reference signals) and, as appropriate, issues forth error signals, u_e. The latter derive from the fact that u_t is not equal to u_r because desirable, quasi-equilibrated physiologic states, u_o, have been victimized by disturbances, u_d. In other words, the human machine is fine-tuned through a variety of complex feedback control mechanisms that maintain, within prescribed limits, variables critical to life. The maintenance of such a carefully controlled environment is called homeostasis. If system outputs, u_o (monitored as u_t), deviate (as a result of disturbances, u_d) from desired outputs, u_r, by some predetermined amount (the operating window), a corresponding error signal, u_e, is generated, which calls for differential (based on the rate of change of u_e), integral (based on the history of u_e), and/or proportional (based on the magnitude of u_e) control.

Feature 5: The control itself is accomplished through controlling systems that respond to u_e by issuing forth control signals, u_c, that attempt to bring u_o back in line with u_r, completing the feedback control loop.

Feature 6: Depending on the nature and tenacity of disturbances, u_d, controlled/controlling systems have the ability to accommodate. Short-term, temporary disturbances are handled by reflexive reactions that do not involve changing either the reference signals, u_r, or the various system transfer functions (input/output characteristics), K_i. More persistent but medium-term disturbances are handled by functional adaptation mechanisms that act to change only u_r, but not K_i. Long-term, continuous disturbances of a permanent nature are handled by changing both u_r and K_i through processes embedded in Feature 7.

Feature 7: The human machine's ability to metabolize and accommodate results in growth, one aspect of which gives the organism the remarkable ability to make other engines just like it, i.e., to reproduce itself or procreate (embedded in the drive for sexual fulfillment). Procreation is not just a simple matter of anatomical cloning of the species; sexual (as opposed to asexual) reproduction allows the organism to breed—to improve on the basic design, to diversify, and incorporate variety as the "spice of life."

All seven of the above features have certain common engineering denominators that may be grouped according to the following six types of physical processes:

Process 1: Morphologic differentiation. This is the process by which newly forming cells in a developing embryo acquire anatomic/physiologic attributes that make them different from one another. These differences allow one to identify some 200 heterogeneous cells that perform individual, specialized functions.

Process 2: Transport. This is a category of highly selective mechanisms that result in movement from one place to another of: mass (actively and/or passively, which includes compartmental kinetics, conduction, convection, and flow), energy (including thermoregulation), momentum (linear and angular), and information (as action potentials).

Process 3: Utilization. This pertains to the utilization of mass (anabolism, catabolism, metabolism), energy (thermodynamics and bioenergetics), momentum (mechanical system outputs), and information (sensory integration, neural networks, etc.).

Process 4: Expediency. This is the process of helping to bring about a desired result more quickly, efficiently, and effectively than it would otherwise occur, which, in this case, addresses such issues as biochemical and enzyme kinetics, catalysis, and activation.

Process 5: Transduction. This is the process, embedded in transfer functions, K_i, of converting from one form to another: mass (e.g., digestion and metamorphosis), energy (e.g., sensory transduction from up to u_r; excitation–contraction coupling in muscle tissue), momentum (e.g., constitutive modeling and material properties of physiologic tissue and inertial dynamics), and information (involving the role of neurotransmitters and synaptic transmission in generating compound action potentials).

Process 6: Homeostasis. As mentioned earlier, this is the process by which certain critical-to-life variables are maintained within narrow limits, governed by the primary human drive for personal survival. These processes underlie the establishment of all u_r's and K_i's and are intimately involved in the body's desire and ability to accommodate.

Within the context of the above common denominators, all of the systems and subsystems of the physiologic organism operate according to five fundamental laws of physics:

- Conservation of mass (the so-called continuity equation)
- Conservation of energy (for example, the first law of thermodynamics, which states that "You can't win")
- The second law of thermodynamics (which introduces the concept of entropy by declaring further that, in fact, "You can't even break even")
- Conservation of linear momentum
- Conservation of angular momentum (the latter two are embedded in Newton's Laws of Motion).

Moreover, the bottom line in all physiologic processes appears to be that they are constrained:

1. Not to generate heat. Indeed, we are isothermal, electrochemical living engines, not heat engines. Our bodies cannot convert heat to work (as can automobile engines). This fundamental consideration constrains and governs the philosophy of how our systems work.

2. To operate on the principle of paired reactions, whereby energy-releasing (exergonic) reactions drive energy-absorbing (endergonic) reactions in coupled fashion. This is a constraint that conserves energy and also helps to minimize heat production.

3. To economize on energy expenditure. The more we learn about the physiology of the human body, the more we realize that it operates according to a minimum energy constraint—an optimization principle. All metabolic processes and mechanical outputs take the path of least resistance in an attempt to optimize performance and at least minimize the rate of entropy production.

4. To economize on the utilization of space for the storage and handling of raw materials and/or information. Thus, the body stores ingredients, not products; and draws upon fractal principles to create complicated geometrical shapes and configurations that fit into tight quarters, yet maximize their functional capacity.

The body does all of the above at essentially three levels of organization: 1) the atomic (ionic) level (biochemistry), 2) the molecular level (biochemistry, cells, tissues), and 3) the continuum level (all of the above, plus organs and systems), and it does so with two very fundamental objectives in mind: a) survival of the self (the first and most fundamental human drive), and b) survival of the species (the second most fundamental drive for sexual fulfillment). The *au fond* ultimate purpose of existence is not quite so easy to address, and requires further consideration.

I would like to suggest that the ultimate purpose of our existence is to move asymptotically toward a physiologic state of cenesthesia and a societal state of utopia. Cenesthesia is the generalized feeling of well-being (euphoria) that one experiences when all of the body's organ systems are functioning normally and in synchrony with one another—a perfect state of health, as reported to us by a sensory neural network of extero- and interoception (ambiensomatic perception). The word originated from the Greek *koinos*, which means "common," and *aisthanesthai*, which means "to perceive." Hence, it connotes a common feeling derived from totally coordinated, properly functioning physiologic systems that are hitting on all cylinders. Utopia, from the Greek *ou* for "not" and *topos* for "place," implies an out-of-the-ordinary place in which perfect justice and social harmony prevail—an ideal society with perfect laws. Thus, the combination of physiologic cenesthesia (a perfectly functioning, healthy human body) and sociologic utopianism (a perfectly functioning, healthy human fellowship) stand as ideal targets to aim for as the ultimate goal of our existence. I am not prepared to discuss here (nor is it appropriate for the purposes of this editorial) the extent to which these idealizations relate to the third strongest human drive, i.e., the need for spiritual fulfillment, except to say that this need (which addresses such esoteric questions as "Why are we here?" and "What is the ultimate purpose of life?") and religion (which involves an affirmation of faith and a respect for what is considered sacred) are not necessarily synonymous with one another. Enough said for now.

Will the *Real* You Please Stand Up?

American Laboratory, December 2002

Back in the good old days, when my class sizes were small enough for me to actually get to know the students enrolled in the course I was teaching, I would begin each academic term by having them write a biographical sketch of themselves. It was very important for me, right up front, to know who I was dealing with so that I could climb into their heads in an effort to communicate with them on their wavelength and frequency.[1] This, however, was no ordinary biographical sketch; I did not want to know where my students were born, where they went to high school, and so on. Rather, I wanted to know what made them tick, what turned them on, how they were likely to react to me, and I to them, and both of us to the material we were about to learn.

So I asked my students to describe themselves by commenting on the following aspects of their personable attributes. The following "'Who are you's?" if you will, are categorized according to whether you are examining yourself from inside out (what you perceive) or whether you are viewing yourself from outside in (what you think others perceive), starting with what you perceive.

First, there's what I call the emulated self, the "who" that we (secretly) would like (or pretend) to be. For me, growing up in Brooklyn, NY, it was Mickey Mantle, center fielder for the New York Yankees. A la Danny Kaye in the 1947 movie *The Secret Life of Walter Mitty*, I would fantasize about all of the great things I could accomplish if I were Mickey Mantle; then, I would daydream that, indeed, I really was him—accomplishing and experiencing all of those exciting things. Most of us have a hero in our lives—an athlete we worship, a political icon, a member of the clergy, a relative we admire, a spouse, a dear friend, a teacher who has influenced us the most, a Hollywood star—someone we look up to as a role model and strive to emulate. One can learn a great deal about a person by knowing who his/her role models are.

Getting back to reality, there is what I have labeled the perceived self, the "who" that we really think we are (as opposed to the individual we would like to be, the emulated self). The perceived self is the person whom, for whatever reason, we envision ourselves to be—genuinely believing that this is the individual we really are. Unfortunately, because of a variety of external pressures (social, peer, family, professional, etc.), we guard the perceived self very carefully, lest it enter the world to become vulnerable to attack, prejudice, judgment, hurt, or humiliation and embarrassment. The perceived self, therefore, remains our own personal secret—just between you and you. It's much safer that way. But should we be fortunate enough to meet someone we really trust—one who will accept us for who we are (human, frail, sensitive, well-meaning folks who just want to love and be loved in return)—then we very cautiously let that perceived self come reluctantly out of hiding, just a little bit at a time, and hope for the best. I believe that the mutual, unconditional acceptance of each other's perceived self is the key to a healthy, honest, and open relationship between any two people, be it a parent and child, student and teacher, or husband and wife. As the expression goes, "A true friend is somebody who knows all about you and likes you anyway." Moreover, to know you are not being judged has a tendency to bring out the very best in you.

But, alas, the above is rarely the case. The perceived self, more often than not, gives way in a functional (social) sense to the persona, the "who" that we want others to think we are. The persona is our protection, the public impression we want to project, our outward appearance as we attempt to express it, our facade—the image behind which we can safely hide. There are two aspects to the persona. One is derived from external pressures, which give rise to the self that we think others (such as our peers, parents, professional colleagues, professors, or prevailing public) want or expect us to be—whether or not we can live up to those expectations (see image self below). The other aspect of persona is derived from an internal motivation driven primarily by the reward system that gives rise to the self we want others to think we are—a role-playing self, if you will, that we attempt to convey to the general public, our friends, and family (see projected self below). This is the self to which William Shakespeare refers in act II, scene 7, of *As You Like It* (thank you, dear readers for keeping me straight on these literary citations), when Jaques declares, "All the world's a stage, and all the men and women merely players . . . and one man in his time plays many parts." Jaques goes on to define these parts as the infant; the whining school boy; the lover; the soldier; the justice (conveying the wisdom that comes with middle age); the lean and "slipper'd pantaloon" (a foolish old man now slipping into senility); followed lastly by a toothless, vision-impaired, senseless second childhood that ends in ultimate oblivion. To the extent that we are able, in each of these seven ages, to play the role that we think is expected of us, and if we are successful actors, life is good, but not necessarily satisfying or fulfilling, because deep down, hidden well below all of the above selves, is the one that few if any of us ever find: the real self.

The "who" that we really are—that concealed self that, like DNA tucked safely away in the nucleolus of a cell, the valuables that we keep securely stowed away in safety deposit boxes, or the queen ant that never leaves the nest—never emerges from hiding. Indeed, this is the self that is so well camouflaged, guarded, and ill-defined that we might not even be conscious of it. And yet, we seem to spend our entire lives in search of this self. Perhaps it is that aspect of "us" that people refer to when they speak about a soul; or maybe the pursuit of this "who" is embedded in concepts such as altered states of consciousness. Could it be that the "who" that we really are exists only momentarily at the instant of birth—to be subsequently buried by experiences that derive from exposure to the outside world? Does this self give way to the ones defined earlier, the "who" that emerges through a process whereby a youngster internalizes the activities of caregivers, and, later, the expectations of the society in which he/she will live out the rest of his/her life? Did a "real" you once exist, briefly, in the womb, yielding to the "now" you, who is just a victim of circumstance? Do we therefore have a subconscious memory of that brief moment in time—a "strange attractor," in the language of Chaos Theory—which drives us to spend the rest of our lives trying to recreate that original, innocent experience in some asymptotic sense? I have lots of questions, but no answers!

Turning, then, away from you *per se*, how about the "who" that others would like you to be, which is the "who" that I call an image self. The image self is the individual that others create for you, a "who" that exists in their minds as they see you, together with their own expectations of you, i.e., the person they think you should endeavor to become, irrespective of whether or not you can live up to their preconceived expectations of you. This "who" is the one that fails your admirers if, for example, you are an athlete who does not live up to your "potential"—potential by whose standards and/or criteria: yours or theirs? More often than not, it is theirs (although, in developing your own persona, you strive to emulate what you think their expectations of you are). The image self is destroyed when we do not live up to others' expectations or fantasies about us, as was the case for people like O.J. Simpson, Pete Rose, televangelist Jim Bakker, and, yes, even former President Bill Clinton. Once they ceased to fit the image the public had created for them, these "heroes" fell from grace; their image was shattered in the eyes of their loyal followers; the role models were no longer models to be emulated.

The image self is very close to (yet subtly different from) another type of self that I call the projected self. The two "whos" are alike in that both have to do with how others perceive us. But, whereas the image self is created in others' minds on the basis of their preconceived expectations of us, the projected self is created in the minds of others based on cues they get from us—how we actually come across to them (based on what we think they are looking for, will accept, and reward). Now, the image we are trying to project (see the persona above—the signals we are sending) may or may not be the same as the image they are getting (how they see us—the signals they are receiving, whether we like it or not). In other words, there may be a significant disparity between what they are getting (as opposed to what they are expecting) and what we are trying for them to get (what we think we are projecting). Therein lies a significant source for the lack of communication that often exists among individuals and, in a more global sense, among governments and nations—especially if that communication is coded into a foreign language. Something just seems to get lost in the translation.

In asking students to write about their experiences in terms of the selves described herein, I know that I have touched on but a few of the many complex aspects of human behavior. Indeed, we are the only form of life on earth who make living so complicated because we conjure up this myriad of behavioral games, with associated rules that we establish to govern how we will navigate the path through the maze that takes us from birth to death. I, personally, have never been able to justify the games or the rules that go with them because, as I mentioned earlier, I see them as being at the root of human conflict, prejudice, lack of communication, deceit, corruption, and lots of other bad things. For instance, although (out of respect for issues related to privacy) I will not mention specific names, you would be surprised (or maybe not) to learn how many students admitted that, given their choice, they would be pursuing another career path (not the one their parents "forced" them to major in); would be doing something with their lives other than what they perceived to be expected of them (or financially rewarding); how they wished their loved ones would just accept them unconditionally (even if that meant "coming out of the closet"); or how happy they were that someone was even giving them the opportunity to express themselves without the fear of suffering any consequences. These students knew—because I promised them anonymity and they trusted me—that they could express themselves openly and honestly and from their hearts. What they wrote brought tears to my eyes then and continues to do so even now as I recall their desperate pleas to have an adult generation just care about them. Just care about them and everything else will take *care* of itself. What a simple concept.

Reference

1. Schneck D. There is no such thing as a learning disability, only teaching disabilities. Am Lab 2000; 32(24):6.

A Musician Views the Human Body
American Laboratory, March 2003

In a related editorial in the February 2003 issue of *American Laboratory*, I described a countdown (7-6-5-4-3-2-1-0) feedback control paradigm that I developed to study human physiologic function from a systems-engineering point of view. That particular paradigm evolved during my 40-year (and counting) career as a biomedical engineer. I have been a musician for much longer than that—40% longer, to be exact—some 56 years (and counting) since I started studying the violin at age 5. So now, let me share with you another countdown paradigm—one formulated from the way a musician might envision physiologic function. That is to say, let us now consider the human body to be characterized by seven basic features that are responsive to the six fundamental elements of music, as interpreted/influenced by five essential laws of perception subject to four primary constraints, imposed at three rudimentary levels of anatomic organization to satisfy two predominant human drives, and one *au fond* purpose. Once again, space will not allow me to elaborate, but here is a brief outline of this musical countdown.

As before, the seven basic features of physiologic function fit nicely into the canonical form of a standard feedback/feedforward control model; to wit:

Feature 1: The entire human organism can be viewed as a controlled system, but one that functions this time as a musical instrument (rather than a mechanical engine). That is to say, we have a controlled system that is animated by breathing (Sanskrit *prana*), just as a wind instrument comes to life when you blow into it. Bodily energy (Chinese *ch'i*), generated in internal organs and systems, combines with the breath of life to resonate along anatomical meridians (lines of energy) and tonification points (access nodes) that resemble in both structure and function all stringed instruments; these also form the basis for the well-established and highly effective acupuncture/acupressure clinical procedures. Moreover, fundamental to all physiologic function are biorhythms—the rhythms of life, which, like the percussion instruments of any musical ensemble, maintain a certain periodicity to the output of this finely tuned, complex human instrument that is, at once, a member of the wind (breath of life), string (vibrational energy of life), and percussion (rhythm of life) families.

Feature 2: The output of this controlled system is emotional expression, one of the most fundamental of all human needs. This instrument emotes; it needs to express itself. Indeed, we are first and foremost creatures of emotion.

Feature 3: All of the instrument's emotional outputs and sensory inputs are monitored to allow for feedback/feedforward control. In the case of music, two major (although not exclusive) adequate stimuli that are tracked continuously for subsequent verification are sound energy (through vocalization and audition) and vibrational energy (through taction).

Feature 4: Verification and, when necessary, calls for responses to transduced, monitored outputs are accomplished through sensory integration, which takes place at a central command post that is most likely localized in the paleoencephalon (the metameric nervous system, which includes neural mechanisms derived from the spinal cord; sensory nuclei; and motoneuronal cell groups located in the brain stem—together with their associated interneurons in the reticular formation—and neural mechanisms that operate through the autonomic nervous system). The command center is where monitored signals are compared against desired operating setpoints, and where decisions are made concerning what to do if the two are not congruent with one another (see Feature 5).

Feature 5: The "what to do about it" is accomplished by controlling systems that respond to error signals generated at the command center by issuing forth corresponding control signals. The latter attempt to bring emotional outputs in line with the emotional needs of the organism, when those needs (quasi-equilibrated emotional states) are victimized by external and/or internal disturbances. Typically, control signals take the form of neurotransmitters (e.g., norepinephrine, serotonin, acetylcholine, and dopamine) and/or hormones (such as corticosteroids, enkephalins, epinephrine, and endorphins), many of which have been shown to be secreted in response to musical stimulation. Indeed, the rapidly growing field of music therapy exploits these responses in an effort to provide effective clinical intervention for a wide variety of medical afflictions.

Feature 6: Depending on the nature and persistence of disturbances to quasi-equilibrated states, controlled/controlling systems have the ability to accommodate. Thus, we have various historical styles and periods of music that paralleled the then-existing state of social/cultural affairs (prevailing emotional needs), which in turn reflected the corresponding state of human existence. When such socio-cultural norms persevered, in a more long-term sense, they secured their place in history through the cultural equivalent of biological evolution (Feature 7).

Feature 7: Corresponding to the gene in the biological Feature 7, which connotes growth, procreation, and inscriptive breeding, we have the *Meme* in the musical Feature 7, which connotes creative emergence into novelty, embraced by a constituency (a cultural "following") that transcends existing norms in favor of a new legacy. In biology, we refer to phenotypes and genotypes; in music, we talk about styles (baroque, classical, romantic, modern, country, jazz, folk, rock, etc.) and forms (suite, sonata, oratorio, opera, fugue, canon, Gregorian chant, cantata, etc.) that define various stages in the evolution of this medium.

All seven of the above features respond to the six fundamental elements of music:

1. *Rhythm.* All God's creations got rhythm![1] It is not surprising, then, that the first and most basic element of music should be rhythm—the beat. Indeed, one could make a good case for the fact that rhythm, in music, is most likely an outward expression of physiologic periodicity.

2. *Melody.* With or without lyrics, melody has evolved as the second most significant element of music, within which is embedded the entire spectrum of human emotions—from the very lowest (despair and sadness) to the very highest (joy and jubilation) and everything in between. Indeed, if rhythm is an expression of physiologic periodicity, melody is an expression of physiologic emotions: It can make us cry; laugh; fall in love; or feel patriotic, lazy, moody, or merry—you name it, there's a melody that can evoke it.

3. *Harmony.* As the superimposition of several melodic lines (sequences of musical tones stacked vertically over one another in patterns known as chord progressions), harmony supports and synergizes with the emotional content of melody, adding color, depth, and richness (sonority) to the sound. One's ability to perceive such depth is called dimensional hearing.

4. *Dynamics.* This refers, quite simply, to the loudness or softness of the music, the sound intensity, as embedded in the amplitude of the sound wave (in contrast to musical pitch, which is embedded in the frequency of the wave).

5. *Timbre*. Sound quality, which is embedded in the wave shape (contour), is a function of the Fourier spectrum of the sound waves. Timbre is what allows you to distinguish a violin from a flute, a flute from a trombone, a trombone from a trumpet, and so on, even though they might all be playing the same exact note at the same exact intensity.

6. *Musical form*. The period-specific envelope within which music takes shape, as mentioned above in Feature 7.

Having invented music as a vehicle for emotional expression, and having embedded into it those physiologic features (elements) we needed to express, we now *experience* music in accordance with five Gestalt laws governing the perceptual organization of sensory information:

- The Law of Proximity, which states that, due to the resolution limitations of sensory transducers, individual elements of adequate stimuli that are received very close to one another in space and/or in time are perceived as a single unit or figure, i.e., we cannot discriminate among them or distinguish one from another.
- The Law of Directionality asserts that, because of the tracking characteristics of the body's information processing systems, absent any discontinuities in incoming information, consecutive individual elements of adequate stimuli that are perceived to follow one another in the same direction tend to be grouped as defining that direction. That is to say, their sequence is perceived to be tracing a smooth (continuous) trajectory in the given direction, such that the next incoming stimulus is expected to follow suit.
- The Law of Similarity maintains that, since the body's information processing systems are capable of extracting essential common denominators that may be embedded in adequate stimuli, those stimuli that share generic features or are otherwise comparable in the attributes that define them tend to be perceptually grouped together into the same object category.
- The Law of Closure derives from our basic desire to avoid loose ends. Thus, if a physical space or region is bounded by a continuous curve that may or may not be closed, it tends nevertheless to be perceived as a self-contained figure, i.e., the brain closes any apparent gaps in information.
- The Law of Pragnanz stipulates that, in an effort to evoke the most effective response to specific adequate stimuli, the body attempts to create the most stable, consistent, and meaningful interpretation of those stimuli, i.e., to glean the essence of the information contained in the stimuli (the spirit of the law), as opposed to its absolute content (the letter of the law).

In music, we deal primarily with sound energy; thus, two obvious constraints are the audible range of hearing, i.e., frequencies (pitches) between 20 and 20,000 Hz, and the range of loudness tolerance, i.e., decibel levels between 0 (the threshold of human hearing) and around 120 (the lowest threshold of ear pain). Two somewhat more subtle constraints involve harmonic consonance—the opposite of dissonance—and tempering of the musical scale. Harmonic dissonance derives from interference patterns (beats) that originate when two tones close in frequency, but not identical, are sounded together. In general, such dissonance is unpleasant to the typical listener, consonance being much more agreeable to the ear. Thus, tempering is an optimization process by which one subdivides the musical scale into the maximum number of equally spaced (for ease of transposition and modulation) notes, containing the minimum number of dissonant intervals, expressed as a percentage of the total number of intervals in the scale.

The three rudimentary levels of anatomic organization can be described by neurologist Paul MacLean's triune brain concept, i.e., a primitive archipallium (brain stem and cerebellum), which contains all survival instincts; an intermediate paleopallium, including the limbic system, which is responsible for emotional responses; and the newest neopallium, which houses intellect. These operate to satisfy the need for individual, personal expression (compare to survival of the self) and the need for social, interpersonal expression (compare to survival of the species). The ultimate goal is self-fulfillment—emotional expression as it contributes to both a perfectly functioning, healthy, euphoric physiologic organism in a state of cenesthesia, and a utopian existence in which perfect justice and social harmony prevail.

I would submit for your final consideration the idea that, if the ultimate goal of cognition (through intellect) is to search for truth, then the ultimate goal of emotional expression (through the arts, in general, and music, in particular) is to search for love.

Reference

1. Schneck D. All God's creations got rhythm! Am Lab 2000; 32(20):6–8.

A Society of Intensive Potentialists
American Laboratory, August 2001

In the opening number "Tradition" from the musical comedy *Fiddler on the Roof* (composed by Jerry Bock, with lyrics by Sheldon Harnick), one of the stars of the show, Tevye, tells the audience about the "little village of Anatevka," where "everyone knows what God wants of them." There are "the pappa" (Tevye, a dairyman), "the mamma" (Golde, a homemaker), "the children" (Tevye and Golde's five rebellious daughters), "a matchmaker" (Yenta, which, literally, means a meddling, rumor-spreading nosibody), a butcher (Lazar Wolf), a tailor (Motel), an innkeeper, a constable, a blacksmith, a hatmaker, musicians, dancers, and, yes, even Nachum, the beggar. Embedded in this musical prologue and developed throughout the rest of the show are philosophies that portray the very essence of what we are as a global society, i.e., survival of the self (food, clothing, shelter); perpetuation of the human species (human sexuality); spiritual fulfillment (including humanitarian and altruistic instincts); control of one's own destiny (the right to life, liberty, and the pursuit of happiness, and the pride and spirit of a people who will not be conquered); creative expression (arts and entertainment, sports, and other forms of sensory stimulation); scientific curiosity (the need to know); and security (which incudes loving, being loved, and the satisfaction that comes with success and recognition). In addressing the issue of control of one's own destiny, even conflict is included, because *Fiddler on the Roof* takes place in Russia in 1905, on the eve of the Russian revolutionary period.

But more importantly, "Tradition" addresses a much deeper concept—that is, the idea that all forms of human endeavor (yes, even begging) are essential to the survival of our society, and that all are equally important ingredients in making up a whole, integrated, complex civilization such as ours. Moreover, no single endeavor is necessarily more or less important than any other, but each has a meaningful, dignified role to play in making our entire system work.

Our own human body is perhaps the best illustration of this concept, and we could learn a great deal about getting along if we spent more time studying how the organs and systems of our "machine" function with a mutual respect for one another. We have a brain, a heart, kidneys, lungs, a stomach, a liver, muscles, nerves, and so on, each organ and tissue being vital to the maintenance of a meaningful life.

Suppose the brain said to the heart one day, "Boy, do you have an easy life! All you do is pump blood all day long, nothing else; and here I am having to do all of this complicated coordinating, synchronizing, data processing, thinking, reacting, storing information, and just plain keeping track of things. My job is so much more sophisticated than yours . . . you should be ashamed of yourself!" To which the heart responds, "You're right. I am ashamed of myself. I'll quit right now! Goodbye!" Where would the brain be then? Or suppose the heart turned to the kidney and said, "Isn't it disgraceful that you wallow around in these waste products all day and night? Look at how high up and powerful I am compared to you, hanging around the catacombs and sewers of our anatomy. You ought to be ashamed!" To which the kidney responds, "You're right. I am ashamed. I'll quit right now! Goodbye!" Where would the heart, the brain, or the rest of the body be then?

The point, of course, of the silly little scenario above, is that the heart is asked only to pump blood, and to do nothing else; the kidneys are expected only to get rid of waste products, and nothing else. Likewise, each organ and tissue has its own unique function, no one being any more or less important than any other. But the real lesson in all of this is that the heart is not judged on how good a kidney it is, nor is the kidney judged on how good a heart it is. Neither organ is ranked nor prioritized in any sense; all of the organs and tissues work *together* to make the whole system go, and each is asked only to do its own individual task as well as it possibly can. So it is that in our society, scientists, engineers, mathematicians, physicists, athletes, artists, actors and actresses, musicians, doctors, lawyers, plumbers, politicians, electricians, teachers, cabdrivers, social workers, butchers, bakers, candlestick makers, and so on, must all be recognized as essential "organs and tissues" of the delicate mesh that makes us what we are as a civilization.

It is time that we put to a stop this archaic and totally foolish obsession we have of tending to judge and prioritize the importance of one form of human endeavor, such as hitting a baseball, over another, such as playing the violin. I never cease to be amazed at how we address with such passion, and make all attempts to eliminate, forms of discrimination based, for example, on physical disabilities, race, creed, gender, age, and nationality while we sweep under the rug obvious discrimination based on one's chosen profession. Thus, we tell athletes that they are worth millions of dollars per year, but pay our elementary school teachers only thousands. Is this not discrimination at its highest? The fact is, each and every one of us is endowed with unique "intensive potentials"—attributes that can be realized in ways that make specific contributions to the entire human experience. Like pieces of a jigsaw puzzle, we each fit into the whole picture (as described by Tevye), but perhaps even more importantly, without each and every piece, the entire jigsaw puzzle falls apart. So it is that each and every one of us has an equally important role to play in all that we are as a global society entering the 21st century.

All forms of endeavor that satisfy every aspect of all of our basic human needs and make us what we are as a global civilization share equal importance in what one might term a "United Nations approach to humanity." This approach is a vehicle for promoting the ideas that united we stand (like the human body), divided we fall; that we are, in fact, greater than the sum of all of our parts, but each part shares an equal piece of the pie; and that if we concentrated less on competing and more on conceding (not to be confused with conceit), we would move with greater dispatch toward making this planet a much better place to live.

Introducing the concept of intensive potentials (which I define to be the unique, individual talents and creative abilities that we all have, and that manifest themselves in different ways, no one way being any more or less important than any other) is a logical first step toward achieving the above goals; it is a prime cause; it is an adequate stimulus; it is a catalyst; it is a major disturbance to the quasi-equilibrated state of social ignorance that characterizes our current place in history, and maintains, much as we refuse to admit it, what still amounts to a caste system. Thus, I propose the establishment of a Society of Intensive Potentialists, which would bring together individuals from all walks of life to walk around in each other's shoes; to learn about what different people in different types of activities do; to appreciate all of the various aspects of a society that make it a functioning whole, and the notion that each is important in its own way. Intensive potentialists would be folks who promote intereaction, learning, experiencing, and becoming an informed society. They would seek mutual respect and appreciation as we launch into a new century of understanding, sensitivity, tolerance, and concern. They would bring a new meaning to the phrase "equal pay for equal work," recognizing that the reward is in direct proportion to the value of the profession, not the level of education required to get there (which is by one's own choice), or the level of responsibility (remember the brain and the heart, or the heart and the kidney), or what the market will bear, or any other criteria that we arbitrarily assign to value and reward our own importance, and recognize that all professions have inherently the same value. Yes, I believe the concept of intensive potentials, long recognized in the scientific community as a means for explaining the manifestation of physical phenomena, now needs to be applied more generically to our society as a whole. I believe the concept of societal intensive potentials is one whose time has come! I can dream, can't I?

What Is This Thing Called "Me"? Part 2: Attributes That Classify the Human Body as Being Alive

American Laboratory News, May 2005

In the first article of this series (*American Laboratory* Dec 2004; 36[24]:4–8), the point was made that "me" is a physical structure organized into various anatomical levels, increasing in size and complexity from atoms to molecules, cells, tissues, organs, and systems. Technically, any such material substance that is composed predominantly of atoms—organized to give the material a certain observable and measurable mass (which is interconvertible with energy) and a constituency that allows it to occupy space—is classified as *matter* (a word derived, interestingly, from the Latin *mater*, for "mother"). But "me" is more than just matter. "Me" is a type of *living* matter, which brings up an immediate question: What is it about this type of matter that classifies it as being alive? What attributes of an assemblage of "living" atoms and molecules distinguish them from inanimate matter?

Well, as we quickly discovered when we attempted to define the concept of "energy" (*American Laboratory News* Aug 2003; 35[17]:4–6), here, too, we find that a similar attempt to define "life"—directly, unambiguously, rigorously, precisely, and unequivocally—is equally elusive and futile. Nor do we have a clue as to when and exactly how certain special atoms and molecules interacted with one another to endow energy with the spark of "life." One theory suggests that life began when a particular class of compounds somehow developed the ability to replicate themselves, but the "somehow" part remains a mystery, as does the "why" aspect that would plausibly explain the reason(s) for this peculiar happening! Some things we *do* know. For example,

1. Humans are the product of a universe that is billions of years old. Its age gives rise to what might be called the Alchemy Principle.

That is to say, it takes a very long time to form and produce the heavier elements that biological complexity requires, and from which derive such processes as protein folding and DNA replication. In fact, the huge time scales involved in making it possible for the complex building blocks of organic life to evolve are often cited as evidence to explain why the age of our universe *must* be so enormous (some 10 ± 2 billion years, perhaps even older!). Moreover,

2. Humans are the product of an environment that developed in accordance with the so-called Anthropic Principle. That is to say, there are unique properties of our very old universe—in particular, its size and makeup—from which derive the necessary and sufficient conditions for the existence, sustenance, and evolution of life forms such as ours (hence, "anthropic," i.e., having to do with humans). I'm talking about such conditions as the magnetic field of the earth, its gravitational field, angle of tilt (between its axis of rotation and the perpendicular to its plane of motion around the sun), thermodynamic milieu (temperature, pressure, humidity, alkalinity/acidity, etc.), atmospheric ambience, stable and cyclic sources of heat and light, and so on—all making for a unique environment of life support. In other words, life exists because an environment conducive to life evolved. If I may take this reasoning still one step further,

3. Perhaps, like gravity and magnetism, life itself could very well be an as-yet unidentified type of "field force," derived from and permeating this conducive environment. If that is, indeed, the case, it is further likely that this field force (prana? ch'i?) could provide the domain from which emerges an intrinsic dynamic order that imprints itself on passive, inert matter, bringing it to "life," a universal principle that is not easily explained by simple randomness, a *logos* that could help to elucidate why this particular collection of complex parts and levels of organization of the human body are harmoniously integrated to transcend the individuality of each. In other words, governed by an Ordering Principle that transcends simple structure, quantity (atoms, molecules, etc.) becomes quality (life), inanimate being (matter) turns into animated becoming (evolving), and an organism is thus produced that takes on a unique essence of its own—an essence not identified with any one of its specific component levels of organization.

And yet, despite all of this knowledge, reasoning, and speculation, there remain unexplained certain very basic phenomena of the human experience—such as consciousness, creativity, memory, paranormal encounters, spirituality, and life itself! Absent such insights, we can only *describe* "life" (as we did "energy"), rather than *define* it. Thus, to describe life is to list certain attributes by which it can be characterized, distinguishing it from inanimate objects by the ability of living things to:

1. *Metabolize.* Derived from the Greek *metabole,* which means "change," metabolism is the generic process whereby living organisms extract energy from the environment (e.g., by ingesting food and inhaling air), and then convert (change) that energy (e.g., the air/fuel mixture) into a stored form via enzymatically catalyzed biochemical reactions. Enzyme-mediated catalysis accomplishes two things: First, it ensures that the biochemical reactions will proceed at a rate compatible with the sustenance of life (in some cases, increasing that rate as much as a trillion-fold!), and second, it ensures that the biochemical reactions can be carefully controlled (the right enzyme, in the right place, in the proper state of activation, is required in order for the reactions to proceed). The term "metabolism" also designates the conversions that take place as the usable portion of that stored energy is subsequently drawn upon to drive all physiologic processes, including those that build things up (anabolism) and those that break things down (catabolism). The nonusable/nonrecyclable portion, as well as the waste products of metabolism, are exhausted back to the environment.

2. *Move.* As I have indicated many times in previous editorials, movement (i.e., kinetic energy) is the very essence of reality, in general, and life, in particular. Thus, metabolic processes convert some of the potential (stored, as in a battery) caloric-energy inherent in the absorbed air/fuel mixture into perceptible kinetic energy of motion. Indeed, the biochemical processes themselves rely on movement at the atomic and molecular scales of perception: Without such movement, no metabolism would be possible. Similarly, the physical processes by which usable energy derived from metabolism becomes "real" at various scales of perception, such as those associated with activities of daily living, derive from movement—which includes such things as posture, locomotion of all or parts of the human body, balance and equilibrium, speaking, hearing, tasting, smelling, touching, hugging, kissing, reproducing, playing musical instruments, etc. Without movement, no perception is possible; it is impossible to take in food, breathe, exhaust waste products, and so on. Indeed, without movement, *nothing is possible*! That's why the output of the controlled system that is the human body is some type of movement at varying scales of perception, ranging from microscopic to macroscopic.

3. *Respond.* Responsiveness, in biological terminology, refers to those processes by which—as a result of being excitable (or irritable)—living systems can perceive (detect) and react to sensory stimulation. Perception involves interoceptive/exteroceptive transduction (by anatomical sense organs) of adequate stimuli. The latter are specific forms of energy (light, heat, sound, etc.) that excite specific sense organs, which, in turn, convert that energy into afferent (sensory) action potentials. These are nerve signals that transmit information to the central nervous system, or CNS, which includes the brain and spinal cord. Reactions to sensory stimulation involve the generation by the CNS of efferent (motor) action potentials that carry commands from the CNS to target organs and tissues, such as peripheral nerve networks, muscles, and glands—either exciting them or inhibiting them, as necessary, depending on the metabolic needs of the organism. In a more generic sense, one can say that living organisms have the ability to process information, which includes such things as consciousness and thinking; moreover, they can store it (which includes memory) and retrieve it (recall). Indeed, the ability to store and retrieve biological information is an important tool for preserving complexity, especially when living organisms are confronted by adverse environments that might temporarily destroy such complexity, or at least threaten it.

4. *Grow and develop.* Growth is the process by which what started out as a single, viable, living cell—a zygote, formed by the union of two gametes, or germ cells (such as an egg and a sperm)—matures into a full-fledged, totally developed, adult organism that I call "me." Growth of somatic cells normally proceeds via a process called mitosis. Notable exceptions include red blood cells (which do not reproduce because they lose their nucleus at maturity); reproductive cells (which undergo a different type of cell division called meiosis, to produce gametes); and certain types of striated skeletal muscle, nerve, and bone cells (although the latter group do have a limited capacity to repair damage to individual cells). In ripening through mitosis, the parent cell of a plant or animal divides to form two new daughter cells, each having the same number of chromosomes as the original cell. The latter then divide again to yield four offspring, which, in turn, produce eight progeny, and so on, until the number balloons to some 100 or so trillion cells in the adult organism.

The concept of growth, as it applies to more complex living systems, goes on to include development as well. The latter introduces two additional considerations: 1) Cellular differentiation—by which the single cell that was originally "me" at conception becomes specialized, so that, as I grow from a fertilized egg . . . to an embryo . . . to a fetus . . . to an infant . . . to a toddler . . . to a child . . . to an adolescent . . . and, finally, to an adult, the 100-trillion-celled organism that is now "me" has been differentiated into more than 200 different cell types that, collectively, can perform all of the functions necessary to keep me and my species alive, and 2) cellular regeneration—by which a living organism can replenish and renew its various constituents, as necessary, throughout its lifetime. Interestingly, as cells develop, they are actually programmed to die, committing suicide, as it were, through a process called apoptosis (derived from a Greek word that describes leaves falling off of trees). The reasons for this are many, but suffice it to say here that of the over 200 different cell types in the human body, some (like certain varieties of brain cells) might survive for virtually the entire life of the individual, while others (like certain types of white blood cells) might survive for just a few seconds. In general, about 0.003% of cells in the body (some 3 billion) die and are replenished (mostly in the skin and blood) *every single minute of every single day*!

5. *Reproduce.* One of the key distinctions between living systems and inanimate ones is the ability that the former have to make more of themselves, i.e., to beget offspring and, thereby, to preserve the species. In the case of humans, the reproductive process is sexual, as opposed to asexual, as is the case in certain plant-like budding mechanisms. The distinct advantage of sexual reproduction is that it is not just a matter of cloning but, rather, of breeding as well, i.e., attempting to improve the species with each succeeding generation. Such improvement might perhaps be accomplished through evolution, in the Darwinian sense of natural selection, or by certain types of mutation, or by other mechanisms, some not yet discovered. Thus, when the reproductive cells of sexually procreating organisms divide by meiosis (from the Greek word for "a lessening"), the number of chromosomes in the daughter cells (gametes) is reduced by half (forming haploid cells). Haploid gametes from contributing male–female adult parents then combine, in a process called fertilization, to produce a zygote—the stem cell that will undergo differentiation to ultimately produce an individual who has never existed before, and who will never exist again (see "Each of Us Is a Minority of One," *American Laboratory* Jan 2001; 33[1]:6–8). The zygote has had the diploid number of human chromosomes (46) restored, and, if all went well, should mature satisfactorily. Unfortunately, all does not always go well, leading to what are called congenital (existing at birth) afflictions, which may be inherited from either or both parents, or which may result from complications *in utero* all the way up to the moment of birth.

The human drive to procreate—to reproduce and therefore to ensure that the species will survive—is the second (survival of the self being the first) strongest human drive, affectionately referred to as the drive for sexual fulfillment. Third is the drive for spiritual fulfillment, and fourth is the need to control one's own destiny. The first two are clearly anatomical/physiological needs common to all living systems. The latter two, alluded to in the opening comments of this article, might be termed egocentric (or anthropocentric) needs, in the sense that they seem to be unique to the human species of animal. Be that as it may, in a much more fundamental way—i.e., at the morphological level that is an attribute of "life"—control is much more basic than just a desire to have input into one's own destiny.

6. *Control, and the maintenance of internal constancy*. Homeostasis is the name given to the process(es) by which the human body seeks to maintain within narrow prescribed limits those variables that are critical for the maintenance of life. In living systems, nothing is left to chance; the potential consequences are too great. Thus, the "window for survival" starts with variables that need to be kept within a desirable range (prescribed limits) that is coded into the body's various operating setpoints, and this state of affairs is maintained by various homeostatic mechanisms—such as those related to the previously mentioned enzyme kinetics, and other sophisticated feedback/feedforward control loops that regulate such things as body temperature, blood pressure, acidity/alkalinity, vital signs, and so on—regulate them, that is, unless the maintenance of these operating setpoints is persistently challenged by external disturbances, in which case, where appropriate, "living" systems can accommodate.

7. *Accommodation*. Briefly stated, accommodation (including sensory and functional adaptation) refers to the ability that living systems have to alter their operating setpoints and/or their systemic transfer functions in order to minimize the amount of control necessary to maintain the life of the individual and/or the species. Having devoted one entire editorial to "Physiological Accommodation" (*American Laboratory News* Sept 2004; 36[19]:4–6), I shall not dwell on it here, except to add that all physiologic function is goal-seeking, or purposeful. That is to say, subject to specific constraints (like optimization or minimum-energy schemes), the "living" system chooses (adapts) its various courses of action out of many possible alternatives. It does this to sustain both its own existence (including "egocentric" needs) and that of its species, with a minimum of effort, under exposure to varying environmental threats and disturbances. As a general rule, this principle seems to apply equally well at all levels of organization of "life" forms, from the most fundamental functional unit of living systems (i.e., the cell) to the entire ecology (bionomics) of the earth's biosphere.

To be continued . . .

Mind/Body—Both or Neither?
American Laboratory, July 2000

In 1917, the great Austrian mathematician J. Radon proved that any two- or three-dimensional object can be uniquely reconstructed from the infinite set of all of its projections into the next lower dimension, i.e., a two-dimensional object mapped into lines, a three-dimensional object projected into all possible two-dimensional planar views, and so on. Indeed, this theory forms the basis for all modern noninvasive medical imaging modalities, such as computed X-ray tomography (CT) scanning, magnetic resonance imaging (MRI), and clinical ultrasound. But there may be more to Radon's discoveries than he, himself, might have realized at the time. That is to say, by inference, Radon introduced the more generalized concept that in order to define and understand (to the point of being able to uniquely reconstruct) *all* of the features of any multidimensional process—when such a process is examined in a domain that has fewer degrees of freedom than does the one in which the process is occurring—then one must take into consideration *all* of the possible manifestations of that process in that next lower dimension (in other words, one must view it from all possible directions).

The point of our recognizing such an extrapolation of Radon's work is this: If we ever expect to derive a comprehensive understanding of the whole of the human phenomenon—viewed as a multidimensional process that is embodied in an infinite number of manifestations (projections), experienced by our limited anatomy, in the limited four-dimensional space–time domain within which it is contained—then we must approach, observe, study, and analyze the phenomenon from *all* conceivable points of view, ascribing to no one of these any more or less importance than is given to any other. In other words, to derive a self-consistent theory that accurately explains all forms of human behavior—everything that is "us"—we must assign equal importance to every projection that reflects every form of human endeavor, lest we create a disproportionate picture by arbitrarily enhancing one point of view at the expense of another. I am reminded, in this regard, of the famous picture that appeared some time ago on the cover of *The New Yorker* magazine, which depicted a New Yorker's view of the city compared with the rest of the United States. In this picture, New York City was shown as a huge metropolis, and the rest of the country was reduced in size to the point where one got the impression that the

George Washington Bridge spanned the distance from New York City to San Francisco, with little or nothing in between.

In very much the same way, we have also taken a disproportionate point of view in defining the role that the arts, in general, and music, in particular, play in the human experience. The arts are one projection that has hitherto been disparagingly minimized in prioritizing the importance of the things we do—most especially in our public education system, and thanks, in part, to the nearly 360-year-old Cartesianism philosophy of another mathematician, the Frenchman René Descartes.

In three major works—his 1637 *Discourse on Method* (short title), *Meditations on First Philosophy* (1641), and *Principles of Philosophy* (1644)—Descartes developed his Theory of Dualism. Dualism separates the mind, which is presumed to reason, objectively, by means of linear, spatial–temporal, cognitive modes of cerebral information processing (Descartes's *Spirit*), from the body, which is presumed to react, subjectively, to holistic, sensory–perceptive, emotional modes of mental function (Descartes's *Matter*). This theory thus ascribes to the former (the mind) a position of authority relative to the latter (the body), the spirit (mind) being capable of interacting with matter (body) but being quite separate from it and, at least in principle, not needing it to exist and/or survive.

By inference, then, dualism suggests that the mind is somehow more basic (yes, in Cartesian philosophy, even "Godly") than is the body (mere mortals are we); that rational thinking is somehow more reliable and justifiable than is emotional reacting; and that, therefore, activities (like the arts) associated with emotional attributes are inferior to those (like the sciences) associated with mental attributes—and so this attitude prevailed as of the end of the 20th century.

Well . . . as we begin a new millennium, perhaps it is time to finally discard dualism as a concept in the same way that Galen's nearly 1500-year-old, but erroneous, conceptualization of physiologic function (in Galen's case, his errant description of the human cardiovascular system) was cast aside following the pioneering work of William Harvey in the early 1600s. More and more, studies of the human brain are suggesting that there is no basis for assuming an anatomical dualism that would allow one to formulate a parallel track set of information-processing networks, in Descartes's either/or sense. Rather, there is growing evidence that our need to satisfy four fundamental drives—

survival of the self, survival of the species, spiritual fulfillment, and self-determination—has resulted in a physiologic organism that is first and foremost a creature of emotion (i.e., reactive)—being rational (reasonable) only when it has the time and/or the inclination to be so. Thus, we now know that the human body processes information *first* perceptually and holistically, and *second* cognitively and rationally. That is, mental function proceeds through neural networks arranged in *series*—in an "and" sense—as opposed to in *parallel*—in an "either/or" sense—and there is no separation between mind and body that would make the body subservient to the mind; in fact, if anything, the situation is exactly the opposite!

Newly developing theories of brain function are therefore now able to shed considerable light on helping to explain the effectiveness of the visual and performing arts in affecting adaptive behavioral responses—so much so that the scientific community is being forced to rethink its long-standing attitude toward the arts as being somewhat less basic than are cognitive subjects such as English, Math, Science, and History. In particular, it is now recognized that there are some very fundamental anatomic, physiologic, and scientific reasons why music originated and evolved to play the major role that it does in satisfying basic human adaptive functions, and with this realization, a whole new field of investigation has emerged: The Biological Foundations of Music. We are starting to take a much closer look at this projection into our domain of existence, and what we are seeing is quite enlightening: Witness the fact that a special conference on this topic was held at the New York Academy of Sciences (New York, NY) this past May, special sessions were dedicated to this subject at the annual meeting of The American Institute of Stress in the fall of 1999, and an international conference devoted entirely to this subject was held at Virginia Polytechnic Institute and State University (Blacksburg) in the fall of 1997. Moreover, the March/April 1999 issue of the *IEEE Engineering in Medicine and Biology* magazine was a special-topic issue that dealt exclusively with Music in Human Adaptation, and hardly a day goes by that one does not see something in the scientific literature that addresses this exciting new area of research. Perhaps Dr. Radon was really onto something!

How Many Brains Do We Have? It's Not Enough
American Laboratory News, September 2003

Over a decade ago, neurologist Paul MacLean (Senior Research Scientist Emeritus, Department of Neurophysiology, National Institutes of Mental Health, Bethesda, MD) proposed that we actually have three brains nested within one another in order of evolutionary development. The oldest, dating back 500 million years or more, is the primitive archipallium (literally, "principal cover"), which is also called the basal or reptilian brain, because it has remained virtually unchanged in our evolutionary progression from reptiles to mammals to humans. This pallium is also regarded as the oldest part of the cerebral cortex, and thus also goes by the names archicortex ("principal bark") and allocortex ("other bark"). The archipallium includes the brain stem, i.e., moving up from the spinal cord: the medulla oblongata (oblong "marrow"), the pons ("bridge"), and the reticular ("netlike") formation that is the mesencephalon ("midbrain"); the tri-lobed, bilateral cerebellum ("small brain"), which is attached to the upper rear of the brain stem; the *globus pallidus*, or *paleostriatum* (an ancient mass of gray matter containing the earliest basal nerve cells); and, since primitive reptiles roamed planet earth relying for survival primarily on their sense of smell, the rhinencephalon ("smell brain," or bilateral olfactory bulbs). This reptilian (or R-) complex of tissues is concerned purely with survival functions: musculoskeletal balance and equilibrium (including posture, locomotion, and coordination of muscular activity), autonomic functions such as breathing and heart rate, levels of alertness (an early-warning system for threatening sensory inputs), and primitive types of survival behavior (often aggressive, mean, and self-serving—traits that prevail even in 21st-century Homo sapiens).

Fast forwarding 200–300 million years, we start to evolve the second in this Triune Brain paradigm—the limbic system, so-called because it comprises a group of interconnected neural structures arranged in border-like fashion (*limbus* is Latin for "a border") surrounding the midline surfaces of the cerebral hemispheres at the top of the brain stem. Also known as the paleomammalian ("ancient mammalian") brain, paleopallium, or the limbic cortex, and, together with the archicortex, forming the paleocortex—the "ancient bark," or paleoencephalon ("ancient brain")—the limbic system connects with the brain stem. It starts its anatomical journey around the latter at the front, stomach-side surface of the cerebral frontal lobe, under the *septum pellucidum* ("translucent partition"), continues rearward, up and over the corpus callosum (a bundle of 300 million nerve fibers that connect the left and right sides of the brain) as the cingulate gyrus (cerebral convolution), and ends as the parahippocampal gyrus at the medial (toward the midline of the body) surface of the temporal lobe. The limbic system includes the hippocampus ("sea horse," because of its appearance), thalamus ("inner room," which receives all incoming sensory information), amygdala ("almond," because the amygdaloid body is shaped like one), parolfactory area, mammillary body, the *fornix* (Latin for "arch"), and the hypothalamus ("beneath the thalamus"), which, together with the thalamus and subthalamus, form the diencephalon ("through-brain," or thalamencephalon).

The limbic system is concerned more generally with homeostasis: the maintenance within an acceptable window of physiologic variables critical to life, such as body temperature, heart rate, respiration rate, blood pressure, blood sugar levels, acid–base balance, sleep/wake cycles, etc. This system also moderates behavior related to survival of the individual and the species, such as thirst/hunger reflexes, the drive for sexual fulfillment, and even competition. Closely connected to the latter are emotional instincts, reactions, and memories, which is why the limbic system is also called the "emotional brain." Research further shows that damage to parts of this system can affect our ability to react to situations that require making life-and-death decisions (or any decisions, for that matter), confirming still further that we are, in fact, creatures of emotion, not reason. Our ability to reason comes much later.

We need to fast forward again, 100–150 million years. At this point in time, we start to develop a cerebrum, covered by a ⅛-in.-thin "new mantle" (neopallium) or "new bark" (neocortex). The convoluted, four-lobed cerebrum (telencephalon, or "endbrain") is also called the neomammalian brain because of its development in primate mammals and, eventually, humans. Many theories (none of them proven) have been offered to explain the systemic increase in brain size that accompanied our evolution. One interesting hypothesis suggests that the neocortex developed as a sort of radiator to cool off blood from the midbrain and hindbrain (the rhombencephalon, or "afterbrain," which includes the pons, cerebellum, and medulla oblongata). This is certainly feasible when one considers that, if laid out flat, this convoluted sheet has a surface area approximating that of total skin surface, measuring some 1.5 m² (about the size of a 5.5-ft-long by 3-ft-wide office desktop). Another theory suggests that longer prey chases along more spread-out landscapes required increased memory, hence the need for more storage space and larger brain size; there are more theories as well.

For whatever reason(s), however, we are now endowed with an organ the size of a grapefruit, weighing about as much as a head of cabbage, and wired with more possible internal connections than there are atoms in the universe (between 10^{78} and 10^{81}). To list but a few of its many functions, the "new" part of this organ receives, processes (somatosensory cortex, mainly for taste, taction, and proprioception), and responds to (motor cortex) sensory inputs (via the parietal lobe); helps us plan, make rational decisions, and follow those with purposeful behavior (via the frontal lobe, which is richly and intimately connected to the limbic system); gives us the ability to perceive, especially through hearing (auditory cortex), and interpret what we experience in life, and commit some of those experiences to memory (via the temporal lobe); and allows us to see (visual cortex) our world of existence (via the occipital lobe). Moreover, because we have a neocortex, we can communicate, think, understand, organize, appreciate, create, learn, manipulate symbols (as in math), formulate theories, and deal with cognitive functions.

Much of the latter we began to develop some 4–5 million years ago, long after we parted company with the chimpanzees, and it progressed in stages that seem to have reached a temporary plateau dating back about 1 million years, with the lateralization of the brain into right-brain–left-brain specialization. That is to say, the popular belief today is that the left brain seems to deal more effectively with temporal/rational/cognitive/linear/verbal types of information processing, whereas the right brain appears to be more comfortable with spatial/creative/integrative/abstract/visual types of activities.

So, what do you think? Do we have: a) one brain (encephalon) with many interconnected functional parts (like the various organs and tissues that make up our one body); b) two brains, one of which (the ancient paleoencephalon) acts like the CPU of a computer system, while the other (the modern neoencephalon) assumes the role of memory and peripheral devices; c) three brains—a 500-million-year-old archipallium that we inherited from our reptilian ancestors, a 250-million-year-old paleopallium that came to us compliments of our mammalian lineage, and a 125-million-year-old neopallium that is uniquely human; d) all of the above; or e) none of the above? I don't know the right answer to the question of how many brains we have, but I do know that, regardless of the number, it is apparently not enough! With all due respect to our outstanding intellectual achievements in science and technology, successful efforts in research and development, advancements in medicine and genetics, etc., we have yet to figure out how to get along with one another. It is the now age-old question: "How come we can send a person to the moon and back, but we can't even . . . (you finish it)?"

Herein lies the irony: While we are busy scratching and clawing each other's eyes out with progressively more sophisticated weapons (the "eye-for-an-eye/tooth-for-a-tooth" philosophy again), we somehow manage to stop long enough to notice, marvel at, admire, and respect the diversity in nature. While, out of one side of our mouths we advocate variety as the spice of life—a good thing to be sought after and savored—out of the other side, as it applies to our own species, we attach negative connotations and adversative associations to words like "race," "ethnicity," "creed," and "religion." All of a sudden, variety is not so good and readily accepted, but fanaticism is (see *American Laboratory* Jan 2001; 33[1]:6).

I became acutely aware of this dichotomy just recently, when my wife and I visited a local nursery to buy some young plants for our home and her garden. There were hydrangeas, nasturtiums, African violets, tulips, morning glories, coleus, geraniums, gypsophilas (baby's breath), dahlias, impatiens—you name it. As we "oohed" and "aahed" at the beauty and diversity of nature's creations, my mind drifted off to bird watchers, who can be mesmerized for hours by the unique, lovely songs and distinctive markings of our fine-feathered flying friends. Birders have a passion for traveling anywhere and everywhere in hopes of catching a glimpse of a European widgeon, Pacific loon, Mexican cormorant, white-winged scoter, Newfoundland hairy woodpecker, Northern bald eagle, red-shafted flicker, broad-winged hawk, or any one of a huge number of rare species of ornithological specimens. I thought further about wildlife—about the zoos and national parks that exist for us to observe and appreciate all breeds of animal that inhabit our planet. I considered aquariums; geological museums; and the thousands of types of insects, trees, and other life-forms that populate our earth. Their sheer number awes us.

Then I thought, "Hey, wait a minute, we, too, are among all of those various forms of life. Why don't we 'ooh' and 'aah' about that?" Not only do we not appreciate and revel in that wonder but, quite to the contrary, all of the diversity and variety exhibited in our own form of life seem to be the very source of great strife, turmoil, and conflict. How odd that we can't learn to accept that diversity as something to be marveled at, to be recognized as the source of our very own identity, in the same way that we are filled with wonder at the assortment of plants, flowers, fish, birds, and so on with which we share this planet. Or, is variety the spice of life *except* when it comes to us? Am I missing something here? Maybe we need to evolve a *fourth* brain, a compatible encephalon, or *futurus* pallium, dedicated solely to humanitarian efforts—nothing cognitive, just pure compassion—a compassionate cortex!

The Physiology of Relativity

American Biotechnology Laboratory, January 2003

"Has it been only 10 minutes? I feel like I've been here for hours!" "Doesn't time fly when you're having fun?" "A watched pot never boils." These are a few of the expressions we use to describe the subjective nature by which we experience time. Indeed, nearly a hundred years ago (1905), Albert Einstein showed that time cannot be perceived objectively. Einstein noted that two events that appear to be simultaneous to one observer, relative to his or her specific frame of reference, might not appear to be so to another observer moving in a different frame of reference. Thus, the physics concept known as the theory of relativity was formulated, and further elaborated upon in the mid-1920s by the Prussian physicist Werner Heisenberg, whose now-famous Uncertainty Principle eventually led to the development of quantum mechanics.

These two brilliant scientists proved, from the point of view of basic physics, that there is no such thing as an absolute, purely objective observation. Rather, any measurement will ultimately depend not only on 1) the extent to which the process of measuring actually disturbs the event being measured, and 2) the resolution capabilities and sources of error in the measuring system itself, but also on 3) the frame of reference of the observer making the measurement, hence the term "relativity." But one very important aspect of the entire concept of relativity involves a question that was never raised by the authors of the physical theory of relativity—that is, to what extent is the observation being processed physiologically, at the same time rate as it is occurring physically in the frame of reference relative to which the measurement is being made? In other words, objective, physical reference frames aside, what about physiologic reference frames and the "relativity" that they introduce into an observation because of individual differences in the ways that incoming sensory information is eventually processed by various observers (i.e., physiologic systems) and the rates at which it is processed?[1,2]

As one approach to answering the question posed above, consider the following: Given that it is impossible to formulate a purely objective measure of time, suppose we define what I will call an intersubjective measure of time, the standard second. The word "intersubjective" is borrowed from Edmund Husserl[3] (a contemporary of Heisenberg), who, in developing his theory of phenomenology (1929), also noted that there is no such thing as a purely objective observation, except that Husserl was talking about it less in a mathematical/physics sense than in a very personal sense. But in order to distinguish phenomenology from solipsism (the theory that nothing but self exists), Husserl spoke of what he called intersubjective phenomena. These are realities experienced by a critical mass of sensing subjects (humans), all of whom report certain similar (or identical) attributes of the event they are describing.

By virtue of this intersubjective consensus, these attributes can presumably be objectively defined, and at least arbitrarily quantified to the extent that they represent common denominators experienced and described in exactly the same way by all subjective observers.

Thus, in the scientific world, we have intersubjective consensus that the standard second shall be defined in terms of the frequency of radiation emitted by cesium atoms when they pass from one equilibrated state into another. More specifically, the standard second is the measurement most commonly described by most observers (consensus of intersubjective experienced duration) when cesium emits 9,192,631,770 cycles of this radiation. This standard second now becomes the unit of time that we all agree to use in describing how long it takes for perceived events to occur; let's call it externalized time, because it is purely arbitrary and not necessarily related on a one-to-one basis to perceived time.

Nevertheless, externalized time based on the standard second is the quantified dimension used to describe the rate at which events in our universe are occurring. This, then, is also presumed to be the rate at which information derived from those events arrives at our sense organs, stimulating them sequentially so that we can perceive the corresponding events taking place in "real" time. Thus, as objectively as it gets, the time history of the corresponding event taking place in the environment external to our senses is described in an arbitrary, physical frame of reference, independent of any specific individual observer, as long as each of them is in the same physical frame of reference.

But we also know that each of us perceives as well the passage of time in accordance with a personalized cerebral information-processing rate, determined at least in part by our individual, genetically inherited ability to handle data at a particular speed. The data to be handled, or information to be processed, derive from the above-mentioned sensory stimulation, which may or may not occur at the same rate as that associated with our own biological clock (internalized sense of time). Thus, in addition to the standard second, we must also talk about our own, unique personal second. The personal second is an individual-specific time interval defined by how long it takes for our own physiologic systems to process discrete pieces of information coded into action potentials, and how we eventually experience that process consciously. I cannot give you a numerical, cesium-based value for the personal second because it is not standard; it is unique for each of us. All I can say about it is that 1) anatomically, we inherit a certain ability to process information at a certain rate; 2) physiologically, we can bias that rate to a certain extent as a function of experience, mood, health, interest in the subject matter being perceived, and a variety of other factors; 3) we think the suprachiasmatic nuclei located in the anterior hypothalamus of the brain have something to do with setting the pace for information processing, specifically, synchronizing and coordinating it with the circadian rhythms of our environment; 4) it is likely that the amygdala (involved in emotional responses) and hippocampus (involved in cognitive responses) of the limbic system are responsible for tagging, sequencing, and processing, at a specific rate, sensory inputs that have gotten past the reticular formation; and 5) information storage and retrieval from primary, secondary, and tertiary memory proceed at rates determined by the synaptic transmission characteristics and neurotransmitter properties of specific nerves and neural networks.

Specific anatomy and physiology aside, the point is that our internalized clock is ticking away at our own cerebral information-processing rate, providing us with a subjective (relative) sense of time, while our senses are being bombarded with inputs that derive from the physics of our universe, arbitrarily timed by an external, scientific (standard) clock, such as the one that resides on your wall or desk. If it so happens that my personal information-processing rate is in phase with the rate at which my senses are being bombarded, then I perceive events in real time in a one-to-one correspondence with the rate at which they are actually occurring; otherwise, I don't.

Let's consider a hypothetical example: Suppose my body receives information coded into, say, 36,000 bits of data, and that it can handle these data at the rate of 60 bits at a time. Then my internalized biological clock ticks off (36,000/60) = 600 of my personal units of time, defined by my own natural rate of information processing. Suppose further, that after I have processed these data, I am told that they represented events that actually transpired in an elapsed time of 10 minutes (600 standard seconds). In order to calibrate my internalized sense of time with the standard, external units of time (i.e., to tell myself that what I was experiencing bore a one-to-one correspondence to what was actually happening), I equate the 600 units of my personal time with the 600 standard seconds and tell my body, cognitively, that it should associate 36,000 bits of data with 600 perceived seconds. In other words, I train my body, through experience, to perceive events coded into 36,000 bits of information as having occurred in 10 standard minutes of time, provided I am in a wakeful state and processing information at my own natural rate. Once calibrated, my body remembers this one-to-one correspondence, whether or not it actually holds in other situations.

For example, suppose I am asleep. My eyes are closed (cutting off visual input), the room is quiet (auditory input is minimized), sensory adaptation has dulled significant tactile input, I am neither eating nor sniffing much of anything, and I am a sound sleeper—not terribly reactive to external stimulation. Under these circumstances, it may actually take as many as eight hours just to accumulate 36,000 bits of information! Furthermore, in this peaceful state of slumber, even my information-processing networks may have slowed (biasing), so that they process information at a rate of only 20 bits at a time. The 36,000 pieces of information will now be processed in (36,000/20) = 1800 units of perceived time (perhaps 30 calibrated minutes), but they will have accumulated during eight hours of clock time. Time has flown: 30 minutes of my time (sleeping, 10 minutes if awake and processing at 60 bits per second) has turned into eight hours of "real" time. You think to yourself, "Where did the other 7.5 hours go?"

Suppose, on the other hand, you are at a very boring party, talking with a very boring person who is firing the same 36,000 bits of information at you in the same 10 minutes of "real" time. But since you are totally disinterested, your body goes into "sleeping mode" (i.e., processes the information at the slower, 20-bits-at-a-time rate). You perceive the same 30 minutes of time to have gone by as you did above when you were sleeping, but when you look at your watch you think, "Has it been only 10 minutes? Time sure is dragging!"

There can be many combinations of these scenarios, but the point is that subjective time drags, flies, or does neither, depending on whether one's personal units of time are greater than, less than, or equal to the standardized units of time. Moreover, natural information processing rates (and hence, subjective perception of time) can be affected by boredom, fear, pain, waiting (whether for some important news or for a pot of water to boil), state of sleep, excitement about an upcoming event, experiencing a surge of acetylcholine (inhibitory) or adrenaline (excitatory), or by any other situation where we are not receiving information in real time at a rate consistent with that at which we are physiologically processing it. Therein lies the essence of a field of study that needs much more attention: physiological relativity.

References

1. Schneck DJ. *There is no such thing as a learning disability, only teaching disabilities.* Am Lab 2000; 32(24):6.
2. Schneck DJ. *Time.* Am Biotechnol Lab 2002; 20(13):4.
3. Husserl E. *Cartesian meditations: an introduction to phenomenology.* (Translated by Dorion Cairns.) The Hague, The Netherlands: Martinus Nijhoff, 1960 (based on work completed ca. 1929).

Creativity

American Laboratory News, November 2001

The best definition of creativity that I have ever heard came not out of the *World Book Dictionary*, or *Webster's Unabridged International Dictionary*, or any other "authoritative" source—it came out of the mouth of a seven-year-old! Several years ago, my wife and I (and the other two members of our string quartet) were invited to be artists-in-residence at a local elementary school for two weeks. The purpose of the residency was to impress upon second-graders the fact that music is as important a part of the human experience as any other type of activity. Students who participated in the program learned how to make, and actually constructed, their own stringed instruments; they were taught all about the physics of sound and the six basic elements of music (rhythm, melody, harmony, timbre, dynamics, and form); they became aware of their anatomical senses and their own unique physiologic responses to various styles of music; we touched very briefly on the historical periods of music; and, after breaking them down into small groups, we helped them compose an original piece of music for a string quartet. The program culminated in the quartet's live performance before an assembly of the entire school, where the original string quartet that the second-grade students had composed was premiered.

During the question-and-answer session that followed our concert, one of the elementary school children in the audience asked the composers of the music, "How did you come up with the melodic ideas for this piece?"

A young lady in our group responded, "It just came out of our head!" Now, if that isn't the best definition of creativity, I don't know what is—the melody "just came out of our head!" What is so satisfying about this definition is that it gets right to the point: We are *inherently* creative; it comes naturally to us; it's intuitive; it "just comes out of our head." The creative process begins by trusting our instincts. Unfortunately, as we grow older, formal education and external pressures inhibit creativity because they make us aware of the word "can't"; they make us conscious of being judged; and they force us to think in a "how to" cognitive mode, rather than in a "what if?" creative mode.

Creative people always dream of "what ifs." They have a vision. They always feel free to think beyond what is obvious or state-of-the-art. They have the ability to conceptualize—to use the power of their education and experiences to go beyond them, rather than to let them act as constraining boundaries. Creative folks either don't know they can't, or, if they do, they don't let it get in their way. I am reminded in this regard of perhaps the most inspiring commencement address I have ever heard, delivered at Virginia Tech (Blacksburg, VA) some years back by one of its most distinguished alumni, Christopher C. Kraft, who was for many years the voice of Mission Control at NASA. Chris was reminiscing about his early years at Tech, and recalled one of his professors proving, mathematically and beyond any reasonable doubt, that it was physically impossible for humans to travel faster than the speed of sound.

"Imagine" he said, "if we had never challenged that premise, and believed it to be gospel." He went on to caution the graduating seniors against closing their minds, encouraging them to recognize that what they had learned during their previous four years was only what we knew up to that point in time. Thus, the knowledge with which they had been endowed needed to be accepted within that framework—constantly challenged, not allowed to constrain or inhibit the imagination. Moreover, the graduates needed to appreciate that the learning process did not end as they departed from the campus. After all, even the great Lord William Kelvin once remarked, "Heavier than air flying machines are impossible"; the world was once thought to be flat; and it was once believed that the atom couldn't be split—indeed, the word "atom" means, literally, "indivisible" (*a–* meaning "without," and *tomos* being the Greek word for "a cutting").

The "what if?" open-mindedness of creative individuals gives them a unique ability to improvise in an innovative way; to extemporize; to invent; to believe in something beyond themselves. They tend to have an adventurous spirit, to be pioneers, and to stray from the "we've always done it this way" mentality. Jazz musicians, of course, are prime examples of the art of improvisation. Through it, they let a piece of themselves surface—something very special "just comes out of their head." Going one step further, really great jazz improvisers never—repeat, never—write out their riffs (melodic phrases or distinctive rhythms). To do so would defeat the whole purpose of improvising, which is to express themselves in a way that is peculiar to that *particular* moment—to the way the artist feels at that time, at that place, about that subject matter. Once written out, the riff captures only that moment in time, whereas the individual's feelings while playing the very same piece of music at another instant might be totally different. To be really spontaneous—to really improvise—is to not write anything out, however great it may seem at the time.

I have a colleague, a recognized expert in his field, who refuses to write a definitive book about his subject for essentially the same reason. As he puts it, "Once it is written down and published, it's too hard to change your mind. As long as I don't publish a book, I am free to modify my theories, to fine-tune my ideas, to continue to develop the formulation, to keep the creative process going. Write it down, and the process comes to a grinding halt; whether justified or not, the public takes you at your word and holds you to what you wrote, unless you then undertake to revise the book and come out with multiple subsequent editions, which is more trouble than it's worth!"

To counter such an egocentric point of view, one might argue that unless the creative process is thus brought to fruition and shared with others (who might, for example, not have been present at the actual live performance of a jazz group), it is essentially an exercise in futility, and dies with its creator, leaving no legacy behind to be enjoyed and appreciated by future generations. Therefore, having the resolve to bring one's innovative ideas to a state of realization is perhaps as important as the creative process itself.

Equally important, in a more practical sense, is to recognize that the creative process needs to be nourished by a conducive environment. It's hard to be creative when one is tired, hungry, stressed out, distracted, and so on. An unhectic environment, proper nutrition, rest, relaxation, and various forms of meditation and exercise all help one to work with the body to free the mind; they provide the energy that drives the creative process, allowing one to focus his or her efforts toward the task at hand. The technical term for this relaxed state of mind is *cenesthesia*, or *coenesthesia*—that common sensation that one experiences when all body parts are functioning in synchrony with one another and the system is hitting on all cylinders. The passiveness of this state of generalized tranquility leads to less random thought processes, an increased mental alertness, and a deeper sense of perception. Thus, imagery, feelings, and hidden thoughts drift more easily into one's awareness, where they might otherwise have been masked, subdued, or lost completely and therein lies the capacity for increasing creativity by exploiting the inherent potential of the human mind mentioned earlier.

Though this short editorial cannot address all aspects of the creative process, I did want to mention one more important attribute that characterizes the creative personality: the ability that such individuals have to stand apart from the crowd. The creative mind has to be a very brave mind, because creativity is a very lonely process. Thus, the creative personality does not fear standing alone, but rather has the self-confidence to believe in the uniqueness and relevance of its particular point of view. This confidence is predicated on a positive attitude, a mindset that is not afraid to be judged, is not fearful of making mistakes, and is open to forging new, hitherto uncharted pathways. The creative mind is an independent mind, which, in our society, frequently faces grave consequences—hence the need for courage, determination, and self-sacrifice in recognizing and addressing, in ways never before attempted, a human need that is not being met. Any inner impediment or restraint that inhibits the free activity, expression, or functioning of the human mind, putting it in a "911 mode," destroys its ability to create.

There Is No Such Thing as a Learning Disability, Only Teaching Disabilities

American Laboratory, December 2000

Several months ago, I attempted to upgrade my computer system's modem-access software that connects it to the Virginia Tech Internet Server. Very confidently, I inserted the brand-new VTNET CD-ROM into my e-drive and waited to hear the satisfying "whirr" and see the flickering lights that assure me something wonderful is happening as the software loads and executes. Instead, after a few seconds, I got back an error message that read, "Setup was unable to connect to the Microsoft site or your administrator's download server to retrieve the Setup instruction file. This can be due to invalid proxy server settings on your computer or other problems with your current Web browser." Thinking of myself as relatively competent to deal with such issues, I began fooling with my system in an attempt to resolve this dilemma, which, of course, messed it up even more. Finally, after several hours of futile effort and a genuine longing for the good old days before computers, I felt humbled enough to call the 4Help service at Virginia Tech's Computer Center. That's when a fine young gentleman named Jeremiah and I met for the first time.

We talked about TCP/IP (Transmission Control Protocol/Internet Protocol) settings, DNS (Domain Name Server) settings, and Configurations for Dial-Up Networking connections. We talked at length about other matters related to the rules and guidelines that allow two programs or computers to interact with one another, so that if one speaks English and the other speaks Spanish, but they both know some German, they can find a common ground along which to communicate. And that's the name of the game: communication.

So, carefully, deliberately, calmly, and with great patience, Jeremiah literally talked me through the tedious, step-by-step process of configuring my system so that it could successfully communicate with other systems. After a considerable period of time had elapsed (I really did mess things up badly and we had to first undo everything I had done before we could move forward), success was achieved. But the story does not end there: You see, at no time during this entire process did we call my computer "learning disabled." At no time did we blame *it* for the problems *we* were encountering. All along the way, we realized that *we* had a communication problem, and *we* had to figure out a way to fix it. Once we did, communication was successfully established and the computer did fine.

Suppose that we too have cerebral "computers" that came with TCP/IP and DNS settings. Perhaps we inherited these hard-wired settings through our DNA computer software, as a form of CD-ROM. Perhaps we acquired these neural-network settings as a result of experiential and environmental programming, as a form of EPROM. Perhaps these settings are some combination of nature and nurture. In any case, suppose, too, that other "computers" (people) with whom we go through life trying to communicate also have their own unique TCP/IP and DNS settings that are quite different from ours. To say, then, that one group of individuals (for example, some students) is learning disabled because their TCP/IP/DNS settings may not be in conformity with those of another group of individuals (for example, some teachers) who are trying to communicate with them is as ludicrous as accusing my computer of being learning disabled because it was unable to communicate with Virginia Tech's download server. It was not the computer's fault, nor is it the student's. Each of us has the ability to learn; the key is to find the proper channels of communication.

As I have professed for the nearly 30 years that I have been in the classroom, there is no such thing as a learning disability; there are only teaching disabilities. It is incumbent upon the teacher to figure out how to reach the student, not the other way around. What our educational system (and, in a broader sense, society) has done is what Rabbi Harold Kushner (author of *When Bad Things Happen to Good People*, New York, Avon Books, 1981) calls "blaming the victim." We have transferred to students, as if it is their fault, our own inability to communicate with them should they happen to have TCP/IP/DNS settings that are different from the ones that we are using in the classroom, thereby accusing them of not being able to learn. It is analogous to (and as ridiculous as) blaming my radio for being at fault because it is tuned to 93.8 FM and is therefore unable to receive a signal that is being broadcast on 101.5 FM.

What is equally ridiculous (and tantamount to a form of child abuse) is that we label individuals as being learning disabled (leading them to actually believe it) based mainly on their ability (or lack thereof) of developing the ill-defined skills presumably required to make a living. We require them to perform up to some arbitrarily determined levels of competence (standards of learning or SOLs) and within what we arbitrarily designate as a reasonable period of time (i.e., by a specific age), cognitive, rational, and verbal and symbolic oriented tasks such as manipulating words and numbers, as if to declare that that is all there is to learning. Be able to do this and/or that by such-and-such a time and you are able to learn; fail to do so, and you are learning disabled. Consider, for example, the case of a brilliant, 40-year-old artist or musician with highly developed visual-perceptive skills, who has well below average aptitude for math and science, much difficulty reading, and cannot seem to learn to write. This individual is labeled by our educational system as being learning disabled and probably goes through life making it a self-fulfilled prophecy. On the other hand, were this a 40-year-old scientist who still draws pictures at the same level as a kindergartener, thus revealing a poorly developed sense of visual-perceptive skills, we would hardly think of calling this individual learning disabled. Quite to the contrary, the very word "scientist" suggests a bright, highly intelligent, well-educated person of respected stature in our society. And yet, such individuals with poorly developed creative/perceptual skills could easily be labeled just as disabled in that respect (if those were the criteria used to define learning) as are those who are inept at developing verbal/symbolic/cognitive skills.

The problem of course in both examples is the feeble attempt that we make to generalize based on definitions that are arbitrary and in fact not really related to the learning process. When we try to teach with little or no appreciation for how people learn, when we establish arbitrary and subjective measures of learning based on arbitrary and subjective standards of learning, when we stress the individuality of people but proceed to develop an educational system that treats them all alike (as a homogeneous group of information processors), then we have developed an educational system that is destined to fail because it operates under the false premises that what is being taught is the same as what our students are learning, and that what we test is in some remote sense a measure of their ability to learn. So I am grateful for the trouble I had with my computer because it reminded me, again, that communication is a two-way street, that everybody has an inherent ability to learn, and that no problem is insurmountable as long as one has the right approach and the right attitude. I derived out of this experience much more than a now-functional computer system. I learned a valuable lesson in life.

Scaling "Unreachable" Heights
American Laboratory News, November 2002

The great Walt Disney is quoted as having said, "Somehow, I can't believe there are many heights that can't be scaled by a man who knows the secret of making dreams come true. This special secret can be summarized in four C's. They are curiosity, confidence, courage and constancy, and the greatest of these is confidence. When you believe in a thing, believe in it all the way. Have the confidence in your ability to do it right. And work hard to do the best possible job."

Case in point: While on the faculty at Radford University in Virginia, my dear wife Judi taught a class that was intended to introduce the string family of orchestral instruments (violin, viola, cello, and double bass) specifically to music education majors who were not familiar with how to play these instruments but who might someday be faced with teaching young children how to play one or more of them. Thus, this course was a required "beginner's" class for nonstring music education students, those whose primary instrument was in the wind family (brass and reed), keyboard, percussion (drums, cymbals, etc.), and so on. To make the class more interesting and fun (as only Judi can), and to promote a bit of camaraderie among the students, she organized them into a small chamber orchestra, which, at the end of the semester, actually put on a performance for the Radford community of faculty and students.

At the end of the performance, one of Judi's colleagues approached her and remarked, "I noticed that Sharon (fictitious name to respect privacy) was the concertmistress of your little chamber ensemble."* "You bet!" replied Judi. "Sharon has been one of the stars of this class. She took to the violin like a duck to water: learned the mechanics of playing the instrument more naturally than anyone else in the class, became technically proficient at it in record time, can read the clef, transpose into or out of just about any key, and legitimately earned the right to sit in the first chair!" "But," continued her colleague, lowering her voice to a hushed whisper, "don't you *know* about Sharon?" "Know what?" Judi retorted. "Well, everyone on the faculty knows about Sharon's 'problem.' She has been diagnosed as being severely learning disabled, and manages to just get by in all of her classes, especially

---

*For those of you who may not be familiar with the term, "concertmaster" or "concertmistress" designates the lead player (who is traditionally the best player) in the violin section of an orchestra. He or she sits right up front, at the head of the section, to the immediate left of the conductor.

her music theory courses, with very great difficulty, and only if she receives quite a bit of private coaching. It's inconceivable that she could master so quickly an instrument as difficult as the violin, much less learn to play it so well so soon. In fact, it would be nothing short of a miracle!" "Well," Judi concluded, "I'm sure glad *I* was not informed of her 'disability' at the beginning of the semester; what's even more important, I'm sure glad Sharon didn't tell me about it and sell herself short! I guess nobody ever explained to her, or (thankfully) to me that she's not supposed to be able to play the violin, so neither one of us could make it a self-fulfilled prophecy. Instead, I guess you just witnessed your miracle."

In fact, Sharon did go on to graduate, and when last heard from, was pursuing a successful and rewarding career in the music business. So much for "She can't do it"!

English poet Edgar A. Guest (1881–1959) explained it this way:

"Somebody said that it couldn't be done
   But he with a chuckle replied
That 'maybe it couldn't,' but he would be one
   Who wouldn't say so till he tried.
So he buckled right in, with the trace of a grin
   On his face. If he worried, he hid it.
He started to sing as he tackled the thing
   That couldn't be done, and he did it!

Somebody scoffed: 'Oh, you'll never do that;
   At least no one ever has done it';
But he took off his coat and he took off his hat
   And the first thing we knew he'd begun it.
With a lift of his chin and a bit of a grin,
   Without any doubting or quiddit,
He started to sing as he tackled the thing
   That couldn't be done, and he did it.

There are thousands to tell you it cannot be done,
   There are thousands to prophesy failure,
There are thousands to point out to you one by one,
   The dangers that wait to assail you.
But just buckle in with a bit of a grin,
   Just take off your coat and go to it;
Just start in to sing as you tackle the thing
   That 'cannot be done,' and you'll do it."

Just like Sharon, it's a good thing that the monarch butterfly that inhabits regions east of the Rocky Mountains in North America doesn't know each fall that it's not supposed to be able to fly as many as 3000 miles as it migrates south to the mountains of the Transverse Neovolcanic Belt west of Mexico City. Various scientific investigations that consider the size, mass, anatomy, and physiological function of monarch butterflies are at a loss to explain how these insects manage to fly that far, and actually gain weight during the trip! One interesting theory suggests that they have a unique ability to find and intercept air currents that allow them to glide huge distances, thereby conserving the abdominal fat stores that fuel the "powered" portions of their journey. If that's the case, then their weight gain could perhaps be accounted for by noting that they do stop periodically for nectar, but there are still many unanswered questions about how these small organisms are able to fly so far under such hazardous conditions. Well, although the answers to those questions remain a mystery to us, they don't seem to be of concern to the butterflies, who neither know nor care about all of those scientific investigations that question their ability to be able to do what they do!

On a daily basis, we too are inundated with "it can't be done" attitudes that constrain our efforts to strive for personal accomplishment and to seek creative solutions to challenging problems. Time and again we are told to "forget it; it won't work." We are constantly reminded of our shortcomings, "disabilities," faults, and limitations. I think to some extent, this mindset derives from the inherent resistance (inertia, conservatism) that all quasi-equilibrated states have to any disturbance that would move them away from their then-prevailing state of existence. The "We've always done it this way; don't rock the boat" mentality is comfortable; it puts us in the realm of the known. We're secure, predictable, and we like it that way. On the other hand, the "How about if we try it this other way?" suggestion has the potential to leave us uneasy; now we're in the uncomfortable, insecure realm of the unknown. The outcome is unpredictable; we feel threatened, and we don't like it that way. We're in 911 survival mode.

There's also the "If it ain't broke, don't fix it" philosophy, which implores us to leave things as they are if there is no obvious reason to fix them. "Stop your foolish experimenting with lights," Ben Franklin was admonished. "What's wrong with our traditional, fabulous oil lamps?" Spanish experts told Columbus (as well as King Ferdinand and Queen Isabella), "Your plans to discover a new, shorter route to the West Indies are both ridiculous and impossible. Why don't you leave well enough alone and stick to the established trade routes, lest your efforts cause you and your men to fall off the edge of the flat world we live in?"

Finally, we are always being held back by the ever-present, dreaded fear of "failing," or, even worse, of being "wrong," for which offenses our society imposes consequences that continue to be totally and mercilessly disproportionate to the deficiencies that presumably precipitated them. Sharon, for example, could have opted to tell Judi of her "severe" learning disabilities, and therefore, that there was no way she could learn to play the violin, even at a beginner's level, without some serious coaching. After all, that is what was "expected" of her (predictability), and she would thereby be living up to those expectations (self-fulfilled prophecy), while avoiding the possibility of failing, or at least providing an acceptable *excuse* for failing. "What can you expect?" people would say, "She is learning disabled, you know." Likewise, Ben Franklin was successful enough without having to pursue his experiments with electric lighting, without risking the possibility of failure and public ridicule. And I'm sure that Christopher Columbus, an eminent astronomer, geographer, cartographer, and navigator, after having been turned down by John II of Portugal (whose nautical and "scientific" experts assured him that Columbus's plans were totally outlandish), could just as easily have trashed the whole idea and gone on to a very successful career doing something else.

But Sharon, Franklin, Columbus, the monarch butterfly, and countless others throughout history did accomplish the "impossible"; they did perform "miracles." They did not opt for the safe, easier alternatives, and so were able to scale those "unreachable" heights. Because of the four C's, they, like the engine in *The Little Engine That Could* (a children's story by Watty Piper, Platt & Munk Publishers, New York, 1930), thought they could . . . thought they could . . . thought they could . . . until they did! Recall that Watty Piper tells of a train filled with toys and other wonderful things that were being delivered to all good boys and girls. The train soon encountered a towering mountain, which the little engine pulling it could not negotiate. The toys on board begged for help from a shiny new engine, which arrogantly replied, "I pull the likes of you? Indeed not!" Next, they pleaded with a big, strong engine, but the conceited engine shook off their pleas with, "I won't pull the likes of you!" Along comes an old, tired, dingy, rusty engine, which would have liked to help, but declared, "I can not. I can not. I can not," as it rumbled off to the roundhouse.

As a last resort, the toys implore a very little blue yard engine to succumb to their desperate request, and so it is left up to the little blue engine to overcome insurmountable odds as it pulls the train up the mountain, repeating to itself over and over again, "I think I can. I think I can. I think I can." Huffing and puffing its way to eventual success, the train makes it over the mountain and into the valley below, bringing great joy to the good little boys and girls of the city.

This story is an inspiring tribute to the power of positive thinking, illustrating that courage, confidence, and persistence (1% inspiration, 99% perspiration) are often what make the difference between success and failure. We all need that confidence, which Disney singles out as the greatest of his four C's. One proven way to get it, as Sharon discovered, is to surround ourselves with people, such as really great teachers, who are positive, encouraging, and selflessly willing to love, nurture, and bring out the very best in us. In fact, the single most important attribute of a great teacher (like Judi!) is having the ability to get students to believe in themselves. Under those circumstances, nobody can ever take your dreams away from you, and success is certainly within reach, if not entirely assured!

Stay Teachable!

American Laboratory, January 2003

When I was a graduate student at Case Western Reserve University (Cleveland, OH, circa 1969–1973), I took a course entitled "Turbulence." The first day of class, after establishing the ground rules for the course, going over how the class would be administered, and outlining the material that would be covered, the instructor ended by saying, "Let's be perfectly clear about this: I'm ignorant, and you're ignorant, but you're more ignorant than I am, and that makes me the teacher and you the student!" He then went on to qualify that statement by explaining that we know a great deal *about* turbulence, but, as is also true of many other things (like magnetism, gravity, electricity, nuclear "strong" and radioactive "weak" forces), we do not really know what it *is*, nor do we really understand it!

Although intellectually I appreciated them at the time, the true meaning of those words became clear to me some 20 years later when I was teaching Physics at Virginia Tech. One day, a student in the class asked, "Dr. Schneck, what is an electric charge? What makes a positive electric charge positive and a negative electric charge negative? Why do 'like' charges repel one another and 'opposites' attract? And why do negative charges always flow toward positive charges, but not the other way around?" I tried to come up with a clever answer to those questions, one that would make me sound like I knew what I was talking about, complete with the proper technical jargon that would throw up an impermeable smoke screen, impress the student with my thorough understanding of the concepts involved, and most importantly, confuse him enough to avoid his pursuing the subject with follow-up questions. The answer suddenly occurred to me: "I haven't got a clue!"

At this point, I was reminded of the words of my Turbulence professor, and then something else occurred to me: "None of us has a clue, but we won't admit it!" The fact is, we know a lot about electricity. We can derive fancy mathematical equations that define various aspects of how it works, we can do neat experiments with it, we can put it to both good and bad uses, we can write books about it, and we can formulate lavish theories that attempt to explain it (electrons, protons, neutrons, and all that good stuff). But let's face it: When push comes to shove, not one of us could have answered that student's questions in a way that would reveal a thorough understanding of what electricity *is*! (Aside: I did, in fact, respond by saying, "I don't know," and the student and I parted as friends. However, in the years that have elapsed since, I have given this matter a great deal of study, thought, and consideration. Asked that same set of questions today, I believe I could explain what I think electricity is, and magnetism, gravity, strong and weak forces, as well, not to mention human nature, but I will share those thoughts with you some other time.) Let's face it: I'm ignorant, and you're ignorant. Wouldn't it be great if more of us had that attitude? But we don't. More often than not, given just a wee bit of information that seems to make sense (and to which we can attach fancy language, Greek terms, Latin definitions, and "in" jargon), we automatically equate that with "knowing." What is even worse, we are adamant in asserting so—so adamant, for example, that the famous theorist A.A. Michelson, mistakenly thinking he was quoting another famous theorist, Lord Kelvin, had the audacity to declare in 1894 that we then knew everything there was to know, and that the future of science would consist merely of "adding a few decimal places to results already obtained." We are so adamant that we even go to extremes in order to defend and preserve those beliefs we cherish and hold sacred. We are willing to destroy those who would dare to question those beliefs, to kill and dispose of those who disagree with us. Indeed, one has simply to examine the history of just about any field of endeavor to see that it is filled with theories and convictions that persisted relentlessly, not just because of inertia (i.e., a natural resistance to change a quasi-equilibrated state), but, more probably, because those who would dare to challenge or question the prevailing dogma feared the consequences of such assertions, including public ridicule, professional rejection, humiliation, personal harm, even death.

A case in point involves the Spanish theologian and physician Michael Servetus. In 1553, he published *Christianismi Restitutio* ("Christianity Restored"), in which he advanced doctrines that were opposed by both the Reformers and the Catholic Church. Among many concerns expressed by Servetus was one that questioned the validity of, what was then, a more than 1300-year-old theory of the human cardiovascular system, one proposed by a Greek physician to the Roman Emperor Marcus Aurelius: Claudius Galenus of Pergamon (131–201 A.D.). The Galenic Tradition, as it came to be known, was so logical in its formulation, so aligned with what little anatomy and physiology were known in Galen's time (and well beyond it), so easy to correlate with the Greek humoral theory, that it prevailed as the physiologic bible during the Middle Ages, through medieval times, and well into the late 16th century. One did not question Galen, even in the face of conflicting experimental findings that could not be reconciled with his theory. Why, then, did the theory prevail? It postulates a unidirectional flow of blood, and relies very heavily on the presumption that so-called nutritive spirits pass from one ventricle of the heart to the other through pores in the heart wall. Nutritive spirits are contained in blood, which is manufactured in the liver and carried to the right side of the heart. There, it trickles through the interventricular septum to the left side, to be mixed with "vital spirits" (air) that were delivered there from the lungs. The ebb and flow motion of the heart drives this mixture out to all body tissues, where it is metabolized (used up), and subsequently excreted; the mixture does not recirculate throughout the body.

In Galen's time, and for centuries later, there was no reason to suppose that blood recirculated throughout the body, or, for that matter, that there was a need for a separate pulmonary circulation. Why would there be? Oxygen was not even discovered until 1774, and capillaries are not visible to the naked eye, so what evidence was there to suggest that arteries and veins are in any way connected to one another? The microscope, through which capillaries were observed for the very first time (William Harvey postulated their existence—he never actually saw them), was not invented until around 1590, 37 years after Michael Servetus was declared a heretic for his "revolutionary ideas" and burned at the stake on October 27, 1553, with a copy of his offending book strapped to his waist . . . oops!

The same fate awaited Giordano Bruno, an Italian theologian and philosopher who became fascinated with Copernicus's theory that the sun, and not the earth, was the center of the universe (Copernicus's theory itself was suppressed for 300 years because it offended the church's inquisitors). Bruno began telling and writing of "multitudes of solar systems, sun-centered universes, scattered among the stars." He envisioned the existence of planets just like earth, with life on them just like ours. He, too, was burned to death as a martyr, on February 17, 1600. I guess the 1500s were not a good time to get creative! Neither, it seems, were the 1700s.

The great composer Ludwig van Beethoven (1770–1827) was very adventurous in the use of tonality. In the opening measures of his First Symphony, premiered in 1800 to a very conservative Viennese audience, he, for the very first time, used what musicians call secondary dominants to delay by three full bars the arrival of the actual tonic chord, upon which is based the remainder of the piece. One critic commented, "Whoever heard of a symphony in the key of C major, opening in the key of F major, and then progressing through the keys of A minor and G major before arriving at its basic tonality?" This unorthodox opening shocked the audience of the day. Although Beethoven was spared from being burned at the stake (beheading and lynching were much more popular at the time), rumor has it that most of the audience walked out on this first performance. The music was just too foreign to their ears. It wasn't "the way it's always been done."

In the 1400s you would never have passed a geography class, not to mention live to a ripe old age, if you dared to suggest that the earth was not flat. In the 1800s you would have flunked physics if you dared to suggest that humans could fly in heavier-than-air machines. ("Heavier than air flying machines are impossible," said the great Lord William Kelvin.) Even as late as the end of the 20th century, around 1980, you would be taking an awful risk to suggest that superconductors were possible at temperatures as warm as liquid nitrogen. They are.

The odds are that if U.S. physicist Allan Cormack of Tufts University (Medford, MA) and Research Engineer Godfrey Hounsfield of the

British firm EMI, Ltd. (Stockport Cheshire, U.K.), winners of the 1979 Nobel Prize in Medicine and Physiology for their development of the computerized axial tomographic scanner, had tried to fund their efforts through conventional channels, their proposals would have been denied. In fact, if memory serves me correctly, I seem to recall their actually saying something to that effect at a press conference following the announcement of the Award. Even after these men were recognized for their achievement, they drew widespread criticism from those who argued that the exorbitant costs involved in applying this technology would render it useless in the clinical community. So much for that argument, and so much for a similar one that surrounded the invention of the automobile, thought to be a "nice toy," but of little practical value.

We humans are a strange breed. We don't take too kindly to those who swim against the tide. Years ago, it was literally worth your life if you so much as dared to question the then state-of-the-art frame of mind on just about any subject; not much has really changed since. Oh, sure, we are not quite as obvious about it, and today we use different methods, but our tendency to condemn, through peer review and public derision, truly innovative thinkers has remained pretty much the same, and continues to inhibit creativity. Despite that, we progress because there are those brave few who, at great personal risk and expense, are willing to slip out of the constraints imposed by the culture of their time; those who are bold enough to keep their mind open to new ideas, alternate explanations, and innovative concepts, those who *stay teachable*! On behalf of all the rest of us, I say to those pioneers, "Thank you."

Bad Stress

American Laboratory News, August 2002

One of my most impressionable experiences in medical school occurred when a professor came into class one day and declared, "Let's get something straight right up front: Cancer does not kill you; heart disease does not kill you; stroke does not kill you . . . *stress kills you*!" He went on to emphasize the point that the deadliest lethal diseases with which we humans are afflicted derive not from the symptoms for which we are clinically treated, but from the stress (mostly psychological, but physical, as well) to which we subject our bodies on a day-to-day basis. And at the top of his list of daily sources of stress were what he called "artificial, self-inflicted, 'bad' stresses"—those that our civilization has *created* for itself.

These bad stresses are as opposed to what he termed "natural, 'good' stresses." The latter—like naturally occurring environmental extremes that irritate our senses (e.g., hot or cold, light or dark, sweet or sour, pungent or bland, and so on)—are indigenous to our instinct for survival. Thus, being exposed to them is actually healthy, in that we are equipped to handle them naturally, thereby helping to maintain our vigilance against potential or impending annihilation. Consider, however, some of the following bad stresses (not necessarily listed in any order of importance) as they contribute to our self-imposed, unhealthy, prolonged and enduring state of fight-or-flight existence.

1. *Meeting deadlines.* For better or worse, we, in an effort to maintain some degree of efficiency in the way our society goes about getting things done, have inflicted upon ourselves the need to hit target dates and times. For instance, the normal filing deadline each year for federal income tax returns is April 15th; colleges and universities adhere to strict deadline dates by which admission applications are due; the same is true for submission of research proposals and/or progress reports to granting agencies—indeed, for just about any activity that has associated with it an application process, always there is a "must be postmarked by (or received by) such-and-such a time and/or date" tagged on to the application form. We race to get to the bank or post office before it closes. Journalists, editors, reporters, and writers race to make publication deadlines. We race to pay bills on time to avoid having our accounts assessed interest and penalty charges, and so on; the list is endless. We impose on just about every aspect of our life some time and/or date deadline that sets off unhealthy fight-or-flight alarms and corresponding bad-stress responses. Maybe that's why we call it a *dead*line!

2. *Taking tests.* We have an obsession with evaluating human performance, which makes test anxiety one of the leading causes of bad stress responses. From the day you are born (and even before that, *in utero*, when you are tested for possible congenital abnormalities and signs of anomalous percentile deviations) to the day you die (and even after that, postmortem, when you might undergo an autopsy to determine the cause of death, lest it be from other than natural causes), you experience continuous testing—testing to determine intelligence; testing to determine aptitude; testing to determine scholastic achievement; testing of your blood, urine, liver function, thyroid function, etc.; testing to get a driver's license; testing to meet the qualifications for a job; testing to obtain academic or experiential credentials for employment. Here, too, the list is endless. Even worse,

testing often combines performance anxiety with the above-described deadline distress, because most of the time examinations are administered with an associated time limit for completion. Thus, with testing, one gets a double whammy of exposure to bad stress.

3. *Competing.* Oh, how we humans love to compete. On the playing field, in sibling rivalries, in marital relationships, in the workplace, in personal interactions with others (especially relatives and neighbors), in capitalistic economies, even in learning how to spell. You name it; whatever we do, the element of competition always creeps in to make the activity stressful. Perhaps the famous Green Bay Packer football coach, Vince Lombardi, summarized best our attitude toward competition when he declared that, "Winning isn't everything, it's the *only* thing." We have this "numero uno" fetish—this need to somehow prove (and *continue* to prove) that we are number one and nobody does it better.

In and of itself, the desire to excel is a noble objective, but when one pursues this objective in the spirit of competition, success comes at the expense of somebody else's failure, and that's the part that bothers me. Inherent to the very essence of competition is the idea that I win because you lose, and so my victory comes at the expense of your defeat. But since there is also the (ever-so-slight) possibility that I might lose in any competitive encounter (after all, even I have had days every so often), being competitive now goes hand-in-hand with experiences that produce bad stress responses, and that's not good.

4. *Diet and exercise.* For years, I have maintained that we concern ourselves more with the fluids and fuels that we put into our cars than we do with the fluids and fuels that we put into our own bodies. There is this tendency to believe that our body, in its infinite wisdom, will extract what it needs from what we feed it, and fix up any disparities that might exist between what it gets and what it wants (and needs to maintain its health). But think about it: Your body has nothing more to work with than the raw materials with which you provide it. Provide it with junk, and it can only produce junk, and junk is metabolically toxic, hence stressful (build a house with inferior materials and your house won't last very long). Junk leads to immune responses, disease, premature aging, and metabolic imbalances; junk can cause wild mood swings, restlessness, sleepless nights, and a whole host of adverse physiological reactions. Yet, we think we know better, feed our bodies junk, and then wonder why we are always getting sick.

The same is true of exercise. The human body was designed to be used—it is a kinematic/kinetic machine, but its engineering design is not intended to be abused. I categorize exercise the same way that my professor categorized the two types of stress: On the one hand, there is the good exercise to which the body should be subjected quite naturally as it is used actively, to perform normal activities of daily living— healthy exercise that keeps us hale and hearty. On the other hand, there is bad exercise that abuses the body by subjecting it to artificial forms of exertion that accomplish nothing more than anatomical wear and tear. Without getting into any more detail at this time, suffice it to say for the purposes of our current discussion, that bad nutritional habits and bad exercise regimens both contribute to a type of bad stress that is artificially imposed on the human body to produce bad results.

5. *Special events.* Not all bad stress is necessarily associated with bad physical and emotional lifestyles. In fact, quite often, we experience the symptoms and complications of bad stress from undertaking activities that we normally think of as being inherently pleasant— though they, too, derive from egocentric needs peculiar to and created by our own form of civilization. Special events such as weddings, bar mitzvahs, buying a new car or a new house, starting a new job, moving to a new neighborhood, and so on all contribute to self-inflicted stresses that promote the flow of stress hormones. Engaged in these activities, our bodies pour into the bloodstream glucocorticoids, mineralocorticoids, thyroxine, epinephrine, norepinephrine, and a host of biochemical agents that mobilize the organism to endure stress.

In the short term, such mobilization, including higher blood pressure, increased heart rate, expanded breathing, activated musculoskeletal function, heightened alertness, accelerated metabolism, etc., is essential for survival, and so is quite desirable (good stress). However, maintained for longer than the short term and/or triggered all too often by a lifestyle that includes all of the above on a fairly regular basis, such mobilization (i.e., the persistent exposure of body organs and tissues to the effects of stress hormones) will eventually lead to gastritis, ulcerative colitis, irritable bowel syndrome, peptic ulcers, hypertension, asthma, migraine headaches, rheumatoid arthritis, anxiety, fibromyalgia, depression, chronic disease/infection, tension myositis, back problems, heart disease, cancer, and stroke—and all of the problems that we think kill us. As my professor pointed out, however, it all begins with bad stress. Absent the bad stress, our body is pretty well designed to go for about 120 years. Enter the bad stress, which can be thought of as a disturbance to a quasi-equilibrated state (see *American Laboratory* Jan 2002; 34[1]:6–8), and an otherwise healthy organism transitions to a new, unhealthy state that, rather than being equilibrated and stable, causes the organism to spiral continuously and relentlessly toward its ultimate demise.

There are numerous other forms of bad stress, among them: 1) those associated with estate planning and managing our personal financial affairs; 2) peer pressure, especially during our most vulnerable juvenile/adolescent years, but more generally, all through life; 3) those we experience while making career decisions (especially when those decisions are made on the basis of what we think others expect of us, rather than on considerations related more appropriately to where our heart leads us, and the lifetime consequences we are destined to endure by not heeding those considerations); 4) those stresses that result from spreading ourselves too thin, overcommitting ourselves to the point of having encumbered too many responsibilities; 5) trying to do the right thing in raising children (according to some rather arbitrary standards that really don't make much sense when critically examined); 6) being the perfect sexual partner (again, by whose standards?); and 7) those stresses associated with being lonely. Once again, the list is almost endless. One could argue *ad infinitum* the pros and cons of all of these self-inflicted bad stresses, but the bottom line is the same: They ain't healthy! Furthermore, they don't really have to be there! *We* put them there. *We* inflict them upon ourselves; and then *we* try to figure out how to live with them, and survive in the process. We don't seem capable of being happy unless we're miserable, fighting, and at war with one another. In fact, I'm getting stressed out just writing and thinking about it, and I'm also trying to finish this editorial by a certain time (deadline stress), so maybe in the interest of maintaining my health, I should stop right here! I think I will.

Food Allergies

American Laboratory News, April 2004

Do you occasionally experience any or all of the following: unusual fatigue/muscle weakness and/or sluggishness, bad breath, painful teeth and/or tender gums, bags under the eyes, blurred or spotty vision, ringing in the ears, arthritislike swollen/painful joints, sudden emotional irritability, problems sleeping, canker sores, heart palpitations, a burning sensation when urinating, or any other symptom(s) for which there seems to be no clinically apparent reason? If so, do yourself a favor by having a complete allergy evaluation. Do any of your children exhibit similar unexplained symptoms that are not allayed by conventional treatment? Have they ever been diagnosed as being hyperactive, learning disabled, or prone to attention deficit disorder and/or behavioral problems? Then encourage them, too, to be evaluated for possible allergies, especially those that may be diet related.

Allergies in general, and food allergies in particular, are among the least understood of all human afflictions. Derived from the Greek *állos*, for "different" (other), and *èrgon*, for "action" (work), the word "allergy" connotes a physiologic response (action) to some stimulant (food, pollen, hair, cloth, or other allergens) that is different from what one would normally expect. The response is different in the sense that the respective allergen, which is ordinarily well-tolerated without significant consequence by most people, triggers in the susceptible individual an immune system reaction that can range from mild and virtually unnoticeable to violent and life-threatening (as in the case of anaphylactic shock and total state of systemic collapse).

Case in point: For more than half my life, I suffered terribly from migraine headaches. I would get at least one whopper per month, complete with nausea, vomiting, vertigo, and photophobia—classic, textbook symptoms that would only resolve after I went to bed and slept them off. If you have ever had a migraine, you know what I am talking about. The feeling is probably akin to having somebody split your head open with an ax; any productive function is absolutely out of the question, and thoughts of euthanasia prevail—you long for somebody to put you out of your misery. When I was not suffering from a migraine, I would still get periodic headaches to a lesser degree, at least two or three disabling ones per week. Even when I was not suffering from a headache *per se*, I always felt "headachy," to the point where I actually forgot what it felt like *not* to have a headache. My mother had the same problem. I can still picture her lying down with an ice pack on her head, moaning in an agony that brought her to tears. My sister, too, was always "head-sick," so it was natural for all of us to assume that the problem was familial. Indeed, we often heard stories of how our grandparents on my mother's side also dealt with this affliction, so we took it for granted that it was a genetically transmitted problem that we inherited and one we would just have to learn to live with. The thought that there might be a connection between the migraines and our diet never occurred to any of us. Back in those days the medical community dismissed any but the most obvious associations between nutrition and human maladies (to a great extent, they still do), and who were we to question the conventional wisdom?

Even during my years in medical school, the subject of food allergies and their relationship to physiologic pathology rarely came up, and when it did, it was casually dismissed as being frivolous and without scientific basis. Perhaps this was because, back then, the belief was that bona fide food allergies affected no more than about 7% of children and 2% of adults (not a terribly significant problem), and that, except in the special case of specific vitamin deficiencies, diet was not causally related to disease. However, knowing what I know now (and what we have learned since, especially from studies in genetics and diet-induced carcinogenesis), I rather suspect that the real reason the subject of food allergies was avoided had to do with how little we know about the body's immune system, how difficult it is to diagnose food allergies, and, even when we can make a proper diagnosis, how difficult it is to treat and manage patients who suffer from these afflictions (short of starving them to death!). Part of the problem in making a proper diagnosis has to do with the fact that we tend to look for allergies only when patients present with classic symptoms, such as bloodshot, itchy eyes; respiratory issues (runny nose, sneezing, wheezing, difficulty breathing, asthma); skin problems (hives, eczema); and so on, most of which are associated with clinically measurable changes in the immune system. Allergic reactions that are more subtle, such as mood swings, general malaise, problems with vision and hearing, toothaches, swollen joints, bouts with depression, and others mentioned earlier, tend to escape notice. This is complicated even further by the fact that allergic reactions to food are not always immediate. Because of the time it takes to digest, metabolize, and react to the suspect allergen(s), and because such reactions can depend on so many contributing factors (necessary and sufficient conditions coming together at just the right time, in just the right combinations, in a cumulative sense), symptoms might not appear until long after the allergen has been ingested—days or even weeks later. Thus, we often fail to realize that what is happening to us now is causally related to something that happened to us quite a while back. (This, incidentally, is not a diagnostic flaw restricted solely to food allergies. It's the old *post hoc, ergo propter hoc* cause–effect syndrome rearing its ugly head again: "[immediately] after this, therefore as a [direct] result of this." We have a problem dealing with the time sequencing of pathological issues.)

Be that as it may, when I joined the faculty at Virginia Tech, the migraines became a real nuisance because they were seriously affecting my performance in the classroom. I decided to take matters into my own hands and, mostly out of curiosity, started to keep a food diary. Soon, I made a startling discovery: The headachy feeling seemed to prevail mostly when I consumed meals rich in dairy products, and the migraines invariably followed my ingestion (within days of one another) of several such meals in a row, including milk, ice cream, cheese, chocolate malteds (I loved these and practically lived on them while working on my Ph.D.), and so on. Encouraged by these observations, I went to a physician and requested that he refer me to somebody who would do a complete allergy series (including blood tests for antibodies) to search for unusual sensitivities to foods, airborne pollen, animal dander, house dust, anything that could be analyzed. He sent me to a specialist who performed this allergy series over a three-day period. The results were quite revealing! Suffice it to say that the list of things I am *not* allergic to is dwarfed by that for which the allergy tests proved to be positive!

What was most interesting to me were the foods found to be particularly offensive: shellfish (which always caused me to wheeze and suffer asthma-like symptoms), dairy products (particularly milk and cheese, the migraine culprits), and certain grains (especially wheat, rice, and corn, all of which caused me to have temperamental mood swings). In this regard, the results were also consistent with what we now know: About 95% of food allergies are due to just seven types of foods, i.e., milk, eggs, wheat, soybeans, seafood, nuts, and legumes, such as peanuts. I met with a dietitian, who put me on a heavily restrictive elimination diet. For what seemed like an eternity, I existed virtually on mashed potatoes, carrots, asparagus, salads, and dietary supplements (the latter to make sure I got enough calcium and protein because the diet did not include many foods rich in calcium, very little meat, and no red meat, even though I did not test positive for any meat allergies except for those processed lunch meats that contained nitrites). To this day, although I am somewhat more relaxed about it, I still watch what I eat very carefully and the headaches are history! That is to say, as soon as I went on the restricted diet (and I mean, immediately), my migraines disappeared. I went from having at least one migraine a month to just one every several years, and even then, only if I was "bad" and indulged in foods (like salami) that were on my no-no list. I also lost 25 pounds in the process, stopped financing companies that manufactured aspirin and stomach antacids, and eliminated that constant bloated, headachy feeling that I had gotten so used to. It was as if I was reborn. Life was worth living again, without head pain.

Now I do not mean to imply that food allergies are the single cause of any of the afflictions mentioned above, nor that cutting certain foods out of a person's diet will magically cure everything that ails him or her. I know better than that, and certainly, by scientific standards, my history would be considered an uncontrolled, "anecdotal" study. But I can state with a reasonable degree of assurance that we pay more attention to the type and quality of gasoline that we put into our automobile engines than we do to the type and quality of fuel (food) that we put into our human engines. The digestive system has become the Rodney Dangerfield of the human body: It "don't get no respect!" We think we can put anything into it and the body, in its infinite wisdom, will "fix up." We are wrong! Indeed, only very recently has the medical community, gradually and reluctantly, begun to admit this and pay much more attention to pathological issues that may derive from alimentary dysfunction.

Helped along by the decoding of the human genome, we are learning more about the intricate enzyme systems that are involved in the processes of digestion and absorption; we are gradually unveiling the mysteries of complicated biochemical pathways; we are piecing together all of the pieces of the puzzle. As we do, the medical establishment is gaining a much greater appreciation for the role of the alimentary system in maintaining human health. For instance, we now know that if one suffers from a genetically determined absence of a crucial enzyme responsible for the breakdown of a specific food substrate (like various wheat products, corn, rice, or dairy products), either that substrate is not digested or absorbed at all (leading, in some cases, to a dietary deficiency, for example, of calcium, with its associated complications, such as impaired muscle and nerve function) or the substrate is only partially digested and therefore absorbed in an unidentifiable "foreign" form, which can trigger a corresponding allergic response.

With regard to the latter, one must distinguish further between bona fide food allergies *per se* (i.e., foods always perceived by the body's immune system to be foreign invaders) and food sensitivities (i.e., foods tolerated well up to critical threshold quantities, or only if not ingested in combination with certain other foods, or only if ingested at certain times of the day or year when seasonal complications such as hay fever are not already challenging the body's immune system to capacity). Moreover, many reactions to food are caused not by allergies, which are directly tied to the antibodies produced by the immune system, but by intolerances, which can produce inflammation and other symptoms (gas, diarrhea, chest pain, etc.) that are often independent of immune system intervention. Common among the latter are intolerances to the milk sugar lactose (due to a deficiency of the lactase enzyme required to digest it); the flavor enhancer monosodium glutamate (MSG); phonolic flavonoid compounds (common especially in red wines); chocolate (what a shame!); and various food additives used for coloring, flavoring, and/or preserving. To make matters even more complicated, add to all of the above the fact that one can outgrow certain food allergies and/or sensitivities and/or intolerances, while being encumbered with new ones with age! Thus, the issue of alimentary-induced causation of specific clinical afflictions, from a medical/ diagnostic point of view, is no easy nut to crack, and I am by no means minimizing its complex elusiveness. The light at the end of the tunnel suggests, however, that we are gaining ground on these issues, at least to the point where we are willing to admit their feasibility and the need for further investigation. It is thus encouraging to know that the future bodes well for those of us who suffer the terrible inconveniences of not being able to eat without consequence those foods we love best, like chocolate malted milk!

Physiological Accommodation

American Laboratory News, September 2004

Whenever I present talks or seminars on subjects related to life skills, leadership skills, etc., many of the same questions invariably come up at the end of the discussion: "How do I manage to accomplish all of the things you have spoken about today?" "Can you give us some 'how-to' tips that will allow us to do what you say?" "How do we go about practicing what you preach?" My response is always the same: "You just answered your own question, i.e., by practicing!" Although I've previously made this point several times in this column, let me elaborate on the physiological basis for that assertion, i.e., the reason that persistent repetition ("rehearsal") works to make the ideal (theory) real (actuality).

Practicing works by exploiting the human body's ability to accommodate or alter either its operating setpoints, the transfer functions of its various subsystems, or both, in response to a persistent stimulus (disturbance to a quasi-equilibrated state). Operating setpoints define the homeostatic reference quantities toward which the body tends to quasi-equilibrate, driven there by its numerous feedback/feedforward control mechanisms. Transfer functions are the input/output properties of the respective subsystems with which we are anatomically endowed (see "A Biomedical Engineer Views the Human Body," *American Laboratory* Feb 2003; 35[3]:6–8). "Practicing" propels the body to new levels of performance;

these levels become the physiological norm if the stimulus that triggered the accommodation process is persistent enough to be dealt with.

As an example of how this works, let's try an experiment. For one entire day, force yourself (disturb your quasi-equilibrated state) to neither say nor do anything negative. Make no derogatory comments about anyone; do not react to unfavorable remarks made to or about you. Avoid confrontations and do not engage in arguments. Make a deliberate effort to find an admirable attribute of any situation in which you might find yourself, and magnify, out of proportion, the positive aspects of that situation. Ignore the down side and concentrate only on the good side. Look for a reason to compliment someone; make one up if you have to.

I can already hear you saying that that's ridiculous and impractical, and is contrary to our instinctive tendencies. I agree. Such behavior is not instinctive because, on a day-to-day basis, we are bathed in negatives, such that our systemic operating setpoints and corresponding transfer functions are specifically coded to protect and defend against attack. We are programmed, both genetically and experientially, to always be on guard, and to be prepared to go on the offensive (or flee) as necessary. We are taught to treat everyone, and every situation, as a potential threat to our safety; we must be suspicious, dubious, cautious.

More than likely, the first word any of us learned was "No." We are greeted every day by newscasters who open with, "Good morning," and then proceed to tell us why it isn't. Dan Rather is quoted as saying, "Hear no evil, speak no evil, see no evil, and you'll never be a television anchorman." We live according to the Laws of Murphy: Nothing is as easy as it looks; everything takes longer than you think it will; and if anything can go wrong, it will; and according to the Principle of Peter: "Mediocrity is encouraged by our consistently promoting people to their highest level of incompetence." Indeed, even many religions preach that all of us are, by nature, sinners, and thus in need of divine salvation.

So, are we conditioned to think in negatives? You bet we are! The wiring, hardware, and anatomical neural networks to think otherwise are basically not there (or are suppressed); certainly, to think positively is not encouraged, which is a classic illustration of the generally accepted "use it or lose it" principle in physiology. That's why I agree with you: It is hard for us, at first, to go through a 24-hour period without succumbing to the tendency to "accentuate the negative and eliminate the positive" (contrary to the words of a popular song). That's exactly why, in our first attempt, we have to force ourselves not to succumb.

Although I agree that your apprehension is perfectly justified, I do so only to a certain degree, because we also know that the "use it or lose it" principle works in reverse as well, and that's where practice enters the picture to exploit the body's ability to accommodate. Each time a particular sensory or motor signal (a disturbing signal, in the language of control theory) passes through a sequence of neural pathways, these pathways become more capable of transmitting the same signal the next time it comes through. This is a physiological process called facilitation, or memory of sensation. At first, the signal might need to be forced through a "potential space" (not yet existing, but possible), thus blazing new information-processing channels. Alternatively, the stimulus might have access to existing but dormant tracks overgrown with weeds from lack of use. The latter will frequently exist as one or more collateral branches of a nerve axon, in which case one might think of facilitation as a clearing of the tracks, opening them up for subsequent use. In the former case (forging new information-processing channels), one could think of facilitation as a type of programmed learning, akin to writing the software that commands a computer to do a specific task it has not done before.

Unlike a computer, however, our body has the ability to convert software into hardware, to build new tracks and neural networks, through an anatomical remodeling capability known as plasticity, provided that the disturbing signal is persistent enough to be reckoned with. That is to say, similar to the organism's immune system, the nervous system, too, "remembers" how, and how often, it responded in a certain way to a certain stimulus. Thus, subsequent responses to that same stimulus, if repeated enough times (practice), become routine. Through the property of plasticity/anatomical remodeling, then, the process of facilitation eventually evolves into a conditioned reflex pathway (as opposed to an inherited instinctive one). The result of this conditioning is that the systemic response to a persistent disturbance (originally in the form of a "software" program or some other type of forcing function) now takes the form of a newly generated anatomical neural network ("hardware") that defines a new systemic operating setpoint, toward which the body is driven through its various control mechanisms.

If the new reference setpoint defines some behavioral pattern (such as not finding fault, in our little experiment), the individual involved finds that he or she can manifest that behavior more easily, and it eventually becomes a habit. Once that has happened, once the new (or rejuvenated) neural networks are in place and the new homeostatic reference quantities are established, we say that the system has adapted to the persistent stimulus. In most cases, this physiological process, called functional adaptation, reaches the point where the original stimulus that started the adaptive process is no longer necessary in order to elicit the response. This is because such stimulation has been replaced by a new operating setpoint that serves the same purpose. The body's desire to function at that new reference level results in its being "forced" to do so by its own inherent control systems. It no longer needs anything else to remind it of what to do; everything is now on automatic.

Getting back to our experiment, I do agree that you might (and probably will) originally experience great difficulty seeing the best in situations and/or people. At first, you will have to work at overriding existing temptations to be negative. However, to the degree that you practice trying it, and not give up, you will prevail, and the physiological process of functional adaptation will eventually prove your original doubts wrong! Indeed, you will find that you no longer have to work at seeing the best in situations or people; it will become your nature to be that way. You will have evolved into a new person (perhaps nicer than the old crabby one) and you will have done it by exploiting your body's inherent ability to adapt to a persistent stimulus. You will have practiced to make perfect.

Going one step further, if you teach your children to develop these same habits and they teach their children, generations later, your little experiment will actually be inscribed into your family's genome. What started out in your generation as a disturbance-driven, forced response that triggered the physiological process of functional adaptation will have evolved into a genetic code that not only permanently resets the homeostatic operating reference quantities of your offspring, but also modulates the very organic transfer functions (input/output characteristics) of the physiological systems that are responsible for the behavioral patterns you instigated. As an inscribed code, then, less control is needed to achieve these patterns, so the feedback/feedforward control mechanisms don't even have to work as hard in order to elicit the desired responses, which are now genetically guaranteed. This might be a better way to look at Charles Darwin's theory of natural selection, i.e., that those species who "survived" were those best able to *adapt* to their changing environment ("disturbances"), and were thus the "fittest" (effectively responsive) in that sense. (Aside: To be strictly accurate, it should be noted that this latter consideration is currently an unresolved issue in the field of genetics, so that it remains somewhat speculative, although feasible. As of this writing, however, a specific mechanism to explain how the *somatic* line of DNA can permeate the *genetic* line of nucleic acids has not been discovered, nor has enough experimental evidence accumulated to support the idea that such a mechanism even exists. Thus, the prevailing conventional wisdom is that the *genetic* line of *inherited* attributes, and the *somatic* line of *acquired* attributes, derive from separate processes, but not all such processes have yet been investigated enough to make this a definitive conclusion.)

The important thing is not to get discouraged about early failures at attempts to learn something new or to change particular behavioral patterns. You need to get out of the programmed "I tried—it didn't work—I give up" mind-set, replacing it instead with trust and faith in the physiology of functional adaptation. You must give the process time to work; don't make a token attempt, only to quit if success isn't immediate. Physiological accommodation is fundamental to the process of learning anything, in that the latter is most effectively accomplished only by persistent repetition, by practice.

In a way, I feel almost silly writing this, because anyone who has ever studied an instrument, participated in sports, or learned to ride a two-wheel bicycle knows and appreciates the value and importance of practice as a means to an end. It seems almost too obvious to write about. Moreover, the physiological examples of functional adaptation are many, for example, the remodeling of bone under stress (Wolff's law, a piezoelectric phenomenon that reverses in a subgravity environment), the ability of the cardiovascular system to (reversibly) acclimate itself to high or low altitudes (involving renal control of erythropoiesis), the evolution of gravity-driven balance and equilibrium reflexes, and so on. Yet, if all of this is so obvious, why am I always being asked the questions posed at the beginning of this editorial? Why, during all my years in the classroom, did I constantly have to impress upon my students the importance of doing their homework, constantly reminding them that homework was practice, and that by practicing, they were responsibly accepting their role in the learning process? "If truth be told, I can't *teach* you anything," I would say. "The human body does not learn that way. The only thing I can do is arm you with information, with the tools and techniques you will need in order to master your craft, and then point you in the (hopefully) right direction. The rest is up to you. The responsibility for learning rests squarely on your shoulders. Learning is an active process, not a passive one. The human body only learns by doing."

The fact that I keep being asked these questions, that I keep needing to remind students to do their homework, that functional adaptation is not a commonly understood concept, all suggest that maybe the role of practice in the learning process is not all that obvious. Maybe we *do* have to read editorials like this one in order to appreciate the fact that, in order to convert theory into practice, we just need to practice the theory and let our bodies do the rest.

Part III: Searching for Relations and Self-Fulfillment—Relating the "In Here" With the "Out There"

Simple Wisdom I: Seven Building Blocks to a Healthy Relationship

American Laboratory, November 2004

I am writing this one week after the funeral of the 40th president of the United States: Ronald Wilson Reagan. President Reagan held office from January 20, 1981, to January 19, 1989. He died June 5, 2004, in Bel Air, CA, at age 93, from the complications of Alzheimer's disease. Last week, I watched, as did much of the world, the news media coverage of this event. What particularly moved me was not so much the legacy attributed to him as a popular politician and world leader, but, rather, descriptions and stories of what has been dubbed one of the great romances of all time.

Ronald Reagan married actress Nancy Davis in 1952. Theirs was one of the exceptions to the rule: Hollywood marriages do not generally last very long. Indeed, the President's first marriage to actress Jane Wyman lasted only from January 26, 1940 to June 28, 1948, ending in divorce after just 8½ years. But the later Reagans's story went beyond being just a persevering nuptual. It was a *true* love affair, in the most faithful sense of a romance novel. What they shared was a mutual affection for one another that set the example for what human interactions should be all about.

Thus, as I watched and listened, I began to ponder: What makes for long and healthy relationships? What are the attributes that define the strong bonds that form between any two individuals, be it husband and wife, employer and employee, parent and child, or "just plain friends," at any age level? I started to compile a list of what I thought these attributes should be, and the list quickly got very long! As I stared at it, however, certain common denominators began to appear, and I ultimately narrowed them down to what I perceive to be the seven most fundamental pillars upon which can be built stable, secure, fulfilling, and enduring relationships.

1. First and foremost, the two of you have to *want it*! There has to be a conscious decision, a mutual agreement, to prioritize the relationship as something desirable and worth working at from both sides. Notice, I said "working at" and "from both sides." One side cannot want it for the other more than the other wants it for him- or herself and vice versa. Unless both of you want the relationship to prevail, it will not. Without exception, one-sided relationships are destined to fail. By

their very nature, they are not balanced, even-sided *relationships*, but rather, oblique, one-sided *arrangements* that tip the scale disproportionately toward only one of the two people involved. In an enduring relationship, there must be a selfless balance of power, but not at the expense of satisfying one's own personal needs, and that has to be appreciated and respected on both sides.

Furthermore, to keep the scale balanced, neither of the two participants in a relationship should get complacent about it, taking it for granted, expecting that it can simply "fly on autopilot," without need for attention. Just like adding logs to a roaring fire, which will fizzle out otherwise, the two participants in a relationship they have chosen to prioritize must keep the flame burning by constantly infusing new energy into it—falling in love all over again, reinforcing their affection for one another, always reminding one another of how important each is to the other, consciously working at it, and never allowing it to get stale. For the relationship to be successful, however, the fuel must be infused in equal proportions from both sides; each partner in a relationship must want it enough to pull his or her own weight, lest the scale tip unfairly to one side.

2. The relationship must be built on trust. In turn, trust derives from honesty and sincerity, both of which identify an individual as being one of integrity. Interestingly, the word "integrity" comes from the Latin prefix *in-*, meaning "not," and the word root *teg-*, meaning "to touch." Thus, to have integrity is to be "untouchable"—whole, complete (from which also derives the word "integrate," i.e., "to make whole"). By extrapolation, then, a relationship is "made whole"—without holes (so to speak), or more holy (if you enjoy a play on words)—when the ties that bind it together derive their strength from the unfailing confidence each partner has in the other, knowing for sure that they can believe firmly in the credibility of whatever interchanges take place between them. No guessing games, no reason to question the truthfulness of any statements made, no doubts, no apprehensions, no suspicions, nothing implied or inferred, just total trust! Blind faith—one in the other.

3. Ronald Reagan was affectionately referred to as "The Great Communicator," which is the third pillar of a healthy relationship: communication. Say what you mean and mean what you say sincerely and openly. Sounds simple enough, but in practice, it may be easier said than done. For one thing, language—humanity's primary form of communication—in and of itself often falls far short of being an effective means for exchanging information (frankly, music, the universal language, works much better). For another thing, our own

human frailties and emotional insecurities may preclude our being able to accurately put into words the exact thoughts we are trying to express in a one-to-one correspondence with that thought. Invariably, something gets lost in the translation. Thus, in a healthy relationship, each of the two participants quickly learns to listen to what the other one *means* ("reading between the lines," as it were), distinguishing it from what he or she actually *says*, literally. That is *real* communication, and it is a very necessary attribute of a healthy relationship.

In fact, taking this feature to its extreme, how often have you heard one member of a partnership say to the other, "You took the words right out of my mouth!" or "I was just going to say that!" These expressions and others, like, "You must have known exactly what I was thinking!" or "We've been married too long!" are typical of relationships wherein the two individuals involved know each other so well that they can "read each other's mind," without ever saying a word. It is believed that identical twins share this attribute (and being parents of such a set, Judi and I can attest firsthand to the validity of that assertion). Indeed, in a healthy relationship, where perception and insight prevail, words might not even be necessary for effective communication—a facial expression, eye-to-eye contact (perhaps accompanied by a wink), a specific type of body language, a soft pat on the arm, a knowing nod, even a brief moment of silence—may suffice to accomplish the same purpose. But the key is to accomplish that purpose, i.e., to communicate, by whatever means works.

4. If one imagines trust to be among the ties that bind individuals together in a healthy relationship (like fibrin filaments forming a netlike mesh to close a gap), then *unconditional* tolerance may be thought of as the glue that seals those binds together, holding them tightly in place. Elizabeth Prophet and Patricia Spadaro, in their book, *Your Seven Energy Centers* (Summit University Press, Corwin Springs, MN, 2000), point out that, "There are two universal truths that we sometimes forget. *Number one*: Not everyone thinks, feels and acts like we do. *Number two*: It's *okay* that everyone doesn't think, feel and act like we do. We don't have to be on a crusade to change anyone." And that's the key: In a healthy relationship, neither one of the two individuals involved tries to change the other; tolerance and acceptance are guaranteed, and unconditional. There is no laundry list of expected behavior; no "I love you because," followed by a long list of attributes; no "You promised me you'd change"; no conditions; no qualifying stipulations. Each member of a healthy relationship accepts the other as is, period! For better or for worse, in good times and in bad, in sickness and in health, for richer or for poorer, for as long as they both shall live. Sound familiar?

5. Continuing with our developing imagery, if trust is one of the ties that binds, and tolerance is the glue that holds those ties together, then what we are building is a net that *supports* the relationship. This connotes the idea that in a healthy relationship, you are always there for one another, supporting each other's efforts; providing a safety net; always being available to stop a fall (literally and figuratively); encouraging one another; lifting each other's spirits; being a friend in need; always making time for each other, regardless of what might otherwise be going on in each of your individual lives.

This "safety net" attribute of a healthy relationship is directly connected to the first one, because when there is a prioritized commitment to make the relationship succeed, there follows the realization that you need one another. Thus, there is a recognized interdependence that leads to teamwork. Each of you knows that the individual success of either one of you automatically guarantees the success of the other, and more importantly, the prosperity of the team. With a "net" under you—absent any envy, one-upmanship, jealousy, and/or a begrudging attitude—you each know that you can depend on one another, no matter what, under any circumstances, with no strings attached. Egotism, self-pride, stubbornness, and selfishness take a back seat to humility, modesty, generosity, altruism, and a spirit of cooperation. Each of you genuinely cares enough about the other to want the very best for him or her. But, going one step further, each of you has also mastered the art of loving with open arms; respecting each other's space; supporting, without suppressing.

6. Know when you have enough! I have often preached that if one owns more than he or she can put into a knapsack and carry off at a moment's notice, then one owns too much. Having said that, I must quickly admit that I don't always practice what I preach. Alas, I, too, am guilty as charged of succumbing to being a pack rat—accumulating and hoarding things. But, in my defense, I must say that I am not alone. We are a "thing" society. We tend to judge success or failure on how many things a person owns or can buy—jewelry, cars, boats, houses, clothing, furniture—you name it. We treasure our worldly possessions; praise them, *ap*praise them; insure them; put them in safety deposit boxes; in some cases, even worship them—to the extent of caring more about them than we do our worldly relationships with other human beings.

Indeed, things can drive a wedge between two people who are involved in a relationship that is built on a foundation of possessions. This is especially true when possessions include the people themselves, and when control of those possessions becomes an end in itself. To be really rich is to "measure wealth not by the things you have, but by the things you have for which you would not take money," said a wise (anonymous) person. I would paraphrase this by adding, "Measure the *health* of a relationship not by the *tangible* wealth that can be attributed to it, but by its *intangible* assets—those that are priceless, and upon which it is impossible to place a meaningful 'thing' value."

7. Learn to say "I'm sorry." No thing or person is totally perfect. Thus, the "net" we have been building to support a healthy relationship might, on occasion, require some repair and maintenance. Enter *super glue*—the all-purpose apology. An apology can fix just about anything that goes wrong in a relationship between two people. It belongs in every relationship repair or first-aid kit. In fact, it should be the first medicine to be tried in an effort to heal an ailing relationship.

When stressed, even the healthiest of relationships gets sick every so often. In the heat of the moment, things are said that are not meant the way they come out; means of communication break down; feelings get hurt; emotions prevail; everyone gets hypersensitive; reason gets compromised; the body shifts into amygdala-driven, "fight-or-flight, 911-survival mode"; the pillars weaken. They bend, but in a strong relationship, they don't break. Rather, when this happens, the universal elixir—the apology—comes to the rescue. Try it, my friends: It works on anyone and can be used for any ailing relationship; it can weather any stormy situation; it requires no advance preparation; nothing can resist it; it can reopen clogged lines of communication; and best of all, it comes with a relationship-back guarantee. Don't take my word for it—the case histories of many successful relationships speak for themselves; those that are healthy invariably consist of two people who say "I'm sorry" on a regular basis. They have found the cure.

The flip side, of course, is to learn to forgive—one of my fundamental "F-words" (see *American Biotechnology Laboratory* Aug 2003; 21[9]:4–8). If your partner apologizes, accept the apology and move on; life starts now and moves forward; what's done is done; what's past is past. So, bottom line: If you truly want a healthy relationship with another human being, and the two of you are equally committed to making it succeed, that relationship must be built on sincere trust, effective communication, unconditional tolerance, mutual support of one another, simple needs, and the ability to both apologize and forgive as necessary. Not a bad start, yes?

Attitude!

American Laboratory News, June 2003

I used to love to hear my late father-in-law tell the inspiring story of how he landed a job in 1930, during the years of the Great Depression. Job opportunities during the years following the Great Stock Market Crash of 1929 were few and far between. For the few opportunities that existed in my father-in-law's field of heating/ventilating/refrigeration and air conditioning, the competition was brutally stiff.

John Kooistra was born in Amsterdam, The Netherlands, in 1902. After being awarded his Bachelor's Degree in Mechanical Engineering (with a major in thermodynamics), he left his entire family back home in Holland, and in 1924, at the tender age of 22, journeyed all alone by ship to the United States to start a whole new life for himself. As his ship sailed past the Statue of Liberty in New York Harbor, John flung his Dutch cap into Upper New York Bay as an expression of his determination to become an American—not that he was ashamed of his Dutch heritage, or that things back home were so bad that he felt the need to get away from it all. To the contrary, John never *left* anything, in a negative sense; he always went to something new, in a positive sense. He always looked for self-improving opportunities; by doing so, John put himself in a position to help others (especially his own family) achieve their goals. He carried that attitude with him throughout his entire 78-year life, inspiring all of us who knew and interacted with him.

John started out in the U.S. with virtually nothing, but managed to get his first job here with the Link Belt Company. That job took him to South Milwaukee, WI, where he also met a young elementary school music teacher, and very talented pianist, Genevieve Jones, who eventually became his wife (and the mother of my dear spouse, Judi). That's the good news. The bad news is that John's arrival to the U.S. was poorly timed, for we all know what happened in 1929. Having very little seniority with the company, and being a "foreigner" and not yet fluent in the English language, John was among the first to get laid off when the economy went belly-up and the country sank into the Great Depression. Things in the Kooistra household were pretty bad for about a year.

But in 1930, John heard that a relatively young company, started in 1915 by "The Father of Cool," Willis Haviland Carrier, together with six other engineers, was looking to expand the workforce at its Los Angeles, CA, facility. Although Carrier did not actually invent air conditioning, his "Apparatus for Treating Air" (U.S. patent #808897, granted in 1906) was the first of several patents awarded to him that would eventually lead to the first practical, truly successful, and safe system of cooling for human comfort (installed in 1924 in the J.L. Hudson Department Store in Detroit, MI). This started a boom that soon spread to other department stores, commercial establishments, and movie theaters (e.g., the Rivoli in New York), and to the eventual development of in-home consumer products. Demand for air conditioning was skyrocketing; the company was growing very quickly; and it needed to add at least one more engineer to its staff in the specific area of industrial/marine air conditioning and ocean-going ship refrigeration. So, John headed off to California to interview for the job.

When he arrived at the location where the interviews were being held, he encountered a packed room—wall-to-wall hopefuls from all over the country, waiting for their opportunities to shine. John panicked at the sight. "I don't have a chance," he thought to himself. Feeling an anxiety attack coming on, he turned around and left the room, intending to head back to Milwaukee, totally demoralized and disheartened by the experience. But something stopped him. "Wait a minute," he thought. "I am no less qualified for this job than anyone else in that room! I have all the appropriate academic credentials; I have a reasonable amount of experience; I am just as (if not more than) capable; I am young and enthusiastic; I have a positive work ethic; I have the confidence to succeed; and I came all the way out here from Wisconsin—well, when you come right down to it, all the way from Holland—so why am I running away? Why am I approaching this interview with such a defeatist attitude? Come on, John, at least give yourself a chance!"

He walked several times around the block to regain his composure and consider his options, finally deciding to "go for it!" Armed with a new, fearless attitude, he marched himself back into the interview waiting room and patiently awaited his turn, which came several hours later. The interview itself was rather routine until the subject of financial compensation came up. "What are your salary expectations?" asked the interviewer. John thought for a moment, and then a voice that sounded remarkably like his answered: "How about if you hire me on a trial basis, and let me come to work for your company for a month? If I disappoint you, you can dismiss me; we'll part friends, no hard feelings, and you'll owe me nothing. On the other hand, if you like my work, if I prove to be of value to the company, and if I therefore convince you to keep me on your staff of engineers, a month from now you can let me know what you think I'm worth, and I'll accept your offer, no questions asked. There's no way you can lose."

The interviewer was noticeably moved by this not-so-routine response to his routine question. Without saying a word to John, he arose from his chair, went out into the reception area (where many applicants still sat waiting for their turns), walked over to his secretary, and whispered, "You can tell everybody else to go home. We've found our man!"

Thus started a 37-year career that saw John's family move coast to coast three times, eventually landing in New York City, where, thankfully, Judi and I crossed paths. During those 37 years, his job responsibilities gradually evolved from straight engineering to the highest levels of sales management. John retired from Carrier in 1967 to accolades, acclaim, and great admiration from all of his staff and professional colleagues. They loved him generally as a person, but mostly they loved his attitude! Right up until his untimely death in 1980, we all loved him as the supreme role model extraordinaire. Everybody wanted to "be like John."

The moral of this story, and the reason I like it so much, is that it serves as a constant reminder of how important attitude can be as the key to unlocking opportunities in life, and how often attitude can make the difference between success and failure. It is of interest to note that the word itself derives from the Latin *aptus*, which means "joined" or "fitted," implying a way of thinking, feeling, and acting that "fits in" with the overall spirit of a corresponding situation or cause. To paraphrase John F. Kennedy (with whom this quotation is most often identified, although he did not author it), John Kooistra's attitude was always, "Ask not what your company can do for you; ask what you can do for your company!" He recognized that when the company benefited from his efforts, so did he. He always got right down to the nitty-gritty, the fundamental issues related to the spirit of any venture, attacking problems head-on and never (even as he faced death) allowing himself to get bogged down with apathy, self-pity, or negativism. John knew that if he approached his co-workers with a kind, positive, encouraging, "We're in this together and I'm on your side" attitude, he could always bring out the very best in them, as well as in himself. He preferred giving to taking, and he lived his life according to the motto of Rotary International, the service organization to which he dedicated nearly 50 years of his life: "Service, Above Self!" To John, it was always about what he could do for you, rather than what you could do for him. It was always about stepping in to try to contribute to the solution, rather than becoming a part of the problem. In the way he handled himself, both professionally and personally, John epitomized William J. Bennett's contention that, "There are no menial jobs . . . only menial attitudes." To John, no job was menial, and no person or activity was beneath him. Is it any wonder, then, that his daughter (my dear wife, Judi) followed in his footsteps?

Lou Holtz will probably be best remembered as the head coach who totally revitalized a struggling Notre Dame football program. In his 27 years there, he amassed a record of 216 wins, 95 losses, and seven ties, taking the Fighting Irish to nine major bowl games and one national championship. He did this despite consistently working with different groups of players, in different situations, with different personnel. The results were always the same: success! When commenting on his formula for success, Holtz attributed it to the following philosophy: "Your talent determines *what* you can do. Your motivation determines how much you are *willing* to do. Your attitude determines how well you do it." Holtz was a great motivator. He got his players to want to work really hard to at least give themselves a chance to succeed. But the success itself was the product of a healthy, positive mental attitude. All the talent and motivation in the world will be of no use if you have a negative attitude, make failure a self-fulfilled prophecy, lose sight of what it is you are trying to achieve, or perhaps even worse, set your sights on the wrong target for the wrong reasons.

"The greatest discovery of my generation," said William James, "is that a human being can alter his life by altering his attitude." Is that an easy thing to do? Of course not! But it never ceases to amaze me that, while we recognize the importance of practice as a means to the end of becoming, for example, a proficient athlete, an accomplished musician, or whatever, we don't extrapolate that same reasoning to the significance of practice in helping us to change certain negative aspects of our behavior. We don't practice adjusting our attitude often enough to make such adjustment a conditioned reflex, a natural approach to experiencing life, responding to its challenges, and facing its inevitable trials and tribulations. Most of the time, we just give up in despair after having given attitude adjustment a token, one-shot chance. "I *tried*," we insist; "it just didn't work," and we are content to leave it at that. But that is as ridiculous as trying to become proficient at riding a two-wheeled bicycle after getting on it just once and falling off.

Speaking as a physiologist, I can tell you that the only way our bodies learn is through repetition. "The only way to get to Carnegie Hall," said my violin teacher, "is to practice, practice, practice!" The athletic coach said, "the only way to make it into the big leagues is to practice—practice until the exception becomes the rule, the extraordinary becomes ordinary, the unusual becomes usual, the unexpected becomes expected, and the isolated physiologic function turns into a habit."

Continuing the logic of this reasoning, then, the only way to succeed in adjusting one's attitude is to keep practicing until it becomes a habit, i.e., to include *practicing* in one's attitude toward attitude adjustment. Just like riding a two-wheeler, once you get it, you never forget it. Indeed, it would behoove all of us to practice being "more like John"!

Let's *Really* Get Back to Basics
American Laboratory News, October 2003

Attention all parents: If you were to conduct a survey of the attributes that employers value most in their employees, and those they mainly look for in individuals being interviewed for employment, what do you think such a survey would reveal? Over the years, I've compiled just such an attributes list, derived from several such surveys, and the results might surprise you: Industrial recruiters and personnel managers place at the very top of this list one's ability to think creatively, i.e., to formulate innovative, practical solutions to problems he or she has never seen before, and sadly, 88% of the 400 employers who responded to one such survey expressed disappointment in the fact that today's college graduates do not fare well in this aspect of their potential for success in the workforce. Some said it took as long as two years or more of in-house training to make new hires "functional." They gave colleges and universities low grades in preparing their graduates to make meaningful contributions to the industry and to solve real-world "messy" problems, emphasizing that curriculums need to be: 1) more deductively oriented than inductive, 2) more process oriented than product oriented, and 3) more generically practice oriented than skills oriented.

Second on the list of desirable attributes is one's ability to communicate, both orally and in writing. Here again, 89% of respondents in another survey gave colleges and universities low grades, saying that, at least in science, technology, and engineering curriculums, there is not enough emphasis placed on communication skills. Students don't express themselves well; when they do come up with original ideas, they are ineffective in conveying them; their writing styles are disorganized and sloppy; their ability to speak in public, give oral presentations, and/or deliver elegant, articulate, and convincing addresses is sorely lacking; they need to learn how to speak and write in different contexts (not just how to construct proper sentences); and they need to realize and appreciate the fact that the ultimate success of any person-to-person interactions (including those, like marriage and parenting, that are not necessarily confined to the work environment) rests greatly on one's ability to engage in dialogue to effect an appropriate exchange of ideas, thoughts, and concepts.

Speaking of person-to-person interactions, third on my list of attributes is one's ability to work in groups. In today's complex society, and especially in the workforce, it is rare that one functions as an island. More likely, an employee will be part of a team charged with accomplishing a specific objective, and again, 94% of respondents said that colleges and universities fail miserably! Let me add quickly that teaching teamwork and social skills is not solely the responsibility of our educational institutions. Certainly, how one is raised at home, the role models one emulates, and many other experiential factors influence how a person relates to and works with others. That having been said, however, I must admit (and my personal experiences confirm) that students are not generally encouraged to develop a collegial relationship with their peers. Quite to the contrary, academic competition is more common than cooperation, especially when it comes to the quest for individual achievement and the ever-popular grade—and once learned, this habit tends to carry over into the workplace. I recall once incurring the wrath of my department head when I gave a take-home exam (in itself, frowned upon) and actually allowed, in fact, encouraged, the students to work in groups (perceived by my boss to be a violation of the university's honor code) to solve the problems. The class loved it! Not only did they do very well on the exam, but each and every one of them expressed their gratitude for my being more concerned with teaching than with being a policeman. They really appreciated my letting them take the exam home and work on it in teams, because, they said, it showed that I trusted them and that we were all in the learning process together. Moreover, they were not about to disappoint me, responding to that confidence by respecting and reinforcing, not violating, the honor code (they even signed a pledge to that effect). All of them also agreed that the exam itself, especially because of the way it was administered, served as a vehicle for learning, and that the experience of having the opportunity to discuss the problems with one another—absent any time constraints, the stress of a monitor peering over their shoulders, the fear of being accused of cheating, and within the spirit of healthy dialogue and positive interaction—contributed very effectively to the entire learning process. Except for my boss, we all agreed that the experiment was a huge success!

Which brings me to number four on the list: honesty, grouped generically with ethical work habits, a sense of right and wrong, and a concern with moral issues. I expressed my views on the topic of ethics in an earlier editorial (*American Laboratory* Oct 2001; 33[20]:6–8), so I will not expound on it here, except to say that 94% of survey respondents confirm that honest employees are highly sought after. More generally, employers look for people of character, being those who have solid, positive value systems as measured by six fundamental traits, i.e., they are 1) trustworthy (reputable, truthful, loyal persons of integrity); 2) respectful (tolerant, courteous, polite, civil individuals who live by the Golden Rule); 3) responsible (persistent, self-disciplined, accountable, cooperative folks who can be relied on to do what they are supposed to do); 4) fair (open-minded, accommodating, just, nonpartisan people who play by the rules, take turns, and share equally); 5) caring (compassionate, kind, grateful, forgiving human beings who are always willing to help others in need); and 6) good citizens (cooperative, well-informed and well-intentioned, environmentally conscious, law-abiding, neighborly members of a community who endeavor to make it a better place to live). Maybe it's a bit unrealistic to expect such hypothetical individuals to exist in real life. Nevertheless, these character traits are certainly worth striving for, and the more of them you can (honestly) boast having, the more likely you are to be hired and to keep your job for a long time.

Number five is an interesting one: Employers look for people who have the ability and are willing to follow directions, cooperate, and be professional about it. Not unrelated to communication skills, social skills, and good character, this attribute is still listed separately because employers view it as being a measure of one's commitment to the company and to its objectives. In other words, as a member of a team, one needs to be a good follower when appropriate as well as a good leader when necessary (*American Laboratory* Mar 2001; 33[6]:6–8).

Number six is also related to those attributes already listed, but deserves to be singled out separately (as I did in an earlier piece that appeared in *American Laboratory News* Jun 2003; 35[13]:4), and that is attitude. There is no doubt that one's attitude can make the difference between success and failure, the former being directly correlated with a positive attitude and the latter often being the result of a negative one. Nobody likes working with someone who has an attitude problem, and negative attitudes tend to be contagious; they are counterproductive, demoralizing, depressing, discouraging, and just plain bad. An employer would much rather have working for the company an individual who sees the light at the end of the tunnel as an opportunity to emerge from the darkness, rather than as a forecast of the doom inherent in a locomotive coming straight toward you at high speed!

Moving down the list, we come to number seven: punctuality. By punctuality, employers are referring not only to one's ability to get to work on time each morning and to be prompt in managing his or her appointment schedule, but, more generally, one's ability to meet deadlines, whether they be target dates for submission of proposals, quotes, reports, estimates, etc., or specific cutoffs established for the timely completion of designated projects. You often hear the words "time management" used in this context. One's ability to manage one's time effectively is viewed as an indication of how one manages his or her life in general.

Number eight addresses the ability to be neat and organized; nine emphasizes awareness and concern for on-the-job safety; ten looks for one's ability to adapt to change, and the versatility to go with the flow; and eleven concerns one's ability to think critically (as a complement to thinking creatively). But have you noticed which items are conspicuously missing so far—ones you might have thought would be right at (or near) the very top of the list? Indeed, jumping to the bottom, we find the five things that concern employers least: basic math skills, basic computer literacy, an understanding of business economics, technical competence, and ambition. That's right, parents: What you have been pounding into your kids' heads all these years about how successful they will be if only they strive to excel in academics is dead wrong! If we can read between the lines, what these surveys are apparently telling us is that employers are looking for the holistic person: well-rounded and having balanced academic achievement with character development, giving equal priority to each, or, if anything, emphasizing the latter more than the former. In other words, if the fundamentals are there, employers can take "good stock" and make achievers out of them, and the fundamentals are not embedded solely in acquiring essential skills for entry-level employment. That's just one category of attributes that employers look for, and it's the least important one.

Much higher up on the list, and what makes good stock, are attributes associated with communication skills, social skills, personal characteristics and attitude, integrative/applied skills, and character . . . so maybe parents should be spending more time drumming that stuff into the heads of their children, rather than the idea that cognitive skills (things like math and science) are all that is required to ensure success. Now I'm not saying that math, science, and other cognitive skills are not important. I'm saying that they are less important than we might otherwise think. Many surveys conducted over the years have verified that such essential skills can be learned more easily than can the other skills listed above. You have to be raised to have character skills; you can always acquire trade and professional skills. That's the easy part, and employers know it. Thus, they would rather start with the former, and teach you the latter, rather than the other way around. That is the lesson to be learned from such surveys, yet it continues to get ignored by our academic institutions (K–12 and higher), which continue (through "Standards of Learning," et al.) to emphasize cognitive skill development over character-building, and by the majority of families that follow suit. Am I missing something here, or is this yet another example of how we continue to strive to distance ourselves from our basic humanness?

Bonding

American Laboratory News, May 2002

As a faculty member at Virginia Tech (Blacksburg, VA), I traveled two or three times a year to various biomedical engineering conferences, most of the time to present a paper, attend a board meeting, or chair a technical session. Whenever it was feasible, I took the entire family along to mix a little pleasure with business, so that by the tender age of seven, our twin daughters were seasoned travelers, having already been to cities such as New York, NY; Atlanta, GA; Madison, WI; Houston, TX; Chicago, IL; Anaheim, CA (of course, Disneyland); Vancouver, British Columbia; Salt Lake City, UT; Washington, DC; and Dayton, OH, to name just a few.

But on this particular day in June of 1979, I was heading off alone to Baton Rouge, LA, to present a paper and chair a session at the annual meeting of the American Society for Engineering Education. My wife, Judi, was driving me to the Roanoke, VA, airport, and we were accompanied by our daughters Patti and Cyndi (out of school for the summer) in the back seat of the car. All of us were making small talk, just passing the time on a hot summer afternoon, when suddenly Cyndi blurted out, "Daddy, please take me with you!"

Total silence. "Please, Daddy, can I come with you?" she said again, as if no one heard her the first time. More silence; but the wheels began turning in my head as I contemplated the various possibilities. Then a voice sounding strangely like mine responded: "Sure, Cyndi, why not? Let's go!" "Cyndi!" exclaimed her horrified sister. "You don't even have a suitcase or a toothbrush! Have you gone completely nuts or something?" Judi concurred, adding, "Dan, are you serious? Look at her. She's only got on a pair of shorts, her T-shirt, and sandals. You sure about this?" "Absolutely," I said, "we can make this work, provided I can get an airline ticket for her. That could be the only stumbling block."

We arrived at the airport, Cyndi squealing with joy, "Yippee!"; Judi still not convinced; Patti thoroughly dumbfounded; and me already second-guessing myself. At the ticket counter we got the bad news: "I can get you to Atlanta," the Piedmont (now U.S. Air) ticket agent said, staring at his computer screen, "but your flight out of Atlanta to Baton Rouge is booked solid. No available seats, sorry." Then he looked into the child's eyes. She was holding back tears, pleading, so full of hope and anticipation. How could any living human being break this child's heart, furiously pounding below those watering eyes? "Of course," continued the agent, "if you are willing to take a chance, you can go down there, check in at the Delta ticket counter and see if you can work something out on stand-by." As I, too, caught a glimpse of Cyndi's face, her grip on my leg tightening, I said, "Okay, let's give it a try," and we all breathed a sigh of relief. "Yippee!" A reprise from Cyndi.

We bought Cyndi a ticket, boarded the plane (she was clutching her hairbrush and a coloring book and crayons that had been in the car), and off we went, leaving Patti still shaking her head in disbelief and her mother waving goodbye as tears welled up in her eyes as well. Arriving in Atlanta, we went immediately to the Delta ticket counter to see about the possibilities for our connecting flight to Baton Rouge. "No available seats," confirmed the Delta employee, "booked solid!" But, as if by some miracle, a gentleman standing nearby had overheard my conversation with the agent and generously came forward to announce that he was willing to give up his seat for Cyndi. "Can't break up a family," he said, giving Cyndi and me an understanding wink as I offered him my sincerest thanks and admiration. With that, we managed to book her all the way through to Baton Rouge and back to Roanoke through Atlanta! "Yippee!" again.

On the airplane, Cyndi and I had a serious discussion about how well-behaved she would have to be if this was going to work. We talked about biomedical engineering, the conference, the subject of my presentation, what daddy does for a living, and how involved I would be during the technical session that I was chairing. I advised her that she would have to sit all by herself while I was on the stage, be quiet, and not create any disturbances or distractions. Most importantly, she was not to leave the room under any circumstances (bathroom needs would have to be taken care of before or after each session, but not during), nor was she to go *anywhere*, with *anybody* but me, understood? Those were the ground rules, which she dutifully accepted, and I knew she wouldn't let me down. She never has!

Arriving in Baton Rouge, our first stop was a shop at the airport to buy Cyndi a brand-new toothbrush and then off to the hotel to call mom and tell her everything was OK. By this time, it was getting rather late and both of us were hungry, so after freshening up a bit, my "date" and I sauntered on down to the hotel dining room for a gourmet dinner. At dinner, she was the perfect young lady, making sure to mind her manners at the table while informing the waiter, "My mom is a pretty good cook too, you know." Being in Louisiana, we, of course, opted for a seafood meal, and Cyndi couldn't wait to get back home to tell her sister, "You haven't *really* had seafood until you've had it in Louisiana!" (Just like I had always bragged, "You haven't *really* had pizza until you've had it in New York.")

The conference went without a hitch. Cyndi abided by all of the ground rules that we had established and really made me proud of her among my colleagues, all of whose hearts (and admiration) she captured, just as she had those of all the airline and hotel personnel. (Why was I not surprised?) She was so well-behaved that she even took personal responsibility for washing and drying the only pair of underwear she had with her for the two nights that we stayed at the hotel, calling her mom and sister each night to check in, and taking her nightly bath. (She loved the plush bathroom in the luxurious hotel.) The only brief moment of panic that I experienced came at the end of the technical session that I chaired, when I looked over to where I thought Cyndi would be sitting, quietly coloring in her coloring book as she had during previous sessions—and I saw nothing! I scanned the entire room . . . no Cyndi! My heart started to race and the sweat broke out around my neck and forehead as I feverishly searched every aisle. Just when I was about to declare an emergency, there, in the very last row, I finally found her, sprawled out across several seats, sound asleep! A colleague of mine, who had joined me in the search, seeing her sleeping peacefully in the back of the room, couldn't help but remark, "Dan, I do believe your daughter got more out of this session than any of us did!"

We started a family tradition on that fateful day in June of 1979. Almost immediately upon our return from Baton Rouge, and taking her cue from Cyndi, Patti started packing for her anticipated trip with her daddy to Denver, CO, later that same year, in October, to attend the Annual Conference of Engineering in Medicine and Biology (ACEMB). Not sharing the same degree of spontaneity as was characteristic of her sister, Patti took three months to get ready for that trip, systematically and carefully packing *everything* she thought she might need (coloring books, reading material, toys, changes of clothes—you name it!). And though space will not permit me to fill you in on the details, suffice it to say that the Denver trip was as successful as was the trip to Baton Rouge. And did her teachers mind that I was pulling Patti out of school to go with me to Denver? "The experience of traveling with her dad is infinitely more valuable than anything she would be learning in school during that same period of time," remarked one of them. "And besides," she continued, "how many kids actually *know*, firsthand, what their fathers do for a living? Patti and Cyndi actually know what a biomedical engineer is, and does!" This teacher was basically expressing the general attitude of the entire school toward the tradition we had started of my always taking at least one girl with me wherever I went, if the entire family could not come along. Such trips didn't really occur often enough (two or, at most, three times a year—at least one of which was always during the summer), and they never lasted long enough (two or three days at a time) to significantly interfere with the girls' schoolwork. Yet there is no way to express or even begin to define the bonds that were formed during those one-on-one trips—the very personal individual relationships that Judi and I were able to establish with each of our girls, separately, and the meaningful time that was shared among us when we were able to travel collectively as a family. Soon my colleagues caught on to this family tradition and they would ask me, "Which girl do you have with you this time, Dan?" (As if they would know the difference—our girls are identical twins!)

Anyway, those were very special, precious times. I thank you for letting me share a couple of them with you.

The Seven "C's"

American Biotechnology Laboratory, February 2004

When one hears the term "The seven seas," what probably comes to mind is the term sailors often use to describe the seven major divisions of the one great body of salt water (the great world ocean) that covers about 70.8% of the earth's surface. These seven seas are the North Atlantic and South Atlantic Oceans (both are really one large ocean that is often considered to include the North Polar Sea as well), the North Pacific and South Pacific Oceans (again, arbitrary compass divisions of one larger mass of salt water), the Indian Ocean, and the Arctic (North Polar Sea) and Antarctic Oceans (Southern Ocean, which is often considered to be the actual source of the Atlantic, Pacific, and Indian Oceans).

That having been said, these seven seas are not what this editorial is about. Instead, what I have in mind is a portion of the "C section" (not to be confused with a Cesarean section, whereby a fetus is extracted from a mother's womb by an incision made through the abdominal wall and uterus) of my "Dictionary of Words to Live By," first introduced in the August 2003 issue of *American Biotechnology Laboratory* (21[9]:5–7). What I am referring to are seven words (in no special order) that begin with the letter "C," each of which provides a solid foundation upon which one can build a positive and constructive philosophy of life.

1. *Conscience.* The great Swedish scientist, philosopher, and religious writer Emanuel Swedenborg (1688–1772) once said, "Conscience is God's presence in man." Indeed, all of us are endowed with this inherent "sense" of right and wrong—godliness, the divine inspiration to be righteous. That this is so is clearly implied by the very origin of the word, which derives from the Latin prefix *com-*, meaning "with, together," and *scire*, meaning "to know" (the same root from which the word "science" derives). Thus, we know instinctively what is just and proper, and inner alarms go off to warn us when we are about to act inappropriately. In the norm, the "hardware" for doing the right thing is already hardwired into our anatomy and physiology, but, as General H. Norman Schwarzkopf told us, "The truth of the matter is that you always know the right thing to do. The hard part is doing it"—so I challenge you to just do it. One thing that will help you in this effort is to practice developing:

2. *Compassion.* This word, too, derives from the Latin prefix *com-*, to which is added *pati*, which means "to suffer." Hence, to have compassion is to be able "to suffer with." What a wonderful word! What better way to show others that you really care about them than to sincerely sympathize with their predicament, share their grief, suffer along with them, and feel for their sorrow or hardship, letting your conscience guide you to empathize with their emotions. Author Bob Goddard reminded us that we need compassion, because we have all been there. "Resolve to be tender with the young, compassionate with the aged, sympathetic with the striving, and tolerant with the weak and the wrong," he says, because "sometime in your life you will have been all of these." The Dalai Lama declared, "If you want *others* to be happy, practice compassion. If *you* want to be happy, practice compassion." Either way, you win. Compassion is just another way of expressing the equally divinely inspired Golden Rule, which, stated simply, implores us to treat others as we would like to be treated.

3. *Confidence.* The great English poet and dramatist John Dryden (1631–1700) said it best: "For they can conquer who believe they can" [emphasis on the letter "C" is mine]. All too often in our lives, defeat becomes a self-fulfilling prophecy; we do not succeed because we do not think we can. Even worse, we surround ourselves with individuals who reinforce that negative way of thinking by constantly criticizing what we do, what we say, what we wear, how we look, and so on. Do not let them—while you are at it, do not become your own worst enemy, either. Give yourself a chance to make your dreams come true, and should it come to pass that those efforts fall short of your expectations, for whatever reasons, do not let one of those reasons be that you failed to try because you lacked the confidence to make it happen.

A contemporary of Dryden's, the French epigrammatist (one who makes short, pointed, often witty sayings) François Duc de La Rochefoucauld (1613–1680), carried this thought yet one step further by declaring that, "The confidence which we have in ourselves gives birth to much of that which we have in others." Simply stated, believe in yourself, and it is much easier to believe in others, but a word of caution is in order: Be careful not to let confidence evolve into another C-word—cockiness. Never let your confidence become conceit and arrogance; your pride in yourself should never turn into contempt for others. In other words, do not become one of the critics you are trying to avoid, lest others avoid you in return. Indeed, one of the hardest lessons we have to learn in life is how to be good winners, and how not to let success spoil us.

4. *Communication.* Like it or not, we are social creatures. This is implicit in the very etymology of the word "communication," which derives again from the Latin prefix *com-* ("together") and *mūnia* ("duties"), i.e., common duties based on social interactions, a connectedness of purpose that is predicated on a mutual understanding of what that purpose is. By inference, then, "communication" suggests an ability to convey—unambiguously, clearly, and without chance of misinterpretation—information intended to define one's hopes and desires, using spoken or written language that accurately expresses meaning and intent. The operative word here is "accurately." I cannot tell you how often my dear wife has said, "Listen to what I *mean*, not to what I *say*." Nor can I tell you how often I have heard others proclaim, "Words fail me," when trying to express a strong feeling or emotion, not to mention, "I didn't mean it that way; you misunderstood." Indeed, our ability to communicate is far more art than science, for it is difficult, if not impossible, to express ourselves in ways that get the message across without ambiguity while remaining totally faithful to its intent. Add to that modes of communication that are accompanied by facial expressions, hand gestures, body language, tone of voice, verbal mannerisms, suggestive innuendos, etc., and further modulated by the receptiveness of the individual(s) to whom information is being communicated and it becomes immediately apparent that the challenge of conveying accurate information is quickly confounded. Yet communication is the key to successful parenting, friendships, marriages, interpersonal relationships, and yes, even world peace. So much so, that if I were to rank these C-words, I think "communication" might be at the top of the list, alongside the next C-word:

5. *Compromise.* What I love about the concept of compromise is that it connotes win–win situations (unlike competition, which presupposes that, in order for someone to win, someone else has to lose, or a prolonged conflict in which, at the end, nobody wins). Compromise requires that the parties involved agree to agree, which already is a noble concession. Moreover, in formulating such an agreement, each side further agrees to settle for less than either side might have originally desired, because if the original situation had prevailed, one of the sides would have been seriously disadvantaged. A compromise is an explicit promise made by each side to the other that they will abide by the terms of a conciliatory settlement that gives neither side everything but both sides something. These are terms that both sides can live with in peace and harmony, with no ill feelings or regrets, which

is crucial to the success of any social interaction or human venture. To compromise is to be sensitive (speaking of compassion) to the feelings and concerns and welfare of others; to respect their rights and privileges (speaking of conscience) as well as your own; to show good faith; and to have confidence in the processes of communication, mediation (if necessary), or, as a last resort, arbitration, and to do so for the benefit of all concerned and for all the right reasons.

6. *Commitment.* Whether it be to <u>c</u>onsummate a <u>c</u>ompromise, realize a <u>c</u>ovenant, fulfill a dream, satisfy a <u>c</u>areer objective, or bring to fruition a lifelong ambition, to make a commitment is to pledge oneself to the ultimate success of any venture. "The quality of a man's life is in direct proportion to his commitment to excellence, regardless of his chosen field of endeavor," said legendary football coach Vince Lombardi. Words, indeed, are cheap. Intentions, however honorable, are meaningless if they fail to result in positive action. Ambitions are wonderful, but as long as they remain just ambitions, without an obligatory <u>c</u>ompulsion to see them become realized, they are just that: unfulfilled aspirations. In order to accomplish anything, one must not only want it to happen, one must endeavor to *make* it happen—persevere, keep trying, never give up, not get discouraged, stay on course (speaking of the seven seas), maintain your resolve, stay committed. To do so will frequently require that you also cultivate the last of the seven "C's":

7. *Courage.* Interestingly, the word "courage" derives from the Latin word for "heart" (*cor*), which, coupled with the suffix *-ous* (as in "courageous," from the Latin *osus*, meaning "full of"), suggests "full of heart." "You've gotta have heart," said Richard Adler and Jerry Ross in their 1955 Broadway hit, "Damn Yankees," which is based on the Douglass Wallop novel, *The Year the Yankees Lost the Pennant.* The song continues, "All you really need is heart. When the odds are sayin' you'll never win, that's when the grin should start. You've gotta have hope. Mustn't sit around and mope. Nothin's half as bad as it may appear; wait'll next year—and hope. When your luck is battin' zero, get your chin up off the floor. Mister, you can be a hero; you can open any door—there's nothin' to it, but to do it!" Indeed, in the face of adversity, one must have the <u>c</u>ourage of one's <u>c</u>onvictions; the guts to stand firm when confronted by opposition to maintaining one's resolve (opposition that might often involve enduring hardship or even being exposed to life-threatening situations), the fortitude to persevere, the willingness to go on, the moral strength to stay on task.

As you can imagine, many C-words can be added to this abbreviated list: words like "children" (the only hope for our future), "consistency," "courtesy" (which I tend to group together with "consideration," "chivalry," and "congeniality," among others), "creed" (you must believe in something), "charity," "culture," and, of course, "citizenship." Once again, I am limited by space and time, but I do want to leave you with one final thought: My dear friends, for the future welfare of our entire planet, we must endeavor not only to *travel* the seven seas, but to *live* by the seven "C's" as well (and I do not mean in the sense of taking up residence by the ocean!).

Simple Wisdom II

American Laboratory News, December 2001

There I was, the proud recipient of a brand-new private pilot's license, the ink on it barely dry. Yes, I felt a great sense of accomplishment, but I still lacked complete confidence in my skills as a pilot, having had not quite 50 hours in the air, only about half of them in the aircraft by myself ("solo," as they say in the flying business). Thus, when Tony Gambino, at the time owner and operator of Deer Park Airport in Long Island, NY, asked if I would be willing to ferry an airplane for him from Teterboro Airport in New Jersey to Deer Park, I felt a sense of anxiety immediately brewing in the pit of my stomach. The plan was for me to fly with an instructor to Teterboro, pick up the aircraft there, and then fly it solo back to Deer Park. Simple enough.

"Sure," I said, "no problem," whereupon I called the weather service to check out conditions between Long Island and New Jersey. Then I went outside and performed a thorough check of the aircraft in which the instructor and I were to fly to Teterboro. Coming back inside, I checked again with the weather service. Then I laid out a round-trip flight plan from Deer Park to Teterboro. "I probably should check the weather, don't you think?" I asked Tony, picking up the phone without even waiting for his response. "Oh, I had better use the restroom before we leave—no toilets in a Cessna 150 you know," I quipped to Tony, with a nervous snicker. Upon my return (deliberately delayed), I thought it best to check once again with the weather service—can't be too careful, you know. "How long do you think the round trip should take?" I asked Tony, realizing at once how ridiculous that question was because he and I both knew that I had just calculated the round-trip travel time and distance in preparing my flight plan. Tony looked up, but didn't say anything. He merely shrugged his shoulders and gave me that, "Wasn't that a rather stupid question?" look. "Better check the weather again," I said, figuring that he would think this to be a much more logical concern, and I followed up quickly with, "When do you think we should leave?"

By now, it was clear that I was stalling, and Tony sensed my apprehension in undertaking this venture. So, in response to my final question, he remarked, "You know, Dan, if you go, you'll come back!" Those words, spoken over 40 years ago, have stuck with me ever since. What a great tribute to the concept of decisiveness, and to the futility of procrastination. Tony's words of wisdom paralleled a similar thought in P.L. Travers's book, *Mary Poppins* (made into a popular 1964 Walt Disney movie), where Mary says, "A job begun is half done!" And of course, how often have we heard that "A long journey always begins with the first step." The point is: Once begun, the most difficult phase of any activity has thereby been successfully completed. I should have realized it at the time because, being a violinist long before I became a private pilot, I knew only too well what all violinists know—namely, that the hardest part of practicing the instrument is opening up the violin case!

I went on to pursue quite an active involvement with flying, eventually being certified by the Civil Air Patrol (CAP) as a search-and-rescue mission pilot and becoming Commanding Officer of a CAP Squadron in Cleveland Heights, OH, while pursuing my Ph.D. degree at Case Western Reserve University in Cleveland. Because I had a friend in the CAP who was a corporate pilot and also a certified multiengine instructor, I decided to work toward that advanced rating by accompanying him on his daily round-trip flights from Cleveland to New York City in the company's twin-engine airplane. One day, as we were cruising along on automatic pilot, I kiddingly said to him, "For this they pay you? To sit up here, cruising along on autopilot, looking out at the scenery, doing nothing?" To which he replied, "They don't pay me for what I *do*, they pay me for what I *know*; and right now, I know how to operate the automatic pilot on this aircraft." That, too, is an expression that has always stayed with me because too often, we fail to recognize and reward people for what they know; we have a tendency to evaluate them only on the basis of what they *do*.

There is an old Arabic apothegm (short, forceful maxim) that identified four types of men: "He who knows not, and knows not he knows not, he is a fool—shun him; he who knows not, and knows he knows not, he is simple—teach him; he who knows, and knows not he knows, he is asleep—wake him; he who knows, and knows he knows, he is wise—follow him." I would add to that last statement, "Follow him—especially if he knows how to operate the automatic pilot on an airplane!"

Having completed my Ph.D. at Case Western Reserve University, it was time to move on. My Ph.D. advisor, Dr. Simon Ostrach, informed me of an opening at Virginia Tech, which he thought would be of interest to me. "Where is Virginia Tech?" I asked. "It's in Blacksburg, Virginia," he replied. "Where is Blacksburg, Virginia?" I asked. "It's a small town in rural southwest Virginia," he answered. "Where?" said I. "Rural southwest Virginia," said he. I paused and thought for a moment. Then I asked, "Do you really think that I, a kid from Brooklyn, New York, having lived all of my life in big cities, could possibly find happiness in Blacksburg, Virginia?" "Dan," Dr. Ostrach said, "just remember this: The trouble with moving is that you always take yourself with you. Wherever you go, there you are! If you are inclined to be a happy person, you will find happiness no matter where you live. If you are inclined to be unhappy, you will fulfill that prophecy regardless of where you go. Happiness has to come from inside-out, not the other way around. If you rely on your environment for your happiness, you will spend the rest of your life looking for the perfect place to live, and, you will probably never find it. So why don't you go down and give Blacksburg a try. It might surprise you." That conversation took place in January of 1973; we came to Blacksburg—18-month-old twins in hand—in August of that year, and we have been here ever since! I learned a big lesson in 1973 from a very wise man.

And speaking of wise men reminds me of a pearl of wisdom that I attribute to my dad, although I am not sure he originated the expression when he said, "Remember, son, when you argue with a fool, so is he." The key is to shun fools (as the Arabs would say), lest you become one of them, and the concept is not all that removed from still another one that is ever so simple, yet exhibits incredible wisdom. The following is often attributed to the famous Missouri clergyman Reinhold Niebuhr (1892–1971), who, in a prayer said to have first been published in 1951, declared: "God, give us the serenity to accept what cannot be changed; give us the courage to change what should be changed; give us the wisdom to distinguish one from the other." An anonymous alternate version of this same thought (which may actually have preceded Niebuhr's version) is, "God, grant me the serenity to accept the things I cannot change; the courage to change the things I can, and the wisdom to know the difference." The key, of course, in any situation where one is confronted with the option of taking action or withdrawing is—in the words of Don Schlitz, made popular by Kenny Rogers in the 1976 hit, "The Gambler"—knowing "when to hold 'em, when to fold 'em, when to walk away, and when to run." Too often, in an effort to appear brave, committed, persistent, and to avoid being labeled a quitter, we pursue exercises in futility that lead us up dead-end roads.

Quitting is not a bad thing if it is the *right* thing to do in a hopeless situation. Several times in my life I have been confronted with such situations, and I thank my dear wife, Judi, for teaching me still another valuable lesson in life: "You can't want something for somebody more than they want it for themselves." As a leader, you can help individuals and/or organizations achieve goals and satisfy objectives; you can guide them along the road to success; you can inspire them and encourage them—but unless *they* want to achieve these things as much as you want it for them, you are probably wasting your time and effort. Algernon Sidney very aptly said, "God helps those who help themselves."

So in closing, let me tell you how I helped myself by heeding perhaps the best advice I have ever gotten about yardwork and gardening. I am not an outdoor person. My idea of a picnic is eating in the dining room with the windows open. Knowing this about me, my former roommate took me aside one day as I was getting ready to be married and said, "Dan . . . always remember this: Don't *ever* plant a vegetable garden bigger than your wife can take care of by herself." I never have!

The Great Equalizer

American Laboratory, November 2001

I am writing this at the airport in Charlotte, North Carolina. My flight to Philadelphia has been delayed almost two hours so far, due to "minor maintenance problems with the aircraft—nothing to be alarmed about," and there's no telling when we will actually depart. To my right sits a young (perhaps 35-or-so years old), executive-type gentleman. He's busy speaking into his cellular phone; he's actually been on it for some time now, making one call after another, but this time he is quite visibly disturbed and very nervous. He also doesn't seem to care much about who's listening in on his conversation, as he impatiently exclaims in a loud, deliberate voice, "My flight's been delayed indefinitely! I've got a huge deal resting on this . . . I can't afford to miss this meeting! Got any suggestions? I need to get there; I can't be late. What should I do?"

My mind drifts off at this point so I don't follow the rest of his conversation. Rather, my attention turns to the middle-aged woman seated to my left. She is frantically typing away on her laptop computer, oblivious to anything going on around her. It looks to me like she's working on accounting sheets of some sort; I can't really tell from this distance and I don't want to appear nosy by obviously leaning over to take a closer look. Besides, I am now distracted again by the mother of two young boys seated opposite me. They appear to have been traveling for some time because they look haggard, very tired, and quite worn out. They are obviously traveling without a husband/father or any other companions; perhaps they are on their way to meet someone somewhere, or maybe they are on their way home. In any event, the boys are quite restless; they're being boys, getting ornery and rather uncontrollable. Mother rummages through a well-used, portable carrying case, finds two candy bars, and offers them to the boys, desperately hoping to keep them occupied, satisfied, and calmer. Her plan doesn't work, though; they're not interested. Finally, sensing perhaps that we are all staring at her, she packs up and goes off for a walk, her two boys reluctantly tagging along.

As the mother leaves, I notice that she was obstructing my view of a gentleman sitting one row behind her, sleeping peacefully, eyes closed, also oblivious to anything going on around him. "There's one in every crowd," I think to myself. "Rolls with the punches; unfazed by anything; able to sleep anywhere, anytime, under any circumstances, no matter what . . . the seasoned traveler who doesn't let anything bother him." I envy folks like him. Somehow, I think they get the most out of life, as opposed to still another woman who sits nervously fidgeting about. She's obviously never flown before (or doesn't do so comfortably) and this whole situation is all rather disconcerting to her. She looks to be on the verge of tears!

By now it's really starting to get late, and everybody is starting to exhibit signs of major concern, especially those who are facing serious problems making connecting flights at the other end. A line starts to form at the ticket counter as distressed passengers start demanding "answers!" One man will miss a connecting flight from Philadelphia to Paris . . . what now? There's no other one going out tonight. Another traveler will miss a connecting flight to Los Angeles, also the last one out that day. What to do? What to do? We are all helpless victims of circumstance, and under these conditions, we are all equals—the technological failure has leveled the playing field.

Mother Nature, too, has a way of being the great equalizer. Our world gets periodically deluged with earthquakes, major winter storms, tornadoes, hurricanes, floods, and other natural disasters of record-breaking proportions. I recall, for example, that when the terrible floods hit the Midwest in that memorable summer of 1993, they brought out the very best in people. Suddenly, neighbors helped neighbors and it didn't matter whether you were Christian, Jewish, Muslim, black, white, Democrat, Republican, Northerner, Southerner, or whatever. What mattered was that there was a job to be done, and everyone pitched in to do his or her fair share. A similar thing happened when devastating earthquakes hit California in the fall of that same year: The day-to-day struggle for success and survival suddenly took on a new meaning, putting everything into proper perspective. Again, what mattered most was common decency, respect for life, aid to those who needed it, and a mutual desire to work together for the common good.

Over and over again, we see in times of catastrophe, dedicated men, women, and children working side by side, together, round the clock, to restore power; clear roads; provide shelters; keep water clean and suitable for drinking; care for the homeless, the sick, the aged, the disabled, the needy; and clean up afterwards. Speaking of the ill-stricken reminds me that disease and disabling accidents, too, are great equalizers. They know no social class. They strike at random, without first examining the résumés of those they afflict.

But getting back to Charlotte, after what seemed like (and was not far from) an eternity, the plane is finally ready for boarding. Over the loudspeaker we hear, "Passengers needing special assistance, and those seated in first class, please come forward to board the plane at this time." The former, "passengers needing special assistance," is fine. I'm all for making allowances for those in need, those traveling with small children, and so on; I don't and never have questioned that policy. The latter, however, "those seated in first class," I take serious issue with. Just moments ago, we were all equals; we were all helpless victims; we were all at the mercy of technology, which held us unwilling prisoners at an airport where none of us wanted to be. It didn't matter who you were—account executive, mother of two, first-time flyer—whomever. We all sat and waited, equally inconvenienced; equally treated by circumstances over which we had no control, circumstances that did not discriminate among those who were being significantly encumbered. Given no choice in the matter, we all tolerated one another in order to make the most of, at best, a very uncomfortable and distressing situation.

But now, suddenly, the prison gates flew open and that equality gave way to a form of caste system. Now it was back to business as usual, the business of establishing social and economic classes. Now the privileged few could go to the head of the line. I'm not big on privileges, especially those that can be "bought," if those privileges are not enjoyed equally by everyone. Try as I may, I just can't justify why someone who is wealthier than I am earns the right to get on the airplane first, to be addressed with reverent "yes sirs," and "no sirs," to be pampered with warm, wet hand towels, to sit in wider seats, with more leg room, while the rest of us get squeezed in like sardines in coach class, unable to "eat, drink, and be merry," or enjoy good food and fine entertainment.

For that matter, I have also never understood why it takes floods, earthquakes, ice storms, and natural disasters to get our attention, to remind us that working together, we can overcome everything and accomplish anything, and to raise our consciousness of the fact that such cooperation should be the norm in how we treat one another, not the exception reserved for our response to crisis situations. Moreover, I have also had trouble comprehending why it takes serious diseases and disabling accidents to remind us of our mortality, of the fact that we are only on this planet for a very brief instant in time, and we should strive to make the most of it in an altruistic sense, to always work together for the benefit of all of humanity.

I guess these are all issues that can be understood only at a higher level. But I do know that if I were wealthy, I would buy first-class seats for everybody, whether they could afford them or not, so that all of us could be the privileged many, instead of the privileged few.

Ethics

American Laboratory, October 2001

When I was in medical school, I was particularly impressed by the effort my professors made to initiate prospective physicians into the profession of medicine—as opposed to merely teaching them the skills required to just practice medicine. Having recently graduated with a Bachelor of Mechanical Engineering degree, I became acutely aware of how skills-oriented my undergraduate education was; how much the curriculum emphasized methods, to the exclusion of purpose and responsibility. Now I found myself in a totally new and refreshing learning environment—one that recognized that it is not enough to teach only the technical expertise required to be a good medical practitioner. Rather, one must teach with equal importance what the physician must *value* in the practice of medicine. Indeed, as medical students, we learned not only what to *do* in order to practice medicine, but also what to *be* as practicing physicians.

There's a message here that goes far beyond the confines of a medical school campus. As the famed endocrinologist and best-selling author, Dr. Deepak Chopra, so eloquently put it, "We are not human doings . . . we are human beings!" And this idea of learning what to value in any human endeavor, starting with a very basic respect and tolerance for one another, is the essence of what it means to be a civilized society. Nobel Peace Prize recipient Dr. Albert Schweitzer, himself a physician, musician, theologian, and philosopher of some prominence, once remarked, "A man is ethical only when life, as such, is sacred to him—that of plants and animals, as well as that of his fellowman—and when he devotes himself helpfully to all life that is in need of help." Thus it is that any system of values, or code of ethics, that professes to establish guidelines for determining what is the right thing to do, and what is wrong, must be predicated on a fundamental reverence for what has come to be known as the Golden Rule. The quote, "All things whatsoever ye would that men should do to you, do ye even so to them," is often attributed to Jesus in his famed Sermon on the Mount (Matthew 7:12, Luke 6:31). But the fact is that Jesus was actually quoting from the Judaic Talmud, wherein it is declared, "That which you do not wish for yourself, you shall not wish for your neighbor. This is the whole law; the rest is only commentary" (Talmud Shabbat 31). Indeed, the Golden Rule shows up in all of the religions of the world, for example, the Mahabharata of Hinduism, where it is written, "Everything you should do you will find in this: Do nothing to others that would hurt you if it were done to you" (5-1517); the Udanavarga of Buddhism, which commands its followers "not to offend others as you would not want to be offended" (5:18); and the Sunnatt of Islam, where the assertion is made that, "None of you shall be true believers unless you wish for your brother the same that you wish for yourself." In all cases, the moral of the story is not to do unto others what you would not have them do unto you.

And what would you not have others do unto you? For one thing, you would prefer that they not lie to you. Few things hurt and upset us more than learning that we have been deceived, double-crossed, made fools of, betrayed, or otherwise victimized as a result of believing something that turns out not to be true. Thomas Jefferson noted that "Honesty is the first chapter in the book of wisdom"; and George Bernard Shaw remarked, "We must first make the world honest before we can honestly say to our children that honesty really is the best policy." Just think of how often we use phrases like, "If truth be told . . ." or "To be perfectly honest with you . . ." or "Truly, Dan, did you . . ." or "Really? Honest?" and so on, and it becomes immediately obvious how important it is to us that we not be deceived by false statements. Of course, the flip side to that is an equally common expression that says, "The truth hurts," which is why honesty must always be tempered with good judgment and sensitivity to another person's feelings. We must learn to be both empathetic and sympathetic to our fellow human beings.

Second, we would all prefer not to be treated unfairly, both in the sense of not being cheated out of what is rightfully ours, and, perhaps even more importantly, not being subjected to various forms of prejudice, partiality, intolerance, and bias. Injustices such as these are unacceptable from a strictly moral point of view; furthermore, they have left behind a long history of barbaric human conflict and suffering. Indeed, Francis Jeffrey once remarked that "Opinions founded on prejudice are always sustained with the greatest violence"; and Gordon W. Allport defined it as "the lazy man's substitute for thinking." The bottom line is that showing favoritism toward certain groups or individual(s), to the exclusion of others for no justifiable reason, only builds negative feelings of resentment, dissatisfaction, hatred, maliciousness, and ultimately, rebellion, none of which can lead to any good.

Third, we don't want others to violate a trust—to disclose to others what we have shared with them in strict confidentiality. All too often, when one expresses an opinion of another's character we hear words like, "I really don't trust him (or her)." Such untrustworthiness does not go a long way toward building goodwill and friendships. George MacDonald, in his novel *The Marquis of Lossie*, writes, "To be trusted is a greater compliment than to be loved." Trustworthiness goes right along with honesty as two of the most sought-after and highly regarded attributes that define the integrity and sincerity of our relationships with other human beings. Absent that trust, we become guarded and reticent. We think twice before confiding in another person. We watch every word that comes out of our mouth. We are not quick to offer opinions.

Fourth, we do not want to be impeded in our quest to achieve the guaranteed right to life, liberty, and the pursuit of happiness. In that sense, we seek the quality of altruism in others, that attribute that allows them to use their own success to ensure the success of their fellow human beings. To have achieved success in life, to get, without giving back so that others might better themselves as well, is to not have deserved getting. Selfish motives and greed are never ultimately beneficial to all concerned; they lead others to be covetous, jealous, envious, and suspicious—all of which, too, lead to no good. The best situations are win–win situations where everybody benefits. And as Albert Schweitzer (again) so aptly put it, "There is no higher religion than human service. To work for the common good is the greatest creed."

Related to all of the above is the concept of being treated with dignity and loyalty. We don't appreciate being destructively belittled, criticized, or reprimanded in demeaning ways that scorn and humiliate us. We much prefer being treated according to a code of ethics that becomes a habit. In fact, the very word "ethics" derives from an ancient Greek word, *êthos*, that actually means "custom," and suggests that the humane treatment of all forms of life on this planet derives from a tradition of respecting the very nature of our existence. But all too often, we forget (or neglect, or even worse, deny) that aspect of our heritage in the way we formally educate our younger generations. I am reminded of the words of Pablo Casals, a world-famous cellist, who once wrote, "Each second we live is a new and unique moment of the universe, a moment that will never be again . . . and what do we teach our children? We teach them that two and two make four, and that Paris is the capital of France. When will we also teach them what they are?" To which I would add, "When will we also teach them how to get along with one another?"

Seven "F-Words"

American Biotechnology Laboratory, August 2003

Got your attention, didn't I? That's because more often than not when people say "F-words," negative thoughts come to mind, thoughts of things gone bad that lead people to vent their frustration by swearing, using profane language (involving several ugly F-words) to express anger and hostility. Well, clear your head of such negativism, because the seven particular F-words I have in mind convey anything but anger, hostility, and frustration. Quite to the contrary, these seven F-words (in no special order) are in the category of "words to live by," expressions of love, compassion, and a philosophy for living a satisfying life.

1. *Friendship:* Derived from the Old English *fréon*, which meant, literally, "to love" (in turn, a derivative of the Sanskrit concept of a "dear one"), a friend is a person who knows everything about you and likes you anyway! All too often, we tend to describe love as if it were a shopping list: I love him or her because . . . followed by an inventory of attributes. Such constraints only serve to choke a relationship (especially a marriage), because they establish criteria that are impossible to live up to consistently. Thus, when the honeymoon stage wears off, and our human frailties emerge, the problems begin, testing the health of the marital relationship. Statistics show that marital relationships are failing these tests at an alarmingly increasing rate. The fact is, true love, and true friendships (especially among relatives), are not predicated on one's ability to meet expectations; they are unconditional, absolute, accepting, understanding, everlasting. In the words of George Santayana, "One's friends are that part of the human race with which one can be human," or as Bern Williams put it, "A friend is a lot of things, but a critic he isn't." So, to have friends, *be* one, and "Judge not, that ye be not judged" (Matthew 7:1).

2. *Forgiveness*: From the German *ver* and the Latin *per* comes the English prefix *for*, meaning "forth" (onward), "through" (by reason of), or "thorough" (complete). Thus, forgiveness is a willingness to move onward, completely, and by reason of giving pardon for another's mistakes graciously and without malicious intent. To forgive might be one of the most difficult things we humans can do for one another, because revenge is a powerful emotion. That is why Alexander Pope refers to one's ability to forgive as being "divine." It is also why Tevye, in the musical *Fiddler on the Roof*, points out that, absent forgiveness, in favor of an "eye for an eye, tooth for a tooth" philosophy of life, the whole world would quickly be left "blind and toothless!"

Part of our reluctance to forgive stems from the implicit notion that the one who has wronged us must initiate the process with an apology; we expect *them* to make the first move. Our pride, vanity, hurt, stubbornness, self-pity, and sense of having been violated and humiliated all get in the way of our willingness to let bygones be bygones. Moreover, in certain instances, such as those wherein a serious criminal offense (perhaps even involving physical abuse and/or death) has been committed, we feel rightfully justified in harboring vindictive feelings, and that's understandable. But vengeance is not a reason for living. Retribution has never brought back a deceased loved one and retaliation has never changed a historical fact. It is difficult if not impossible to find the right punishment to fit any specific crime, and rarely does "evening the score" bring closure to a real tragedy. Thus, the Lord's Prayer challenges us to "forgive those who trespass against us." In other words, as much as we would hope to be forgiven for our human failures ("forgive us our trespasses"), it would behoove us to return the compliment by extending that same courtesy to others. Indeed, in most instances, life would be more pleasant, healthier, and even longer if we would practice liberating ourselves from the burdens of carrying grudges in favor of learning to forgive and forget. So much more could thus be accomplished in a positive and rewarding lifestyle.

3. *Fitness*: Speaking of a healthy lifestyle, the word "fitness" comes to mind, which, interestingly, derives from the same root as "fact," i.e., the Latin *factum*, "a thing done," and by extension, "that which one can do, and those who do it" (as in "faculty"). In common usage, fitness is most generally thought of in terms of physical well-being, a state ("thing done") wherein neuro-musculoskeletal and cardiovascular performance are optimal. But I prefer to think of fitness more generically as a physiologic state of cenesthesia, the generalized feeling of well-being that one experiences when all of the body's organ systems are functioning optimally and in complete synchrony with one another. Achieving this state requires a good mental attitude (psychological fitness), proper eating habits (nutritional fitness), and enough rest (including sleep) and recreation (R&R fitness), balanced carefully with other activities (including work) of daily living (ADL fitness). In other words, it's not just about exercise, and certainly not about artificial exercise. The latter abuses the body and wears it out, as opposed to natural physical activities that use the body in an optimal way, maintaining tone, endurance, and resilience. As it relates to the way exercise is misconstrued today, I am inclined to agree with American educator Robert Hutchins, who said, "Whenever I feel like exercise, I lie down until the feeling passes," or with Chauncey Depew's observation, "I get my exercise acting as a pallbearer to my friends who exercise."

4. *Fairness*: The word "fair" has an interesting etymology. It derives from the Latin *fanum*, for "temple," the symbol of all that is righteous, honest, just, and unprejudiced. As an extension of that concept, "fair" became associated with beauty (fair maidens, fair weather), unblemished physical features (fair skin), joyful occasions (county fairs and festivals), and so on. In principle, I think most of us would agree that it is admirable to have the ability not to show favoritism, bias, or prejudice when dealing with other individuals, or with situations where a necessity might arise to make some sort of decision or value judgment. In practice, however, to display that

ability is not so simple. We are so impressionable, so easily influenced, so impassioned in our beliefs and convictions, so subject to persuasion, so fearful of retribution . . . so human . . . that when it comes to matters requiring some degree of rational objectivity, our ability to be totally impartial is perhaps unrealistic. But that should not, indeed must not, stand in the way of our attempt to strive for fairness as an attainable goal of civilized behavior. The more secure one is in one's self-image, the more informed and confident he or she is, the more selfless—kinder, gentler, more caring, more open-minded—the greater the probability that he or she will also be brave enough to be a fair person.

5. *Fantasize*: Never relinquish your power to imagine. Never stop dreaming. Never let anybody take those dreams away from you. Never stop saying, "What if?" even as those around you bombard you with all of the reasons "why not." There's an old Sanskrit word, *bhāti*, meaning "it shines," which became the Greek *phaos*, or *phōs*, for "light," *phainein* ("to show" or "appear"), and then the French *phantazein*, which connotes "making visible to the mind"—a fantasy. (This eventually led to fancy, which also derives from the Latin *focus*, the word for "hearth," the center of home life.) "I like the dreams of the future," said Thomas Jefferson, "better than the history of the past." As I mentioned above, there's not a thing you can do to change the past; it's historical fact, a done deal. Time spent dwelling on its injustices is time wasted.

On the other hand, the future is yet to come, and subject to your discretions, aspirations, hopes, and dreams. Anything is still possible in the future, and your dreaming of those possibilities gives you a reason for living! "I have learned this at least by my experiment," said Henry David Thoreau, "that if one advances confidently in the direction of his dreams, and endeavors to live the life which he has imagined, he will meet with a success unexpected in common hours." And the best reason for having dreams, as Ashleigh Brilliant put it, is that "in dreams no reasons are necessary." Fantasize a life for yourself, and then go for it!

6. *Frugality*: In going for it, however, don't be wasteful. The word "frugal" actually derives from the Latin *fruì*, meaning "to enjoy" (which also became fruit). But could the connection between the words "fruit" and "frugal" imply that one should enjoy but not overdo it? I think so. As is true of anything, going to extremes rarely achieves desirable results, whereas balancing things toward a happy medium almost always does. Achieving

balance implies use of proper perspective, proportioning, compromising, making concessions, ensuring that there will be enough for everybody. Mahatma Gandhi is quoted as saying, "There is a sufficiency in the world for man's need but not for man's greed." Indeed, ravenous desires quickly deplete limited resources, whether they be natural, physiologic, economic, or political. We must learn to satisfy our needs responsibly.

7. *Faith*: Last, but certainly not least, is faith, which comes to us from the Latin *fidere*, meaning "to trust." Although I am very respectful of the importance of faith in satisfying the human need for spiritual fulfillment (in the sense of believing without proof whatever it is that keeps you going), I am using the word "faith" here in a much broader sense. I am talking about being faithful to one's convictions ("keeping the faith"), having the confidence to succeed and refusing to give up; just knowing deep inside that you can make your dreams come true—not just fantasizing, but making those aspirations self-fulfilled prophecies. I'm talking about believing in yourself as well as in whatever spirituality drives you to persevere. I'm talking about knowing that you are better than your critics would have you believe, releasing yourself from paralyzing doubts, fears, and concerns about your abilities, just taking as a given the fact that you can do it. I'm talking about a positive mindset, an optimistic attitude, a confident resolve, a firm commitment, a determined vigor, and all of these for no particular reason that you can specifically put your finger on, except that you just know you can make it happen! I'm talking about trusting that things will work out for the best and then, in Miguel de Cervantes's *Man of La Mancha* style, forging ahead with visions of glory (as does Don Quixote) to battle evil and right all the wrongs of the world. You can make a difference—believe it!

Not a bad list of F-words to live by, don't you think? I'm sure you could add many to this list, like family (which I tend to include under the more general concept of friends because I see them as sharing many of the same attributes), fate ("How a person masters his fate is more important than what his fate is," said Wilhelm von Humboldt), femininity, fun, fervor (passion), finesse ("As I grow older, I learn to live with finesse," said a colleague of mine), fellowship (sharing), foresight, fulfillment.... In fact, over the years, I have amassed a kind of "Dictionary of Words to Live By," which goes through the entire alphabet in much the same way as I have done here specifically for F-words. I probably ought to think about publishing that dictionary someday. Anybody out there know a good literary agent?

To Err Is Human, to Forgive Divine

American Laboratory News, March 2002

The story goes that two old-time high school chums meet at a class reunion. One is a married father of three, the other still single. "How come you never married?" asks the friend. "Well," answers the bachelor, "I've actually had three opportunities to tie the knot, but none of them worked out. I met a woman many years ago who was gorgeous, extremely intelligent, and quite exciting. We fell in love and planned to marry, but she had such a Jekyll-and-Hyde personality that her inability to get along with people soon caused us to part company. Several years later, I met and fell in love with another young lady who was kind, considerate, and had the patience of a saint. She could get along with anybody, but was so indecisive in the way she approached situations in life that I soon lost my patience with her and we, too, went our separate ways. Then one day I met The *Perfect* Woman: a beauty queen and ex-college cheerleader and an academic scholar with good common sense and brains to spare who was decisive, enthusiastic, extroverted, warm, thoughtful, unselfish—you name it, she had it all going for her. And to top it off, she was a gourmet cook! Man, we are talking perfect here; a 'ten' in every way." "So, what happened? Why didn't you marry her?" asks the friend. "Well," the bachelor responds, his voice lowering, becoming sad and despondent, "as it turned out, she, in turn, was also looking for the perfect man!"

Moral of the story: If it's perfection that we seek in others, then we might as well stop looking, for we are not going to find it—in them, or in us! As Alexander Pope (1688–1744) so aptly put it in his *An Essay On Criticism* (from which the title of this editorial was quoted), "To err is human." To make mistakes is what we are all about. What is divine, on the other hand, is the ability to *forgive*. I discovered firsthand just how rare that ability is when I erred in my editorial "On the Seven Elements of Knowledge" (*American Laboratory News* Jul 2001; 33[15]:4), when I inadvertently and carelessly referred to a light year as a unit of time, rather than the unit of distance that it is by definition. To date, that blunder has generated more feedback from readers than any other of my more than 200 publications! Telephone messages, snail-mails, faxes, and e-mails came pouring in from everywhere! Normally, I try to respond to all of those from whom I hear, because if they make the effort to contact me (with *constructive* criticism and/or praise, ideas, and/or suggestions), then they deserve the courtesy of a response. In this case, however, I just couldn't keep up with the tsunamic flood of reaction that the error in this editorial generated, and so I apologize publicly for not getting back to all of you (although a correction was published on page 2 of the September 2001 edition of *American Laboratory News*).

Now, some of the feedback was constructive, in the sense that the respondent was willing to give me the benefit of the doubt, prefacing his or her remarks with something like, "I know you know better, and I'm sure it was just an oversight, but I wanted to call to your attention an error that appeared in your editorial . . .." (In fact, for the record, I *do* know better, and indeed, it *was* an unfortunate oversight that just "fell through the cracks" in a weak moment of haste.) A very small percentage of readers wanted me to clarify what I meant, just to make sure that *they* were not under the wrong impression in their understanding of what a light year really was (I must admit that for them, I was tempted to make up a story like, "I really did that on *purpose*, just to see how carefully you read these editorials and to test how much you really know about a light year," but my conscience would only force me to admit I made a foolish mistake). By far, however, the overwhelming majority of responses to the editorial came from those who seemed to revel in having "caught" me in my errant ways. "Gotcha!" was the essence of their message; and now I felt what an athlete must feel when he or she makes an unfortunate error on the playing field, only to have that unfortunate blunder caught on tape (or, in my case, recorded permanently in print), and to be replayed a hundred times on TV ("Let's take a look at *that* one again!"), from every conceivable camera angle, over and over again. The error is also virtually destined to make the highlight clips for the rest of the sport's season and, if bad enough, that one mistake may even become archival, coming back to haunt that athlete years later, when in a totally unrelated situation, sports announcers will replay the video again, reminiscing, "Do you fans remember when so-and-so made that critical error that cost his (or her) team the ball game and knocked them out of the playoffs way back when? Let's take another look at it." That thought gave me nightmares in which I envisioned my great-grandchildren pulling out that ill-fated edition of *American Laboratory News*, commenting to their great-grandchildren, "This is to remind you of a serious blunder that one of your relatives (who shall remain unidentified for the shame he caused us offspring to endure) made generations back, when a reputable scientific journal indiscreetly chose to publish some of his work. We don't talk about him much anymore, and when we do, it's only in a hushed whisper—he was such a disgrace to our family name!"

Silly as the above may sound, it is intended to make us aware of how preoccupied we are with mistakes, and how intolerant we are of those who make them. In and of itself, that lack of tolerance is admirable if we are talking about the consequences of errors such as those that blow up manned spaceships, or cause patients to die on operating tables, and so on. I am not suggesting that we routinely accept slipups in a cavalier fashion, laughing them off as "just human." But, in a less serious context, it did concern me that, of all the responses I received to that editorial, a mere fraction addressed the significance of the points made, or chose to comment on the "spirit of the law," as opposed to its "letter." Most of the responses were so absorbed with the mistake that they lost sight of the forest for the trees. And so my point is that there are times to seek perfection and times not to, as was the case for the bachelor in the story above, and the bride he was not destined to have. Even knowing that "to err is human," we continue to be obsessed with *denying* that humanness.

In the New Testament (John 8:7) the story is told of a woman who had been caught committing adultery. The woman is brought before Jesus, who is told, "This woman was caught in the very act of committing adultery. In our Law, Moses gave a commandment that such a woman must be stoned to death. Now, what do you say?" Jesus replied, "Whichever one of you has committed no sin, let him cast the first stone at her." Following this, one by one (the older ones first) the captors left, leaving Jesus alone with the woman standing before him. "You may leave," Jesus said to the woman, "but do not sin again." (This passage is sometimes quoted as "Go, and sin no more.") Now, by recounting this story, it is not my intent to justify adultery (please, no letters!) by shrugging it off as a simple example of the human tendency to err. Rather, the point of the story is to stress that none of us is without sin, and to emphasize the divine nature of forgiveness. Again, as with spaceships blowing up or patients dying in surgery, given our society's moral and ethical standards, some mistakes in judgment are more serious, and perhaps should have graver consequences than others, but the point, quoting once more from Pope's *An Essay on Criticism*, is that "Whoever thinks a faultless piece to see,/Thinks what ne'er was, nor is, nor e'er shall be." In everyday language, what Pope is saying is, "Nothing ever was, or is now, or ever will be perfect!"

The English poet Robert Browning (1812–1889), in his "La Saisiaz," takes this idea one step further when he declares, "Good to forgive;/Best to forget." In other words, burn the videotapes; blot out the printed errors. Don't only forgive, but also don't carry a grudge; put it behind you; move on, forgive and *forget*. As far back as 500 B.C., Confucius declared, "To be wronged is nothing unless you continue to remember it." You see, we have this bad habit of not only emphasizing what people do wrong (to the exclusion of what they do right), and of doing so in a destructive (as opposed to constructive) way . . . but, too, we tend never to let them forget it! It is branded in their reputation forever.

So we should remember, instead, that all of us err. Yes, we should be made aware of it when we do; and granted, some errors are significantly more serious than others, and have drastically worse consequences. But, since we all do it, how about also keeping in mind the Lord's Prayer, which says, "Forgive us our debts as we forgive our debtors." And for heaven's sake, be kind! You can point out an error without making people feel like they never should have been born if they were to be less-than-perfect specimens of the human species!

On the Importance of Putting Things Into Perspective

American Laboratory, July 2001

When I was young, I practiced the violin a great deal: an hour a day through elementary school, two hours a day through junior high school, three hours a day (and often even more) throughout my years at the prestigious High School of Music and Art in New York City, and up to six hours a day when I was a student of the famed violin teacher Dorothy DeLay, of the Juilliard School of Music. My mother was a real slave driver, not allowing me, as a child, to do anything of a recreational nature until I had done my practicing for the day.

One day I was watching a New York Yankees baseball game (I remain, to this day, an avid fan) and enjoying myself to the point where I was procrastinating in getting my practicing done, much to the dismay of my mother, who kept nagging me to "practice, practice, practice!" My father, the more laid-back of the two parents, listening to my mother badgering me, finally had enough. Coming to my defense, he put the whole issue into perspective, saying, "So what? What's so terrible if he becomes a great violinist one day later?"

Those words have always remained in my fondest memories, and I always recall them when I start to suffer guilt if I am doing something I enjoy, putting off in the process some other chore (like spending more time at the office?) that needs to be done. My dad had a wonderful way of always being able to pause, step back, and reflect upon a situation before jumping to conclusions and leaping to hasty decisions. I am very fortunate to be married to a wonderful woman (also a violinist) who has that same gift of always being able to put things into perspective.

Case in point: our twin daughters, Patti and Cyndi, reach puberty. Sex hormones start circulating wildly, controlling all bodily functions and destroying rational thinking. Any sense of reason becomes history, and the Mr. Hyde aspect of Dan Schneck's personality takes over completely. "No (expletive) guy is gonna get anywhere near (much less lay a hand on) MY daughters! I'll kill him! I will personally escort the girls on their dates. If I can't, I'll hire private detectives to tail them; I'll have them followed. I'll remind them that when they were three they promised NEVER to show an interest in boys. THEY PROMISED! A promise is a promise! You can't go back on a promise. I'll remind them. They can't do this to me; I'M THEIR FATHER!! If they really love me, they will never date—NEVER!"

Judi—middle-of-the-road, never-get-excited, take-things-in-stride, calm, cool, and collected Judi—sits me down one day and says, "Dan, you're a physiologist, aren't you? Tell me, how old is the human body?" "Aha!" I exclaim and, being ever the diplomat, I respond, "It depends on whether you are an evolutionist or a creationist" (figuring to myself, "That will put her in her place and end this conversation"). "Either way," she continues, never skipping a beat. "Well," I cautiously and pensively consider the question, stalling for time, "if you are an evolutionist, the human body is estimated to be about two million years old. If you are a creationist, well, probably around 10 thousand years or so." "Good!" says my dear wife. "In either case, that's a pretty long time, isn't it?" "Well . . . I guess so," say I, sheepishly starting to put my tail between my legs. "Did you ever wonder," continues Judi, "how civilization managed to make it this far without you?"

End of conversation. The dating years went by uneventfully, Judi continually reminding me that thousands of generations survived to perpetuate the species and they all did it successfully without my help, as would the present generation (she also reminded me of our own dating years and humbled my concerns about all possible outcomes). Furthermore, she went on to observe that thousands of generations would follow long after we're gone.

See, that's the incredible ability people like Judi and my dad have to immediately see the whole picture and put things in perspective. Here's another example: Several years ago, I was invited to present the keynote address at the annual meeting of a major health-care facility, which was held at a very exclusive resort hotel not far from here. I was both honored to have been chosen and thrilled to have this opportunity to advance my professional career. After dinner, the master of ceremonies was in the process of introducing me, and chose to elaborate on how impressed he was by the many papers I had published in scientific journals. As my head gradually swelled to enormous proportions, Judi (who was my invited guest at this elaborate affair) leaned over and whispered in my ear, "Well, dear, if you had gotten it right the *first* time . . .." CRASH! My ego suffered instant deflation, and the entire matter was put immediately into perspective as she went on to remind me later that God only published one book! (Incidentally, I also reminded *her* that God would never have gotten tenure by today's university standards.)

People who have the talent to view things in perspective typically have their "So what?" moments. Faced with any type of crisis situation, they always say, "So what?" ("So what if he becomes a great violinist a day later?") Whenever something happens that has the potential to be blown out of proportion, Judi always asks, "So what?" Given the worst-case scenario in answer to her query, she again asks, "So what?" Given the devastating consequences of the worst-case scenario, she replies again, "So what?" Given the dreadful outcome of those consequences, she still inquires, "So what?" And so the iterative process continues until, after enough "So what's?" it becomes apparent that the situation that caused the concern to begin with was never really as bad as it originally seemed. In most cases (92%, according to most studies dealing with worry), all of the potential consequences—even if they all *did* materialize—would still not create an insurmountable problem. In fact, things really are never as bad as we make them out to be, and according to folks like Judi and my dad, if those things do not pass the "So what?" test, they are not worth worrying about.

There are, of course, exceptions to this rule—the remaining 8% of situations that may involve serious health issues and other matters that warrant genuine concern—but in the overall scheme of things, the exceptions are few and far between. Moreover, even serious situations benefit greatly by being subjected to the "So what?" test. "So what?" lets you put things in perspective, forcing you to keep them from being blown out of proportion, and, in so doing, makes even the worst scenarios comfortable to deal with. "So what?" helps you adjust, or at least *better* adjust, providing for you a comfort level that promotes health and well-being; it eases the burden, the fear, the guilt, the pain, and the anguish. It lets you develop an attitude that "Whatever is going to happen is going to happen. If it's going to happen anyway, then there's nothing I can do about it; and if it doesn't happen, then it was not worth worrying about in the first place; and if there is something I can do about it, then let me get on with it and stop all this fretting about what 'might' be . . . so what? Que será, será! Whatever will be, will be."

So the next time you get overwhelmed, or life seems to be dealing you a bad hand and you can't seem to see the light at the end of the tunnel, just think of Judi and ask, "So what?" And *keep* asking until you realize that after enough "So what's?" there's nothing left to worry about. And then the problem goes away, as I am now.

The "I's" Have It!

American Laboratory, September 2004

I'm not referring to the "aye's" that signify affirmative votes, nor the "eyes" that are the organs of sight, nor the "-ize" that is the suffix added to adjectives and nouns to form verbs (like harmonize, categorize, and colonize). And I'm most definitely not referring to the improper slang contraction of "I is," as in, "I's going to the movies, y'all wanna come?" What I have in mind are words that begin with the letter "I." The seven I-words listed here provide a pretty good set of principles and guidelines to live by.

Individualize: Literally, this word means "to make something indivisible, incapable of being divided." In common usage (and the way in which I am using it here), it also connotes giving a distinctive character to a person, thus making each one of us a different individual. We should cultivate, exploit, and be proud of the fact that the exceptional talents and abilities with which each of us has been endowed allow us to stand out alone. We should be happy to be recognized and appreciated for those attributes, not ashamed of or embarrassed by them, as is too often the case. I have addressed our personal individuality and uniqueness at least twice before (see "Each of Us Is a Minority of One," *American Laboratory* Jan 2001; 33[1]:6–8, and "Will the *Real* You Please Stand Up?" *American Laboratory* Dec 2002; 34[24]:6–8), but I cannot stress enough how important it is, for the sake of your health and happiness, to be your own person and not succumb to external pressures to be otherwise. Indeed, although his doctrines were later abused by Hitler, German philosopher and writer Friedrich Wilhelm Nietzsche (1844–1900) had the right idea when he said, "At bottom, every man knows well enough that he is a unique being, only once on this earth; and by no extraordinary chance will such a marvelously picturesque piece of diversity in unity as he is, ever be put together a second time." In other words, there never was and there never will be anybody exactly like you. Don't give up (and don't let anybody take away from you) your unique privilege to be you, and to enjoy being you. It's a great adventure, a stimulating voyage of discovery; it's inspiring, invigorating, and best of all it makes life worth living! So why, as Arthur Schopenhauer (1788–1860) observed, do "We forfeit three-fourths of ourselves in order to be like other people"?

Indulge: At first, it might seem strange to have a word like "indulge" in this list, because one thinks of indulging as yielding to temptation, not having the self-discipline to control one's passions, being selfish, and these are not considered to be particularly desirable attributes. However, the Latin *indulgére*, from which this word derives, means not only "to yield" in the above sense, but also "to bestow," as in a favor to a friend, to be too kind or agreeable, to give in to another's wishes or whims (as opposed to your own) without being critical of those wishes. So you see, in that sense, being indulgent is not that bad, after all.

But the idea goes even further than that. Years ago, my wife Judi and I were fortunate to be invited to the ordination ceremony of a dear friend of ours who had chosen to pursue a life of service through the ministry. The person presiding over the liturgy gave one of the most inspiring sermons I have ever heard on the subject of service. She ended, however, with this profound caution: "Don't be so busy serving others," she said, "that you fail to leave something for yourself. You can't really help anybody if too many of your own needs are not being met."

Indeed, Monica Tuma Brown, a health spa development consultant, speaks of the "pampering factor," all of the positive spinoffs that result from your taking time out from this "techno-crazy" world to recognize your own need to nourish body, mind, and soul, and to attend to them. As a type of pampering, then, indulging responsibly, in moderation and without feeling guilty, transports you physically, mentally, and spiritually to a better place. Indulging is thus quite acceptable, even necessary, in order to help you become a better person, with batteries recharged, more energized and effective in being able to help others. So go ahead and treat yourself every once in a while; you're worth it.

Introspect: When not pampering yourself or using your unique talents to help others, take time out of your busy schedule to also look deep inside yourself. Introduce yourself to yourself; get to know *you*. Pretend that you are a person you have just met. Would you like to be that person's friend? *Are* you a friend of yours? Are you your best friend? Do you like you? Do you accept yourself for what you are, or are you constantly thinking: "I should've done this ... I should've done that ... I shouldn't be that way"? What don't you like about yourself? Why? And if that concern is legitimate, are you willing to change? If not, why not? If so, how are you going to go about it? What are your strengths? What are your weaknesses? Are they real or imagined? What turns you on? What turns you off? What do you believe in and are willing to fight for? What's really not worth fighting for? How good are you at prioritizing? Are you wasting a great deal of your time on things that don't really matter? Do you anticipate and take steps to prevent problems before they become an issue, or do you compromise your effectiveness by spending too much time trying to solve problems that could have been avoided with just a little forethought?

As a process, introspection can be both revealing (about what makes you tick) and cathartic (cleansing). Take time to examine your innermost thoughts, feelings, and motivation. Are you honest with yourself? Do you routinely forgive yourself and others, or are you vindictive? By what principles do you live? How would you like to be treated by others? Do you treat *them* that way? Are you happy with what you are doing with your life? Do you have a plan? Are you following that plan? Are you pursuing your dreams and passions? Do you have dreams and passions? Is life just happening to you, or are you steering the ship in the direction in which you want it to go? When all is said and done, how would you like to be remembered? As you practice introspection, learn also to be inquisitive and insightful. Always question, and in accordance with the title of a previous editorial, always "Stay Teachable!" (*American Laboratory* Jan 2003; 35[1]:6–8). An open mind is a bottomless pit of possibilities.

Improvise: To express your individualism, trust your innate instincts and intuitions. This, too, is a subject I have addressed at least twice before (see "Creativity," *American Laboratory News* Nov 2001; 33[23]:4 and "An Experiment in Creativity Through Improvisation," *American Laboratory* Aug 2004; 36[16]:4–8). One of our greatest attributes as human beings is the ability to fantasize, to imagine, to invent. Yet, ironically, helped along by our nation's educational system, we are taught very early in life to suppress those natural tendencies. For the most part, we grow up experiencing many potential consequences, and very little incentive to freely express our unique individuality. The process of improvisation, on the other hand, exploits it! To improvise is to not be afraid of being impulsive; to succumb to those sudden ideas that come to us instantaneously, without warning, to allow ourselves to be enticed into following our hunches; and to yield to our urge to capture the feeling of that moment and to act on it, purely on faith, just "knowing" that it is the right thing to do in that situation. Indeed, if necessity is truly the mother of invention, then the ability to improvise is what fertilizes the egg!

Integrity: None of what I've said so far would be particularly meaningful as a philosophy of life were it not predicated on the attribute of integrity. The expression of your individualism, what you choose to indulge in and believe in, how you view yourself, and what you create must all be based on an inherent commitment to do the right thing, for all the right reasons, and furthermore to stand firm in that commitment in the face of adversity and temptation. In fact, the word "integrity" derives from the Latin prefix *in-*, meaning "not," and the root *teg-*, meaning "to touch"; hence, to have integrity is to be "untouchable" in your convictions (which, in common usage, are presumed to be noble, honest, and sincere).

As an aside, to be untouchable also implies to be indivisible, whole. Thus, we have the words "integer" (a whole number) and "integration" (making whole through inclusion on an equal basis). Alternatively, the Latin *in-* can also mean "on," and an extension of *"teg-"* to *"tegere"* implies "to touch all over," as in "to cover," such as the natural outer cover or skin of an animal, hence our own integumentary system.

To have integrity is to be impeccable, irreproachable, and resistant to temptation, not like Faust, who, according to German legend, sold his soul to the Devil in return for youth, knowledge, and magic powers; or like armchair athlete Joe Boyd (alias Hardy) who, in the Broadway musical *Damn Yankees*, sells his soul to the Devil so that he can become a baseball superstar to help the sad-sack Washington Senators finally defeat the invincible New York Yankees to win an American League Pennant. In the end, Joe manages to win back his soul, proving that love does, indeed, conquer all!

Improve: Likewise, none of what I've said so far would be purposeful were it not for an ultimate desire to improve, inspire, and influence others in a positive way. We are, after all, only human, and to be human is to be imperfect, a work in progress. We need to operate from that premise and move on! The idea is to learn from our mistakes, to "profit" (the root of the word "improve") from them so that we are not destined to repeat them. Today, more than ever before, we appreciate and stress the importance of lifelong learning as a means for self-improvement, as a way of keeping up with changing times, and as a path that leads to a meaningful life. Christina (1626–1689), Queen of Sweden, a liberal of uncommon intelligence and great brilliance, had a keen interest in learning, self-improvement, and the rewards derived therefrom. "It is necessary to try to surpass one's self always," she said. "This occupation ought to last as long as life." Enough said.

Implement: Last but certainly not least, one needs not only to be aware of all of the above, but to also make it happen, i.e., to implement in one's everyday life the principles of individualism, indulgence, introspection, improvisation, integrity, and a sincere desire to improve. It does absolutely no good to just think about these things and talk about them, without taking constructive action to bring them to fruition. Indeed, from the Latin *implére*, for "to fill" (as in a need), to implement is to carry out, to get things done, to convert theory into practice. (Note: An implement is an instrument or device that helps you get things done.) To actually accomplish a goal often involves taking the initiative to lead the way, becoming impassioned about what you are doing, working hard (and diligently, i.e., being industrious) in that effort, and practicing (iterating) what you preach (ideate).

All who agree, please say "Aye!"

"L"-Ementary, My Dear Fellow!

American Laboratory, April 2005

The title of this editorial was the phrase often used by author Arthur Conan Doyle's (1859–1930) legendary fictional detective character, Sherlock Holmes, when his trusted friend and assistant, Dr. John Watson, would express amazement at Holmes's incredible deductive powers. "L"-ementary, indeed, my dear friends! That phrase also comes to mind when I think of how fundamental—*e*lementary—the following L-words are in helping one sort through the complexities of one's existence in order to find a vocabulary to live by—one that will guarantee ultimate personal success and fulfillment. Let's begin with the most obvious L-word: *love*!

It might interest you to know that the words "love," "leave," "leaf," "believe," "libido," and even "furlough" all share the same etymology, being derived from the Sanskrit *lubh* for "to desire." Thus, we have the Old English, "by your leave," expressing one's desire to seek your desire (and willingness) to grant him or her permission to do something—like be absent—which became "take a leave," hence, "furlough," which is what leaves do when they fall from the trees in autumn, and so on. To "believe" is to desire that something be true or real; and what we desire to be just so is what we *love*—from the Anglo-Saxon *leof*, for "dear," the Latin *lubet*, for "it delights," and *libido*, for "a strong (sexual) desire to be pleased." In modern usage, "to desire"—*lubh*, to love—has come to mean one's expression of a sincere and passionate affection for just about anything, but especially for other people—to desire, selflessly, what is best for them, and in so doing, derive great personal satisfaction and benefit.

"Love is a game that two can play and both win," said the famed actress Eva Gabor. In Paul's First Letter to the Christians at Corinth, he writes, at the end of Chapter 13 of the *Phillips Translation of the New Testament*, "In this life we have three great lasting qualities—faith, hope and love. But the greatest of these is love." (Note: In some translations the word "charity" is used instead of "love," but I think it is meant in the same spirit and context.) Personally, my favorite expression of this virtue is sung by Nat "King" Cole in the last line of his rendition of the song, "Nature Boy"—"The greatest thing . . . you'll ever learn . . . is just to love . . . and be loved in return." Second only to those emotions related to the instinct for survival of self, love prevails as a great expression of human sensibility, be it manifest in the drive for sexual fulfillment to meet the human need for survival of the species; the strong attachment that binds a parent to a child; or the unconditional (the operative word here) devotion and loyalty one has to family, friends, or whatever. Love trumps all other feelings (except, perhaps, fear, which is directly related to one's personal instinct to survive); it is, as English poet Philip Bailey (1816–1902) states in *Festus*, "The sweetest joy, the wildest woe."

One of the finest attributes that characterize those who have the ability to love, unconditionally, is their ability to *listen*, as well. I distinguish, here, the difference between *hearing*—which derives from the anatomical architecture that gives us the ability to receive and process sound energy in the range 20–20,000 cycles per second—and *listening*—by which we eventually ascribe meaning to what we hear. If the anatomical architecture is working properly, one will be able to *hear* sound. But if one does not attend (hopefully, accurately and without bias) to what he or she *hears*—if one does not *listen*—the meaning embedded in the sound he or she *hears* can easily be lost in the translation, if, indeed, it is translated at all, and not merely perceived as background noise! "Listen to what I *mean*, not what I *say*!" is a phrase I hear so often from my dear wife, Judi, who implores me to attend to and digest her words, rather than merely hear them and take them at face value. And, as author Doug Larson so aptly observed, "Wisdom is the reward you get for a lifetime of listening when you'd have preferred to talk." Paraphrasing this thought, I might add, "It is very difficult to *receive* when you are too busy *broadcasting* (i.e., transmitting)!" *Learning* (L-word number 3) to *listen* is as easy as making up your mind to do so, and then practicing (one of my very favorite P-words) the technique! Eventually, it becomes a habit, and the rewards inevitably follow—as do those that come from a lifetime of *learning*, in general.

Learning is a great passion (*love*) of mine, one that I have written about (both as a process and as an ultimate goal), not only many times in this column, but also in several of my published papers and books. I cannot emphasize enough the importance of open-minded learning as a means for solving many of the problems of the world, for I believe that closed-minded ignorance is to blame for most of them. Whether it is in an academic setting that addresses such subjects as math, physics, chemistry, history, biology, earth science, nature, psychology, sociology, world literature, etc.; in "real life" experiential situations that involve such human features as the performing and visual arts, wardrobe and architectural styles, religious beliefs, cultural customs and traditions, ethnic traits shared by members of a given group as a product of common factors such as race, family heritage, nationality, etc.; or in more personal encounters involving a friend, foe, sibling, spouse, relative, etc.—regardless of the circumstances, the more we *learn* about some*thing*, or some*one*, the less fearful we are of that thing or person. Furthermore, the less amygdala-driven fear we experience, the more likely we are to be hippocampus-driven rational (and thus, less prejudicial) in our approach to dealing with that thing or person (and, parenthetically, the greater also is our capacity to *love*). And finally, the more rational we are, the less likely we are to be easily intimidated, confrontational, aggressive, and unable to accept—for those are all symptoms of the fear that derives from both the unknown, and from perceived threats that are all too often based on sheer ignorance!

Among the attributes displayed by a successful *learner* are: 1) the right "attitude" (*American Laboratory News* Jun 2003; 35[13]:4), which includes 2) realizing that "there is no such thing as a learning disability" (*American Laboratory* Dec 2000; 32[24]:6–8). In other words, once you make the conscious decision to make learning an ongoing, established priority in your life, don't become your own worst enemy. Then (3) set your sights high (*American Laboratory News* Nov 2002; 34[23]:4), and 4) don't let anybody *else* become your enemy by allowing them to discourage (and perhaps deter) you from reaching your goals. Having thus set yourself up to succeed, 5) "persist and persevere until you prevail" in your efforts, 6) always "stay teachable" (*American Laboratory* Jan 2003; 35[1]:6–8), and for heaven's sake, have fun! Learn to *laugh* at yourself—the fourth L-word.

Ethel Barrymore is quoted as saying, "You grow up the day you have your first real laugh—at yourself!" Elsa Maxwell, in *R.S.V.P.: Elsa Maxwell's Own Story*, adds, "Always laugh at yourself first—before others do." Here, the operative word is "yourself." I am not advocating that you laugh at others, unless you are laughing *with* (as opposed to *at*) them. Indeed, not only is such an amusing form of self-mockery a sign of maturity, but, in a more generic sense, so, too, does having oneself a good belly laugh contribute significantly to his or her health! The healing power of laughter is well documented in the medical literature, punctuated by the highly successful 1998 motion picture *Patch Adams*, starring comedian Robin Williams as the medical doctor upon whose humorous exploits the film is based.

Another famous comedian, virtuoso pianist Victor Borge, notes that "Laughter is the shortest distance between two people." How true! Especially when, in the midst of a heated argument, those involved burst into hysterical laughter when they realize how utterly ridiculous the argument is, and oh how incredibly cathartic is that realization and the hysterical laughter that follows! "So many tangles in life are ultimately so hopeless that we have no appropriate sword other than laughter," said Gordon W. Allport. Indeed, that ability to find something to laugh about—to not take yourself too seriously—in the midst of all of the trials and tribulations of life, is fundamental to the maintenance of your physical and psychological health and well-being! Try it . . . you'll like it!

But a word of caution: While you're having fun and laughing at yourself, don't take it to the extreme of becoming *lazy*! One must *learn* to balance *laughter* with *labor*, our next L-word. Anything worth doing (the "one percent inspiration" that Thomas Edison claims is the essence of genius) is worth doing well (the 99% perspiration that, according to Mr. Edison, brings genius to fruition). To *labor*, in accordance with a good work ethic, i.e., to "take your work seriously but yourself lightly," in the words of C.W. Metcalf, is to display a properly proportioned sense of balance between, on the one hand, the effort (*labor*) and commitment required to successfully accomplish anything meaningful in life (the 99% perspiration) and, on the other hand, the humility (taking yourself *lightly*, or *lowly*, from the Latin, *humus* for "earth") that should accompany that accomplishment. Indeed, those individuals who are *lucky* enough to have perfected (through practice) this delicate balancing act between laborious achievements and self-obsession are role models who display, as well, many of the attributes of our next L-word, *leadership*.

As is the case for *learning*, I have also written a great deal here and elsewhere on the general subject of *leadership* and what makes for a good leader. Suffice it to say, for the purposes of this editorial, that, among other things: 1) "There's a big difference between ruling and leading" (*American Laboratory* Mar 2001; 33[6]:6–8); 2) a good leader recognizes "the importance of putting things into perspective" (*American Laboratory* Jul 2001; 33[14]:6–8); he or she displays several key 3) "leadership skills" (*American Laboratory* Dec 2003; 35[24]:6–10); and 4) "decision-making skills" (*American Laboratory News* Feb 2005; 37[4]:4–6), including, again, 5) a great "attitude" (*American Laboratory News* Jun 2003; 35[13]:4), and skills related to 6) "creativity" (*American Laboratory News* Nov 2001; 33[23]:4), not to mention 7) "ethics" (*American Laboratory* Oct 2001; 33[20]:6–8). The bottom line, however, is that to *lead*, one has to have the ability to "go to the head of the pack," set a good example, and motivate others to follow. Whenever I speak or write about this "going to the head of the pack" aspect of leadership, I am reminded of a humorous cartoon that I saw years ago that showed an Eskimo dog being followed by a team of Siberian huskies. The caption under the cartoon read something like this: "If your quest in life is to always be a follower, you limit yourself to only one view of the world!" I think you get the point.

A *leader* is a role model who *lives* his or her life accordingly, which brings me to the last L-word that space and time allow me to consider: *live*! Whenever I think of the word "live," I associate it with one of my favorite anonymous quotations: "I expect to pass through this world but once. Any good therefore that I can do, or any kindness that I can show to any fellow creature, let me do it now. Let me not defer or neglect it, for I shall not pass this way again." The word "live" also brings us back full circle to where we started—*love*—for, as Khalil Gibran reminds us in *The Prophet* (1923), "Life is indeed darkness save when there is urge, And all urge is blind save when there is knowledge [*learn*], And all knowledge is vain save when there is work [*labor*], And all work is empty save when there is love." My friends, your life is not a dress rehearsal! You only get one shot at it—make the most of it, and do it *now*!

There's a Big Difference Between Ruling and Leading!

American Laboratory, March 2001

Many of us either already have been or will someday be placed in a position of authority—one that may also require us to manage people. Some will have attained that stature as a result of distinguished achievements in their professional careers or personal lives; others will have climbed the ladder according to the famed Peter Principle (which asserts, somewhat tongue-in-cheek, that employees advance until they are promoted to their highest level of incompetence); still others will get there by pulling the right strings, knowing how and whom to influence when, being in the right place at the right time, and so on. But very few will actually possess the qualities of leadership that make for a successful boss, because, consciously or subconsciously, they will fail to recognize the subtle differences between *leading* and *ruling*.

When I was in the Corps of Engineers at Fort Belvoir, VA, I was very fortunate to have a Commanding Officer who was a true leader. Over the years, I have remembered him with great admiration, both for the influence he had on me personally, and for the ability he had to get the most out of his people. What gave him this ability? First and foremost, this man genuinely and sincerely cared (dare I say loved?) each and every one of us. In a recent *Sports Illustrated* editorial about the legendary Penn State football coach Joe Paterno (vol. 93, no. 20, Nov. 13, 2000), the writer Rick Reilly quotes the father of one of Coach Paterno's ailing players as saying, "You see this man on television, but you don't know him. I know him now" (referring to how genuinely concerned—to the point of tears—the Coach was about the seriousness of his player's injury). "His caring isn't an act." Contrast this genuine concern with what I once heard a department head say at a faculty meeting during which the departure of an ill-treated, disgruntled research superstar was being lamented by his colleagues. Without the slightest remorse, the department head pronounced that, "I don't consider any member of this faculty to be irreplaceable!" Which of these two individuals would you rather work for?

Coupled with my Captain's bona fide concern was his perception of us as people. He recognized that we had feelings, that we were not machines, that we were human; and he savored that humanness rather than condemn it, as we are so often prone to do. He appreciated that to be human is to sometimes make mistakes and exhibit frailty; to reinforce that appreciation, he would never shy away from or ignore an obvious delicate situation that might fester or worsen if left unattended. Instead, he would always confront issues head on, resolving them quickly and effectively, and move on. I remember once, when I was going through a tough period in my life, he called me into his office and closed the door. "Dan," he said, "I've noticed recently that your performance has not been quite up to par, up to your usually high standards. Is it anything you care to talk about, and is there anything I can do to help?" I poured my heart out to him that afternoon, knowing that he would listen without judging, that I could trust him, that I could level with him honestly and openly, and that I could depend on him to offer constructive, positive advice. He was prepared to walk in my shoes, to see my point of view, and I knew that he was on my side. Guess what the outcome of that encounter was?

One of the greatest qualities of a good leader is having the ability to bring out the best in those that he or she leads, and that means offering words of kindness and appreciation in the process of suggesting positive means for further improvement and accomplishment. Charles Schwab once said, "I have yet to find the man, however exalted his station, who did not do better work and put forth greater effort under a spirit of approval than under a spirit of criticism." Praise and encouragement will always get results; intimidation and reprimand never. The old adage of getting much further with people by saying two nice things about them for every concern that you have was one that my Captain lived by. This approach inspired us and made all of us *want* to do better.

There's another old expression that says, "The acorn does not fall too far from the tree." By implication, the expression suggests that we tend to follow role models, and so an individual in a position of authority must lead by example. Moreover, this individual should never ask of his or her subordinates anything that he or she would not be willing to do himself or herself. I am reminded of an incident that occurred in our company that required disciplinary action. Such discipline frequently was administered in the form of having us do pushups. Angered by what happened, my Captain sternly said to the perpetrator (not me!) of the offense, "Give me ten, mister!"—meaning, "Get down on the floor and give me ten pushups." Whereupon the Captain got down on the floor and did all ten pushups together with the individual being punished. How's that for earning the respect and admiration of your constituents?

Those you lead take their cues from you. You have the ability to bring out the best in them, or the worst. And one tried-and-true method for bringing out the best in people is to reward them for their efforts. "To say, 'well done' to any bit of good work is to take hold of the powers which have made the effort, and strengthen them beyond our knowledge," said Phillip Brooks. We all want that pat on the head, that feeling of approval that makes it all worth it, that recognition which shows our efforts are not being taken for granted. As Mary Kay put it, "Everyone has an invisible sign hanging from their neck saying, 'Make me feel important.' Never forget this message when working with people." The good leader knows how to reward in ways that encourage people to believe in themselves. Nothing (good or bad) that happened in our company at Fort Belvoir went unnoticed. The bad things were acknowledged, corrected, and forgotten; the good ones were rewarded, praised, and compensated—but never was one made to feel unimportant or unappreciated. Each one of us in the company felt needed. Whether it was true or not, our Captain made us feel that the entire company would self-destruct if it were to lose any one of us. Did that reinforce commitment? You bet it did!

Our Captain valued *people*, not *things*. He expressed more concern for our success than for his. He never imposed on us unrealistic expectations; rather, he always established reachable goals and benchmarks. He was prudent, patient, and proud.

But perhaps most importantly, our Captain taught us that *real power is* the power we have over *ourselves*, not over others. By example, he taught us that the power to lead derives from an inherent self-respect, self-discipline, self-confidence, and personal satisfaction that says, "I have nothing to prove. I'm O.K." One's ability to project that self-confidence in a meaningful and sincere way, without being arrogant, rude, or self-imposing, gives that individual an aura that, like a magnetic field, attracts a following that is loyal and committed to a common cause.

Our Captain taught us that respect for others begins with respect for oneself, and when we respect others, we gain their trust, their confidence, their allegiance, and their willingness to serve. Are these values, in fact, not the formula for success in any situation of authority? No matter whether you are a parent, a college dean, a corporate executive, the president of a society, the leader of a group, etc., the common denominator for the effective management of people comes down to your ability to recognize the difference between ruling and leading, between forcing people to conform to your will, and making them want to!

Leadership Skills
American Laboratory, December 2003

A long time ago, just for fun, I started to collect and save memoranda, correspondence, announcements, notes (more recently, e-mails), and various other forms of written communication. To the casual observer, what appears to have been accumulated is a useless collection of unrelated trivia, with no apparent reason(s) for why these particular pieces of literature should be grouped and filed together. But a further, more careful examination reveals that they do, indeed, share a common denominator that links them together—one that is perhaps subtle and not immediately obvious if you are not looking for it specifically. You see, they all begin with a phrase such as: "I should like to call your attention to Section XXIII, pages 25–26, of the *Department Handbook of Committees, Procedures, and Policies*, where it clearly states that . . ." or "Pursuant to Dean Jane's memorandum of June 16, we have been advised to . . ." or "According to university regulations it is incumbent upon us to . . ." or "In keeping with the guidelines set forth in the *University Faculty Handbook*, we are required to . . ." or "Jane Doe has asked me to . . ." or "Virginia State Law mandates that we . . ." or "In accordance with Article XVI, Subparagraph 13.6 of the State Code on Buildings and Grounds, you are hereby directed to . . ." or any one of a long list of related catch phrases that say, in essence, "Look, don't shoot the messenger! Yes, I am the person who is ordering you to do something you might or might not like, but hey, don't blame *me*—I'm just following orders! It's not my fault."

"Don't blame me. It's not my fault!" These few words reveal the fear many of us have of taking personal responsibility for our actions, lest the finger be pointed squarely at us if those actions produce less than desirable results; this fear does more to destroy one's ability to lead than (perhaps) any other single cause. "Don't blame me. John asked me to do this. Don't blame me. I'm just carrying out policy. Don't blame me. I'm just operating according to the letter of the law. Don't blame me if things go wrong or if the consequences of my actions lead to adversity among the individuals who are affected by them. It's not my fault. Don't blame me!"

I forget who originally said, "Wherever you see a successful business, someone once made a courageous decision and accepted full responsibility for its potential consequences, good or bad." I do know that President Harry S. Truman had a sign on his desk bearing the words,

"The Buck Stops Here!" ("Passing the buck" is a poker-playing expression, referring to a marker that can be passed along by someone who does not wish to deal.) These same philosophies are embedded in a principle I have always tried to live by: "I have never made a *right* decision in my life—I have made a *decision*, and then I have endeavored to make it right."

Indeed, the ability to be decisive is one of the most fundamental skills of leadership. Being unable (or not wanting) to make decisions, or fearing the repercussions and culpability that may result, often causes us to handle situations in one or a combination of three basic ways: First, we close our eyes to the need for taking decisive action at all, hoping (in some cases, even praying) instead that the situation will go away or otherwise resolve itself without our having to do anything. If that doesn't work, we look for some precedent in the form of someone or something to blame (an existing law, an edict, an unsuspecting scapegoat, etc.). We thus distance ourselves from the situation and certainly exonerate ourselves from the responsibility for any decision we are "forced" to make ("Don't blame me"). If that isn't possible, or if we cannot find a precedent, we assign the problem to a committee in order to get consensus—to get a group decision or recommendation that lets us off the hook. Although we may not necessarily be bound by their deliberations and conclusions, the fact that a committee was involved nevertheless ensures that any decision made, if it results in some cause for blame, will allow that blame to be shared, rather than encumbered by a single individual. Of course, more recently, if all else fails, there's always the "Don't blame me. Our computers are down and we have had system failures" approach. Computers (like deceased persons) cannot defend themselves, and thus make the ideal target for blame.

Leaders understand that being wrong need not be feared, nor should being blamed. It is not wrong to be wrong, provided you act responsibly, sincerely, and motivated by the best interests of all of those concerned. Being wrong takes courage, and courage is a second basic skill of great leadership. Great leadership is what it takes to move forward, and moving forward, in today's world, is prerequisite for survival—whether it be a corporation, an organization, a profession, a nation, or whatever.

Case in point: the symphony orchestra. If you have had occasion to visit my Web site (www.schneck.bizland.com), you know that I have a rather extensive background as an orchestral violinist. Such musical ensembles are great illustrations of the essential concepts of leadership because they contain the three basic elements that are embedded in this concept: the leader (in this case, the conductor of the orchestra), the followers (the musicians who play in the orchestra), and the mission of the group (in the case of an orchestra, the successful performance of a piece of music, faithful to the intent of its composer).

The conductor of an orchestra must have the ability to define its mission (i.e., a successful performance), interpret the objective(s) of the mission (or its purpose, which is formulated in a way that is faithful to the intent of the composer of the music), and stay focused on those objectives while figuring out an expedient way to meet them. The latter will definitely require that he or she have the technical competence to guide and direct the followers (the group of musicians). In orchestra parlance, we talk about this competence in terms of stick skills—clarity of beat, absence of distracting mannerisms, eye-to-eye contact, etc. The conductor must (of course) be able to read orchestral scores and have a thorough knowledge of the instruments of the orchestra—their pitch range, timbre (sound quality), how they balance against one another, how to get a desired sonority, musical blending of sounds, and so on.

To be a good leader, the conductor of an orchestra must display initiative. Great conductors develop a uniquely recognizable style, a signature sound. While attempting to remain faithful to the intent of the composer, leaders of musical ensembles do, nevertheless, add their own interpretation to the music—specific tempi, phrasing, sonority, and other musical characteristics that define the conductor's vision of what the composer had in mind. Listen to a big band and you can tell almost instantly that it is Glenn Miller rather than Benny Goodman. Listen to an orchestral recording of a symphony, and the trained ear can instantly tell whether it is that of the (now-defunct) NBC Symphony Orchestra under the direction of Arturo Toscanini; Eugene Ormandy conducting the Philadelphia Orchestra; the New York Philharmonic under the baton of Leonard Bernstein; the Boston Symphony led by Seiji Ozawa; the Pittsburgh Symphony under the direction of Andre Previn; or the Israeli Philharmonic, with Zubin Mehta on the podium. Each of these great conductors (leaders) has his own distinctive style, which is immediately recognizable and directly attributable to him. In this sense, orchestras are not unlike sports teams, which typically take on the personality and playing styles of their respective coaches or managers.

Really great conductors (leaders) are also great communicators, not only orally and on paper, but through unspoken body language as well.

They have the ability to express themselves in ways that the musicians understand; they get their point across so that everybody in the orchestra is on the same wavelength. If problems emerge during rehearsals, good conductors know how to resolve those problems; they are good at problem-solving. In fact, they can do even better than that: They often anticipate potential problems and take appropriate steps to prevent them from ever becoming realized. In other words, good leaders are *pro*active, as opposed to *re*active. They exercise good judgment, having an instinctive feel for when it is best to go with the flow, take the helm and steer the ship in its intended direction, or initiate a midcourse correction, thus changing the path altogether.

Good leaders are self-driven, self-motivated, self-confident, and self-disciplined, but not self-serving. They never put their own interests ahead of those (the mission) of the organization, and most certainly never ahead of those (the followers) they lead. (See "There's a Big Difference Between Ruling and Leading!" *American Laboratory* Mar 2001; 33[6]:6–8, which addresses this point in much greater detail, and which was touched upon as well in the Ingersoll-Rand seminar.) That is to say, good conductors develop (or instinctively have) good people skills to go along with their academic technical skills, and those leadership skills we have been discussing here in a somewhat theoretical sense. They adhere to strict ethical standards; are trustworthy, honest individuals of great integrity; are good role models; and make clear their expectations of those they lead.

"All well and good," says somebody in the audience, "but how do I convert the theory into practice? How do I learn to *apply* in my everyday life and professional career these leadership skills and principles, which you just even admitted, we are talking about here in a somewhat theoretical sense?" "Well," I respond, "you just answered your own question when you used the word 'practice.'" What musicians, orchestral conductors, athletes, and all good leaders appreciate is the notion that practice makes perfect! They know that to achieve success, you must do the same thing over and over again until you get it right. Speaking from an anatomical/physiological point of view, repetition is the only way our bodies learn anything! I can teach you the mechanics of playing the violin, but I cannot make you a violinist; only *you* can do that—so musicians practice hours a day to master their respective instruments. The Juilliard School of Music in New York City has instructors that can teach you the principles of conducting an orchestra, but they cannot make you a conductor; only *you* can do that—so conductors practice constantly to develop good stick skills. Orchestras rehearse, over and over again, to become proficient; so do sports teams: football practice, basketball practice, soccer practice, etc.

It never ceases to amaze me how we appreciate the concept of practice when it comes to musical or athletic skills, but fail to make the connection that it applies equally well when it comes to developing leadership skills. So, you need to think of this seminar as a class in leadership, and you need to *practice* the skills we have talked about in the sense of doing your homework for this class. I can teach you what you need to do to become a leader, and—recognizing that there are naturals in any field of endeavor—I am here to tell you that *anybody* can become one, contrary to some popular beliefs, but *I* can't make you one—only *you* can do that, by being committed to becoming one (I can't want it for you more than you want it for yourself), and, like an Olympic athlete, by *showing* that commitment, i.e., being dedicated to the practice that is required to be one.

Decision-Making Skills

American Laboratory News, February 2005

Decisiveness refers to one's ability to be decisive—to make decisions. When all is said and done, is that not what life (literally and figuratively) is all about? Just think: You would not be reading this right now if your biological parents had not *decided* (intentionally or otherwise, voluntarily or not, unilaterally or unanimously) to have a very specific type of intimate physical relationship with one another, and to carry that relationship to its ultimate successful realization—hence, the source of your very existence (life!). You might also not be reading this if you *decided* not to subscribe to *American Laboratory News,* and there was no other way for it to come across your desk, or if decisions you made early on in your academic and professional career led you into a field far remote from one that would even cause you to have the slightest interest in a periodical such as this.

Indeed, from birth to death, we travel through the maze of life making constant decisions that dictate the path we take from beginning to end. Sometimes those decisions are momentous ones, with a significant impact on others and us. In different situations, they might perhaps be less critical and influential, but nonetheless, still have potential consequences. Sometimes we make choices consciously and deliberately, and at other times subconsciously and unintentionally, or even unconsciously! Yet, as critical as making an effective decision is, in shaping what route our journey through the maze of life will take, we pay little or no attention to actually promoting and teaching the fundamentals of effective decision-making skills. This is an interesting paradox, not unlike the subjects of my editorials on "Enlightened Neurosis" (*American Laboratory News* May 2003; 35[11]:4) and "Let's Really Get Back to Basics" (*American Laboratory News* Oct 2003; 35[21]:4–6).

What, exactly, does it mean to make an effective decision? One clue to answering this question might be gleaned from the interesting history of the word "decision" (we'll get to the "effective" part later). It, like "incision" and "excision," derives from the Latin *caedere*, which means "to cut." Thus, "incision" means "to cut *into*" (Latin *in-* = into); "excision" means "to cut *out*" (Latin *ex-* = out); and "decision" means "to cut *off*" (Latin *dé-* = away, in the sense of disconnected or off). To make a decision, then, connotes settling a matter by 1) "cutting away" those considerations that are either totally irrelevant or, at most, only peripherally germane to its resolution so that 2) you can "cut off" deliberations that serve merely to *delay* the resolution of the issue and thereby impede the decision-making process. The latter might result, for example, from inordinate attempts to find all possible solutions to the problem under consideration, and to evaluate each and every consequence of each and every possible solution before even attempting to make a decision. "A man would do nothing if he waited until he could do it so well that no one could find fault," said John Henry Cardinal Newman.

Having accomplished nos. 1 and 2, you can then proceed to 3) "cut off" the umbilical cord that keeps you tied to the issue—make up your mind to take a course of action that will resolve the matter, take that course, and be done with it and move on! Turn your attention to how you will handle the results and possible consequences of that decision. (Note, in each of the above three points, the significance of "cutting off," of literally *de-ciding*.)

Okay, I can hear you now: I know the essential features of making effective decisions; I've heard them all, and they are pretty standard and straightforward. First, you carefully *define* the problem you are trying to solve. Then, you clarify what objectives you are trying to achieve in solving that issue and the criteria you will use to satisfy those objectives (i.e., the rules by which you will play the game). Then, you list (brainstorm) as many alternative solutions to the problem as are feasible within the framework you have established to constrain these solutions, such as economic considerations, time constraints, initial and boundary conditions, resources available, and so on. You then evaluate 1) how well each of these solutions satisfies your objectives; 2) what potential consequences might result (and how you will handle them); 3) what tradeoffs might be required if it is necessary to compromise, should it turn out that not all of the objectives can be satisfied simultaneously; 4) what level of uncertainty might affect the outcome of your decision; and 5) how all of these factors are related to your risk tolerance, as compared to the benefits that are likely to be achieved (i.e., the risk-to-benefit ratio). Finally, you evaluate the cascading effect that this decision might have on related issues and future considerations. Putting it all together, you are then in a position to make an informed decision (we are not yet to the "effective" part), which is to say, a decision that is based on complete knowledge of all of the facts and potential consequences (avoiding, of course, the "my mind's made up—don't confuse me with facts" syndrome).

You are right, and I agree. The above, indeed, *are* the essential pillars upon which informed decision-making processes can (and should) rest comfortably. But this editorial is not about making *informed* decisions—it's about making *effective* decisions, by considering somewhat more subtle aspects of the decision-making process, aspects that the rule book does not always address.

1. The dramatist Eugene Ionesco (1909–94) reminds us that, "It is not the answer that enlightens, but the question." In other words, at the very first step in the decision-making process, which is to formulate and carefully define the issue in need of attention, it is more important to ask the right questions than to wind up expending a great deal of time, energy, effort, and resources into answering the wrong ones. The skills involved here include being able to separate symptoms from causes, isolated anecdotal/circumstantial evidence from generic trends and universal tendencies, narrow-minded views from broadband perspectives, and fact from fiction. Absent these skills, what happens all too often is that one winds up sidestepping the real issues, solving instead a different (often easier) problem to avoid tackling the less obvious, harder ones.

Case in point: Although Isaac Newton's (1642–1727) empirical Law of Gravitation was generally accepted without significant controversy, nobody quite understood why it should take on the special form that it does, i.e., why the gravitational force between two masses should be proportional to the inverse square of their separation in space—nobody, that is, until the German philosopher Immanuel Kant

(1742–1804) asked a question that had never been asked before: "Why does space have three dimensions?" Attempts to answer that very insightful question led to research that showed, for the first time, that the *form* of certain basic laws of nature bears an ($n-1$) power relationship to the corresponding number, n, of dimensions of space in which those laws apply. Thus, since we live in a three-dimensional space ($n = 3$, because it takes three independent measurements to uniquely locate a point in space), gravity (as well as electrical and magnetic forces) falls off as the inverse square ($n-1 = 2$) of distance. Brilliant! I wonder how much more we would learn about physics if a greater effort were made to answer similar soul-searching questions, like the one I posed in an earlier editorial ("Stay Teachable!" *American Laboratory* Jan 2003; 35[1]:6–8): "What, exactly, *is* an electric charge?" I also wonder how much more we would learn about a person's real IQ (intelligence quotient) if we knew how to formulate and ask the *right* questions on an IQ exam. But I will leave that topic for another time, except to emphasize that in order to make *effective* decisions, one must learn to ask the right questions.

2. The expression "paralysis by analysis" comes to mind when I think of the various steps in the decision-making process that involve formulating alternative solutions and evaluating them. Don't overanalyze! "The man who insists upon seeing with perfect clearness before he decides, never decides," said Henri Frédéric Amiel. The word "gridlock" also comes to mind, indicating a complete stoppage of activity due to information overload. Skills that are needed to circumvent the problem of gridlock include being able to stay focused on your goal; addressing only those issues that have direct and first-order implications on the results of your decision (i.e., not getting sidetracked by issues that are only peripherally related); knowing when enough is enough, thus truncating any further deliberations in favor of deciding; and, to paraphrase Abraham Lincoln, recognizing that you can satisfy all of the people only some of the time, you can perhaps satisfy some of the people all of the time, but you definitely cannot satisfy all of the people all of the time! Therefore, you must learn not to overanalyze a situation in search of the perfect solution. As author Marilyn Moats Kennedy put it in *Across the Board*, "It's better to be boldly decisive and risk being wrong than to agonize at length and be right too late." Going one step further, in the decision-making process, you must stop trying to be all things to all people; it is impossible to make decisions that will always satisfy everybody. (For more on information overload and gridlock, see a related editorial, "All God's Creations Got Rhythm!" *American Laboratory* Oct 2000; 32[20]:6–8.)

3. Studies have shown that doctors deprived of sleep and rest are much more likely to misdiagnose a patient, prescribe the wrong medication, and/or dictate the wrong dosage for that individual. Tired pilots, too, are more prone to serious errors in judgment, with life-threatening implications. All of us will most likely err in making effective decisions if those decisions are made when, physiologically, we are not "running on all cylinders" due to fatigue and/or malnourishment. Thus, properly nourishing the body, mind, and spirit with good habits that relate to diet, rest, sleep, and relaxation increases the chances that your decisions will be effective ones. Drug, alcohol, and tobacco abuse do not help either.

4. Trust your instincts—that is to say, let decision-making be a human experience, a natural activity derived from natural abilities. Indeed, the nice part about trusting your instincts is that it is an ability that does not have to be taught; the only skill required is to have confidence in your evolutionary heritage. The hardware is already there, and it derives from generations of experience; all you have to do is let it go and have faith that more often than not it will not betray you. It helped us get this far!

5. Be prepared to improvise. There is an old Yiddish expression that goes (phonetically) something like this: "*Der Mentsch Tracht, und Got Lacht,*" which essentially translates to "Man plans, and God laughs." In other words, despite painstakingly careful planning, recognize that things can still happen that you had no way of anticipating—"acts of God," for example, such as blizzards, hurricanes, tornadoes, and unforeseen natural disasters, or sudden illness, or an accident, a discontinuous sequence of events, etc. Realistically, there is really no way to take these kinds of situations into account in the decision-making process. The skills required to deal with them if they do occur include being spontaneously creative ("If life deals you lemons, make lemonade"); having enough flexibility to go to a Plan B (even if you might not know *a priori* what that particular alternate plan might have to be); knowing how to diversify (not "putting all of your eggs in one basket," lest you not allow yourself options just in case you do encounter unforeseen circumstances); and learning to have faith that all decisions are not necessarily irreversible. In the majority of cases, you can change your mind later, if that becomes necessary—"As long as there's a tomorrow, there's always another chance for success." In the decision-making process, we tend to agonize too much, fearing that whatever we decide will be etched in stone. More often than not, this is not the case.

6. Don't assume things that are not there. How often have you heard people say, "I guess I automatically assumed that . . ." only to find out later that there was no basis for that assumption? This goes back to getting your facts straight and doing your homework before jumping to conclusions. In making decisions, we frequently fall into the trap of imposing fictitious and sometimes conflicting imaginary constraints. Don't do it! If you cannot identify the source of your assumption—if you cannot confirm it, if you cannot justify it—do not use it as a constraining factor in the decision-making process. Period. The neglect of unfounded and often misleading assumptions goes a long way toward maximizing the effectiveness of decisions we make.

7. Finally, make your decision a self-fulfilled prophecy. Expect things to go as planned as a result of the decisions you have made. Live by the adage, "I've never made a right decision in my life. I have made a decision, and then I've made it right!" Don't procrastinate—which is to say, *decide to decide*, lest somebody else decides for you—and have confidence that if you followed the guidelines suggested in this editorial, chances are your decision will have been an effective one, which is to say, one that has optimized the outcome(s) of your decision, and is right for the issue it set out to resolve. I guarantee it!

"Enlightened" Neurosis!

American Laboratory News, May 2003

The Enlightenment generally refers to the period of time during the 17th and 18th centuries when the human spirit could finally be liberated from the medieval thinking that dominated from about 500 to 1450 A.D. Fueled by the Renaissance movement that began in the 1300s and reached its climax from around 1420 to 1580 A.D., during which there emerged a great revival of art and learning, the Enlightenment Paradigm, as it is sometimes called, declared that all problems could and *should* be solved by reasoning. Indeed, according to this paradigm, the *only* path to truth and knowledge (cognition) is rational thought; reason must be the absolute ruler of human life; there must be an intellectual basis for all that we say and do; emotions are bad and must be suppressed; "mind" must be separated from "body,"[1] and all "valid" knowledge can be derived only by adhering strictly to the scientific method. The latter demands that: 1) a problem be precisely defined; 2) all pertinent data related to the problem be carefully gathered; 3) a working hypothesis be formulated to explain the who, what, where, why, when, and how aspects of the problem; 4) accurately designed and properly executed experiments be performed to collect relevant and meaningful data that can be used to test the hypothesis; 5) results of these experiments be objectively analyzed and interpreted; and finally, 6) conclusions be drawn that follow directly and logically from a meaningful and unbiased discussion of the results obtained. Sounds reasonable enough.

Well, in fact, it *is* reasonable—so reasonable that French philosophers, including René Descartes, Charles de Montesquieu, François Voltaire, and Jean Baptiste Rousseau; British empiricists and theorists such as Sir Francis Bacon, Thomas Hobbes, John Locke, and Lord Ashley Shaftesbury; German and Dutch writers including Gottfried Leibnitz, Hugo Grotius, Christian Wolff, Gotthold Lessing, Johann Herder, and Immanuel Kant; and American statesmen such as Benjamin Franklin, Thomas Jefferson, Alexander Hamilton, and Thomas Paine (to name just a few) influenced virtually all aspects of our present-day lifestyle, including religion, law, government, politics, philosophy, literature, the arts, science, sociology, medicine, and so on. Indeed, the influence of the Enlightenment movement can be seen even in our own American Constitution.

But, as frequently happens when we solve one problem (in this case, medieval thinking), we create, or significantly contribute to, another one, such as "enlightened" thinking. That is to say, the Enlightenment Paradigm reinforced and continued what has been an evolving trend to distance ourselves from our humanness. We are intent on progressing asymptotically toward a totally neurotic state of existence. By this, I mean that we have an abnormal fixation to repress and deny what is factually real—i.e., that we are first and foremost human, with all of the frailties and imperfections that being human is all about—in favor of creating a hypothetically "perfect" person that is only intellectually real—i.e., a figment of our imagination; a "don't you wish it were true" mental construct that has validity only as an abstraction; an illusion that, if anything, creates expectations that are irrational, rather than rational.[2] The result is a societal preponderance of individuals who suffer from various self and socially inflicted mental and emotional disorders characterized by depression, anxiety, abnormal fears, and compulsive behavior (in short, neuroses) because they are trying to live up to some fictitious character that is portrayed to us on stage and screen as being the optimum human; somebody that we must all strive to be, as futile as the effort to do so might be.

The optimum human keeps "a stiff upper lip," a phrase first used in the early 1800s to allay the fears of fishermen who were about to go out in rough seas. We are advised to "hold your chin up high"—be brave, be strong, and whatever you do, *don't* let your emotions show! The optimum human does not "wear one's heart on one's sleeve," a phrase attributed to Shakespeare, implying an ostentatious display of one's limitless devotion. The Bard of Avon actually coined this expression as an extrapolation of a custom of his 1500–1700 era, wherein one would pin on one's sleeve various displays or trinkets to advertise his or her exploits and accomplishments. This is not altogether different from what we do today, as we still wear medals and pins to show others our perspectives or accomplishments.

We are taught further that "real" men don't cry: to display emotion is a sign of weakness, for which we should feel guilty; we must endeavor to suppress our feelings; to maintain a "poker face" in situations that provoke us to react; to "fake it" when we are genuinely moved by some experience; to pretend we don't care, when we really do; and to stay cool under any circumstances ("never, but never let them see you sweat!").

The optimum human is very discreet when slipping out of a meeting or public gathering in order to take care of "nature's calls." Using the toilet is always referred to as "going to the restroom"; and certainly, this person never says "toilet paper" in public (he or she just whispers "T.P." in the softest voice possible). I will leave it to your imagination to fill in the blanks on the obvious directions in which this aspect of our discussion can go. Suffice it to say that the very subject that is the essence of this essay precludes my being able to talk about certain aspects of our humanness that one simply does not discuss "in public."

The optimum human practices "anger management." Indeed, the outward display of anger, displeasure, or hostility is, like crying, considered to be immature. Never mind that it is a perfectly normal human reaction to feeling threatened; normal human reactions are not an acceptable form of "civilized" behavior. Not to belabor the point, let me just summarize by saying that the optimum human, by 21st-century standards, is the consummate neurotic human.

Just to cite one example of our continuing efforts to dehumanize ourselves, I note that we constantly refer in very impersonal ways to organizational structures and activities that involve people. We say things like, "Wall Street reacted quite favorably to the Fed's announcement that interest rates would be reduced by a quarter percent." The last time I looked, "Wall Street" was a street in lower Manhattan. I don't think of inanimate streets as "reacting" to things like humans do. Moreover, if by "the Fed's," we mean a spokesperson for the Federal Reserve, why not identify that individual by saying instead, "Investors (*people*) reacted quite favorably to the announcement by the Chairman (a *person*) of the Federal Reserve that interest rates will be reduced by a quarter of one percent"? What does, "The White House issued a statement today" mean? The last time I looked, the White House was a big house in Washington, DC. Do houses "issue statements"? And what does, "Turkey reached an agreement with Washington" mean? How do geographic locations reach "agreements" with one another? I never knew the National Weather Service could issue a storm advisory, or the Centers for Disease Control could warn of an impending epidemic, or the IRS could reorganize itself. Then, of course, there's the old standby: "Your problem cannot be resolved today because our computers are down," as if computers solve problems, or make errors. (Certainly, people don't! And don't even get me started on, "If you want . . . press 1.") The bottom line is that computers, Wall Street, the Federal Reserve, the White House, the Centers for Disease Control, and so on, are all *things*—things to which we refer as "it," and not "I," "you," "me," or "we." These are things that have no personality, no identity, no beating heart, no pulse, no emotions, nothing to make them tangible in a human sense. They are just abstract objects behind which we can hide, from which we can distance ourselves, and thereby maintain anonymity.

Now don't misunderstand me, I have nothing against science; the objective search for truth is a noble quest. I have nothing against cognition; the desire to know is just as human as the need to emote. I have nothing against modesty, Victorian morals, humility, or even vanity; in their own way, they too are very human. But as I once told a class of mine, "When computers start thinking like human beings, we will have made significant progress. But as we human beings strive more and more to think like computers, we are seriously regressing, and taking huge steps backwards in our journey toward ultimate maturity." In other words, as science and technology consume us, the pendulum starts to swing too far in the direction of repressing and denying our own humanness, thus causing us to become neurotic in the name of "Enlightenment." We, not nature, have separated our minds from our bodies in the name of an "enlightened civilization." We have opted to suppress our natural human drives, instincts, and emotions, creating instead this tough, emotionless, "I don't need anybody," not-bothered-by-anything, totally independent "super-human," in the name of what we arbitrarily call rational thinking, whatever that is. In so doing, we have put science on a pedestal above all else, virtually worshipping it as the panacea for all that ails us, and considering it, through "enlightenment," to be the only path to "truth."

We have further relegated the arts to some obscure place in the human spectrum of experience, denouncing them as some inherent form of evil and justifying this on the basis of this "enlightened" philosophy. We have made the arts the Rodney Dangerfields of humanity—"They don't get no respect!" Subconsciously (or perhaps deliberately), could it be that we fear the role of the arts as a means for humans to satisfy their fundamental need for emotional expression as being too threatening to "scientific thinking"? Well, the fact is, given a choice between how we feel and what we *think*, we will invariably go with how we *feel*. As documented in scientific literature, it is more naturally and inherently "us." We are *emotional* creatures who think, not the other way around.

And so, it is we who continue to distance ourselves from our very human nature, which we perceive to be weak and feeble. In the words of Pogo Comic Strip writer Walt Kelly, "We have met the enemy, and it is us!" (As an aside, I wanted to mention that, so far as I know, we are the only member of the animal kingdom that has become so estranged from our own bodies, perhaps even ashamed of them, that we deem it a crime to expose them in public. But my dear wife Judi, always the more diplomatic one, made me promise not to go there, lest I be accused of advocating public nudity, which I do not. I'm just making an observation. But I did want to cite this as still another example of our reluctance to talk openly about things that are human and natural to us, because we don't talk about them; that's being too human.)

Rabbi Harold Kushner, author of *When Bad Things Happen to Good People*,[3] tells of a young boy who comes home late from school one day. "Why are you late?" asks his mother. "On my way home from school," answers the lad, "I stopped to help my friend, whose bicycle had broken." The mother questions, "What do *you* know about fixing bicycles?" The boy replies, "Nothing! I just stopped to help my friend cry." Not a bad idea. Every once in a while, we all need somebody to "just help us cry." It's a humanly normal, nothing to be ashamed of, "enlightening" reality that defies rational justification. And sometimes, kindness is wiser than truth.

References

1. Schneck DJ. Mind/body—both or neither? Am Lab 2000; 32(14):6–8.
2. Schneck DJ. To err is human, to forgive divine. Am Lab 2002; 34(6):4.
3. Kushner H. When bad things happen to good people. New York: Avon, 1981.

We're So Busy Being Busy!

American Biotechnology Laboratory, August 2002

When I get reincarnated, I want my soul to be reborn into the body of a household pet. I came to this conclusion after an experience that gave me a whole new perspective on what we human beings are all about. Recently, my wife and I visited our daughter and son-in-law, and their wonderful pet dog, Maisy. After enjoying a delicious dinner, we all retreated to the living room, accompanied by Maisy, who was perfectly happy to settle down in the middle of the living room floor and amuse herself with all of her dog toys. This, of course, was after communicating her affection by giving all of us a tongue bath to let us know how happy she was to be in our presence, and how totally she trusted us. I stared in envy at this scene of total contentment—just an animal and her toys, experiencing the pleasures of life, flourishing in her secure environment, lacking any worldly concerns, surrounded by a family who she knew loved her and would care for her. I stared and I stared, and I thought, Wow! (not to be confused with bow wow).

Maybe it was the timing (this event occurred around a festive holiday season); maybe it was the mood (I was feeling particularly serene and comfortable that evening); maybe it was the company (all of us get along quite well with one another and seemed especially relaxed and at ease following a gourmet dinner). I'm not sure how many things came together in just the right combination that day to trigger it, but as I sat silently staring at this animal entertaining herself, I thought, "Why can't it be like that for all of us? We're so vain, so enamored of our own importance, so driven to spend so much time keeping track of our life instead of living it, so preoccupied with being busy!" Indeed, humans are the "keep-trackiest" bunch of obsessive pack rats and workaholics in the entire animal kingdom. This would not be all that bad were it not for the fact that we pursue these passions to the exclusion of taking time out to search for the real pleasures in life. As the expression goes, how many people do you know who, lying on their deathbed, would look back on their life and exclaim, "Gee, in retrospect, I wish I had spent more time at the office!"?

So as I continued to stare at this content animal, I began making a mental list of the causes of this "busyness." Jealously, I thought, "Come April, this dog will not be at all concerned with her income taxes. How much time, Dan, do you spend tracking expenses so that you can report those figures to Uncle Sam on an annual basis, in an effort to keep as much as possible of what you earn? We won't even mention the time spent in actually filling out those income tax forms each spring, and the effort you expend in trying to read as much as possible about the income tax code, so that you can avail yourself of all of the strategies that allow you to pay no more in taxes than you legally have to, and the time spent in maintaining at least five years' worth of income tax records—on the outside chance that you might be audited.

"How much time, Dan, do you spend annually updating your résumé and/or curriculum vitae in order to document all the wonderful things you have accomplished over the course of your entire life/career? We won't even count the additional time you devote to updating all of the various versions of your résumé that are used for different purposes, for example, the abbreviated version required in research proposals (each proposal, of course, requiring a different format), the comprehensive long version required to be kept on file at the University (listing everything you have ever published, every talk you have ever given, every course you have ever taught, every student you have ever advised), the more moderate yet somewhat detailed version that you routinely send out to those who ask for it, and the special five-year-synopsis version used in the departmental accreditation process. Then, of course, we have to fill out an annual faculty activity report; let's not forget that!

"Look at this dog, Dan. Does she worry about health insurance, or home insurance, or auto insurance, or any insurance? Is maintaining a car of any interest to her? How about landscaping, or cutting the lawn, or building a deck onto her house, or even paying off a mortgage? Does she occupy significant portions of her time addressing such issues? Is Maisy concerned about what earrings she will wear with her evening dress, or what shoes will go with the color of her dress (maybe she should wear a pants outfit instead of a dress?), or whether to wear heels (and, if so, how high?) or flats, or whether to wear her hair up or down? How about doing her nails? What perfume to use? What deodorant? I mention these things first because Maisy happens to be a female. We men are no better and, in many ways, much worse when it comes to matters involving clothing, accessories, jewelry, grooming, and 'keeping up with the Joneses.' So, how much time does Maisy spend in shopping malls buying clothes, or dressing herself in the morning (only to change several more times during the day), or grooming herself, or feeding her vanity? How much of that time would have been spent more productively living her life, as opposed to pampering herself?"

I sat, I stared, and I contemplated, coveting this animal's lust for life; the more I thought about it, the longer the busy-list got. "Why are we so obsessed with keeping track of history," I mused, reflecting on the number of museums, libraries, archives, chronologies, and galleries there are out there, and the time, effort, and resources we expend in maintaining and updating them. Maisy certainly doesn't care if one of her ancestors was King of the Canines, or if centuries ago there was an earthquake in Christiansburg. Maisy doesn't hold on to things for "sentimental value," reminisce about the "good old days," or pore nostalgically over old picture albums. She couldn't care less about the history of the family that adopted her, her canine heritage, or when this planet was born. Moreover, she certainly does not seem any the worse for wear because of her apparent apathy toward memorabilia. Could this interest in our history be vanity raising its ugly head again? Certainly it can't be because we learn from it, for history itself proves that we seem destined to keep making the same mistakes over and over again.

I pondered even further: "Speaking of history, why do we have this passion to immortalize criminals of some prominence, while the rest of us languish in obscurity?" One hundred years from now, nobody will have ever heard of Dan Schneck, but Al Capone, Billy the Kid, Adolf Hitler, Napoleon, and others who have left behind a legacy of carnage and a life dedicated to breaching public law will still be household names. I am not aware that any significant crime has been deterred as a result of television networks running a week's worth of biographies detailing the exploits of the world's most famous criminals, yet we continue to watch, and such programs continue to prosper. Now before you get the wrong impression, please note that I am not denigrating the subject of history, nor am I advocating that we remove the subject from all academic curricula. I am just observing that we expend a great deal of effort keeping track of things, and that perhaps we do so to an extent disproportionate to that expended doing other things that might make our lives just a bit more meaningful.

The list goes on: I am not aware of the existence of a Canine Bureau of Vital Statistics. Maisy really doesn't care how many dogs there are in the world, or how many of them in Asia came down with hip dysplasia. As far as I know, dogs don't keep track of their dead, either. Nor do they spend hours reading instruction manuals to learn how to use new software packages, packages that become obsolete in less than a year anyway. But Maisy did know how to deliver her own babies, no ob/gyn necessary, no birthing classes, maternity wards, how-to books, or Dr. Spock books afterward. Maisy did openly, candidly, and without the slightest reservation display her affection for us—honestly, without prompting, and without resorting to the "games people play." Maisy does trust her instincts and could take care of herself quite independently if she had to. Maisy does enjoy every ounce of her life and will someday die having experienced as much of it as she could. Indeed, I suspect that her daily to-do lists of busy-time well-spent would ultimately look much more impressive than mine. And we call ourselves the most intelligent of the animal kingdom? Who's smarter?